Transport Law in Spain

Transport Law in Spain

Second Edition

Juan-Luis Pulido-Begines
Maria-Victoria Petit-Lavall
Achim Puetz

This book was originally published as a monograph in the International Encyclopaedia of Laws/Transport Law.

Founding Editor: Roger Blanpain
General Editor: Frank Hendrickx
Volume Editor: Eric Van Hooydonk

Wolters Kluwer

Published by:
Kluwer Law International B.V.
PO Box 316
2400 AH Alphen aan den Rijn
The Netherlands
E-mail: international-sales@wolterskluwer.com
Website: lrus.wolterskluwer.com

Sold and distributed in North, Central and South America by:
Wolters Kluwer Legal & Regulatory U.S.
7201 McKinney Circle
Frederick, MD 21704
United States of America
Email: customer.service@wolterskluwer.com

Sold and distributed in all other countries by:
Air Business Subscriptions
Rockwood House
Haywards Heath
West Sussex
RH16 3DH
United Kingdom
Email: international-customerservice@wolterskluwer.com

Printed on acid-free paper

ISBN 978-94-035-0073-7

e-Book: ISBN 978-94-035-0074-4
web-PDF: ISBN 978-94-035-0075-1

Printed in the United Kingdom.

The Authors

Juan-Luis Pulido-Begines is a Spanish citizen and has been a lecturer in the University of Cádiz since 1992, becoming a Full Senior Professor of Commercial Law at the University of Cádiz in 2007. He holds a Law Degree (1989) and a PhD in Law (1995) from the University of Cádiz, for which he received the outstanding doctorate award. He has authored more than sixty publications (monographies, articles in law reviews, contributions to collective books) on different subjects of Commercial Law (Company Law, Banking Law, Insurance Law, and mostly Maritime Law).

These include the following monographs: *Los contratos de remolque marítimo*, Barcelona, 1996; *El derecho de información del socio en la sociedad de responsabilidad limitada*, Madrid, 1997; *El derecho de información del accionista*, Madrid, 1998; *Seguro de mercancías y seguro de responsabilidad civil del porteador terrestre*, Barcelona, 2001; *Las averías y los accidentes de la navegación marítima y aérea*, Madrid, 2003; *La responsabilidad frente a terceros de las sociedades de clasificación de buques*, Vitoria, 2006; *Instituciones de Derecho de la navegación marítima*, Madrid, 2009; *El concepto de porteador efectivo en el Derecho uniforme del transporte, La transición incompleta*, Madrid, 2012; *Curso de Derecho de la navegación marítima*, Madrid, 2015; and *Cruise Ships Law*, en *Hamburg Lectures on Maritime Law 2011–2013*, Hamburg, 2015.

Prof. Pulido has been a speaker at numerous courses, masters, PhD courses, seminars and conferences in Spain and abroad and has been a visiting Professor at the Universities of Messina (Italy), La Habana (Cuba), and Gabriel René Moreno in Santa Cruz de la Sierra (Bolivia), among others.

He is a member of the Editorial Board of the following journals: *Anuario de Derecho Marítimo*; *Revista de Derecho del Transporte*; *Studia Iuridica Toruniensa* and *Diritto dei Trasporti*.

The Authors

Maria-Victoria Petit-Lavall is a Spanish national and has been working at the University since 1990, being a Full Professor of Commercial Law at Jaume I-University, Castellon (Spain) since 2008. She holds a Law Degree (1988), a Business Studies Degree (1990) and a PhD in Law (1993) from the University of Valencia. Mrs Petit has also been substitute Judge at the Castellon Court of Appeal for fifteen years. She is the author of some one hundred publications, among monographs, articles in scientific reviews and contributions to collective works on various subjects of Commercial Law (Company Law, Banking Law, Insurance Law, Competition Law, Intellectual Property and mostly Transport Law). She has also edited and/or coordinated eleven collective works.

These include the following monographs: Legal status of auditing of financial statements, ICAC, Madrid, 1994; Consumer protection credit: abusive credit terms, Tirant lo Blanch, Valencia, 1996; Agreements between airlines in the Community legislation liberalizing the air transport sector, Tirant lo Blanch, Valencia, 2000; Liability for damages in international air cargo, Comares, Granada, 2007; PETIT-LAVALL/SÁNCHEZ PAVÓN, Future prospects of airport management in Spain, Galician Institute of Transportation Studies and Infrastructure, A Coruña, 2008; Air and Space law, Marcial Pons, Madrid 2014 (co-authored with MORILLAS JARILLO & GUERRERO LEBRÓN).

Prof. Petit has participated as a speaker at numerous courses, masters, PhD courses, seminars and conferences in Spain and abroad, and she has been a visiting Professor at the Universities of Bologna; San Carlos (Guatemala), UTEM (Santiago de Chile); Gabriel René Moreno (Santa Cruz de la Sierra, Bolivia), Autonomous University of Mexico, among others.

She is a member of the Editorial Board of the following scientific journals: *Revista de Derecho del Transporte*; *European Journal of Commercial Contract Law*; *Revista Aranzadi Civil doctrinal*; *La Ley Mercantil*; and *Diritto dei Trasporti*.

She has also formed part of numerous tribunals to judge PhD thesis and of different boards of examination for future professors and lecturers, and she has been a member of the research group or the director of more than fifteen competitively funded research projects. Since 2014, she is the Director of the Institute of Transport Law at Jaume I-University.

The Authors

Achim Puetz is a German citizen resident in Spain. He holds a Law and a Masters degree in Transport Law and Administration (2006), as well as a European PhD (Law) from Jaume I-University of Castellon (Spain) in 2008, for which he received the outstanding doctorate award. Bilingual in Spanish and German and with an advanced knowledge of English, French and Italian, he is a senior lecturer of Commercial Law at Jaume I-University since September 2012. He has also lectured as a visiting professor, mostly on transport law, in degree, Masters and PhD studies at other higher education institutions in Spain (Complutense University, Madrid; Catholic University of Valencia) and abroad (Université Catholique de Lille, Università degli Studi di Cagliari, Universidad de San Carlos de Guatemala). He is the author of a monograph on rail wagon law (Madrid, 2012) and has published numerous research articles and contributions to collective works, both in transport matters and in other areas of commercial law (company law, antitrust and unfair competition law, insurance and factoring contract, insolvency law). Dr Puetz holds the position of the academic secretary of the Institute for Transport Law (IDT) at Jaume I-University and is the director of its Master in Transport Law. He frequently participates as a speaker in conferences and seminars on transport law and has carried out research stays at renowned institutions in Germany, such as the Max Planck Institutes for Comparative and International Private Law (Hamburg) and for Intellectual Property, Competition and Tax Law (Munich), or Prof. Dr Ingo Koller's chair at Regensburg University; in Switzerland, at the Swiss Institute of Comparative Law (Lausanne); and in Uruguay, at the University of the Republic (Montevideo).

The Authors

Table of Contents

Preface

This monograph constitutes an introduction to Spanish transport law, providing an overview of the private law regulation of domestic origin in Spain, avoiding whenever possible issues of public law. Nonetheless, reference will naturally be made to the most important International Treaties or Conventions and to EU regulations in the field of transport law, to the extent that they affect national commercial law and private law matters.

Consequently, this monograph aims at approaching Spanish transportation law to readers from abroad. Although transport is characterized nowadays by its uniformity, it is nonetheless true that, together with international and/or European provisions, domestic law continues to play a very important role. On the one hand, because international or EU regulations usually fail to provide a complete legal framework for transport and leave many aspects to domestic law. On the other hand, it is almost always national courts that will have to apply both national and international rules.

It should be highlighted that, during the last years, Spain has made an important effort to profoundly amend and reform the national law relating to transport, in particular, with respect to road, rail and maritime transport. There is, however, still an urgent need to reform the domestic law applicable to air transport, especially the carriage of goods by air.

The present contribution is a result of the research Project entitled '*Transport as a Motor of Socio-Economic Development: Protection of the Weak Contracting Party and Progress as regards Transport Sector Regulation*', (DER2015-65424-C4-3-P), financed by the Ministry of Economy and Competitiveness (*Ministerio de Economía y Competitividad*), cofinanced by the European Regional Development Fund (MINECO/FEDER).

Cadis & Castellon de la Plana,
June 2017.

List of Abbreviations

ANA	Air Navigation Act (Act No 48/1960, of 21 June, on Air Navigation (*Ley de Navegación Aérea*)).
AOLTA	Administrative Organisation of Land Transport Act (Act No 16/1987, of 30 July, on the Administrative Organisation of Land Transport (*Ley de Ordenación de los Transportes Terrestres*)).
AP	Court of Appeal (*Audiencia Provincial*).
Art. / Arts.	Article / Articles.
B.O.E.	Official Journal (*Boletín Oficial del Estado*).
CMI	International Maritime Committee.
CMR	Convention on the Contract for the International Carriage of Goods by Road, signed in Geneva on 19 May 1956.
COGLA	Carriage of Goods by Land Act (Act No 15/2009, of 11 November, on the Contract for the Carriage of Goods by Land (*Ley del Contrato de Transporte Terrestre de Mercancías por Carretera*)).
COTIF	Convention concerning International Carriage by Rail, as amended by the Vilnius Protocol in force from 1 July 2006.
ECJ	European Court of Justice.
EU	European Union.
LLMC	Convention on Limitation of Liability for Maritime Claims, done at London on 19 November 1976.
MARPOL	International Convention for the Prevention of Pollution from Ships, adopted on 2 November 1973, as amended in 1978.
MC	Convention for the Unification of Certain Rules for International Carriage by Air (the Montreal Convention), of 28 May 1999.

List of Abbreviations

MLC	Maritime Labour Convention, 2006, as amended.
MNA	Maritime Navigation Act (Act No 14/2014, of 24 July, on Maritime Navigation (*Ley de Navegación Marítima*)).
O.J.	Official Journal of the European Union.
RAMB	*Registro de Abanderamiento y Matriculación de Buques* (Maritime Register), as regulated in Royal Decree 1027/1989, of 28 July, on the Flagging and Registry of Ships, as well as on the Maritime Register.
RSA	Rail Sector Act (Act No 38/2015, of 29 September, on the Rail Sector (*Ley del Sector Ferroviario*)).
RSR	Rail Sector Regulation (*Reglamento del Sector Ferroviario*), approved by Royal Decree 2387/2004, of 30 December.
SPMNA	Consolidated Text of the Act on State Ports and Merchant Navy (*Ley de Puertos del Estado y de la Marina Mercante*), approved by Royal Legislative Decree 2/2011, of 5 September.
SDR	Special Drawing Right of the International Monetary Fund.
STCW	International Convention on Standards of Training, Certification and Watchkeeping, 1978, as amended in 1995.
TS	Supreme Court (*Tribunal Supremo*).
UNCLOS	United Nations Convention on the Law of the Sea, of 10 December 1982.
WC	Convention for the Unification of Certain Rules of Law on International Transport by Air, signed at Warsaw on 12 October 1929 (The Warsaw Convention 1929).
YAR	York-Antwerp Rules

General Introduction

by Maria-Victoria Petit-Lavall

§1. Geography

1. The Kingdom of Spain is located in the southwest of Europe.[1] Most of the territory of Spain is situated, along with Portugal, on the Iberian Peninsula. Covering an area of 506,030 square kilometres, it is among the fifty largest countries in the world, the third European country in extension and the fifth in population. Its total extension includes both the peninsular territory and adjacent islands, as the archipelagos of the Canary Islands in the Atlantic Ocean and the Balearics in the Mediterranean Sea, other smaller islands and the autonomous cities of Ceuta and Melilla, located in the north of the African continent.

The Spanish coastline is 5,755 kilometres long, bathed by the Mediterranean Sea in the east, from the Pyrenees to Gibraltar; by the Atlantic Ocean in the south, from Gibraltar to the Portuguese border, and in the west (Galicia); and in the north by the Cantabrian Sea. The Atlantic Ocean is connected with the Mediterranean Sea by a narrow channel called the Strait of Gibraltar.

To the north, Spain limits with France and Andorra, finding its natural border in the Pyrenees. To the west, it limits with Portugal.

The surface of Spain is extremely diverse and is characterized by a relatively high average altitude of over 600 metres above sea level. This is due to the presence at the centre of the Peninsula of a vast plateau, known as the *Meseta*, divided into two smaller plateaus by the *Sistema Central* mountain range. A series of other mountain ranges around the plateau and others located on the edges of the peninsula complete the topographical analysis. There are two depressions (the Ebro and Guadalquivir river valleys) located between the *Meseta* and the peripheral ranges.

Its main rivers are the Duero, Tajo, Guadiana and Guadalquivir on the Atlantic slope and the Ebro on the Mediterranean.

§2. Demography

2. In 2016, the Spanish population was nearly 46.4 million people. Of this total population, 4.4 million are of foreign nationality. Madrid is the capital of the State

1. Data have been obtained from: *http://www.lamoncloa.gob.es/Paginas/index.aspx*; *http://www.ine.es/*; *https://www.fomento.gob.es/mfom/lang_castellano/default.htm*.

and the largest city with more than 3 million inhabitants. Other large cities are Barcelona (1.6 million), Valencia (790,200) or Seville (690,500).

§3. Information on the Political and Legal System of the Country-Form of Government

3. The Kingdom of Spain is a sovereign country, member of the European Union since 1 January 1986. Established as a social and democratic State of Law, it is subject to the rule of law, which advocates freedom, justice, equality and political pluralism as highest values of its legal system. The political form of the Spanish State is the Parliamentary Monarchy. The King is the head of State and symbolizes the unity and presence of the State. He arbitrates and moderates the regular functioning of the institutions and assumes the highest representation of the Spanish State in international relations. Since 2014, Felipe VI, King of Spain, occupies the throne.

The Parliament (*Cortes Generales*) represents the Spanish people, exercises the legislative power of the State and adopts its budget, controls the action of the Government and has other competences assigned to it by the Constitution. The *Cortes Generales* comprise two Houses: the House of Representatives and the Senate. It is, therefore, a bicameral parliamentary system, of the type called 'imperfect bicameralism'.

The Government shall consist of the President, Vice-Presidents, when appropriate, Ministers and other members, as may be created by law. It exercises executive authority and the power of statutory regulations in accordance with the Constitution and the laws. The Government shall conduct domestic and foreign policy, civil and military administration and the defence of the State.

4. The Constitution of 29 December 1978 is the fundamental rule of law, based on the indissoluble unity of the Spanish Nation. Nonetheless, at the same time, it recognizes and guarantees the right to self-government of the nationalities and regions Spain is composed of and the solidarity among them all. More specifically, the Spanish territory, with its capital in Madrid, is organized in seventeen Autonomous Communities and two Autonomous Cities (Ceuta and Melilla), with the consequent redistribution of political and administrative power between central and autonomous authorities. This redistribution of power has turned Spain into one of the most decentralized countries in Europe. Each Autonomous Community has its Statute of Regional Autonomy, which is the basic institutional regulation of the Community.

Furthermore, Spain is divided into 50 provinces and 8,117 municipalities. The institutions of government and administration of the provinces are provincial councils (*diputacionesprovinciales*) those of municipalities are councils (*ayuntamientos*), and those of the islands the island councils or *Cabildos* and *Consejos Insulares* on the Canary Islands and the Balearics, respectively.

Castilian or 'Spanish' is the official language of the State, although there are other languages that are co-official in some Autonomous Communities in accordance with their Statutes, such as Catalan, Valencian, Basque and Galician.

Spain forms part of the group of countries with the most advanced level of development. It plays an active role in the main international forums and organizations, such as the UN, the NATO, the OECD and the G-20.

§4. Population and Employment: Social and Cultural Values

5. The recent economic crisis (the 'Great Recession') has had severe adverse effects on the Spanish labour market, although in 2014 the economy slowly began to undertake the path of recovery that has led to the creation of 440,000 new jobs.

However, the data for 2016 show that, from a working population of 18,508,100 people, almost one-quarter is unemployed. The unemployment rate varies between 14.9% in Navarre and 34.2% in Andalusia, and is particularly high among those under the age of 25 (51.8%).

6. The Spanish economy is characterized by a high weight of the services sector and by a low presence of the industrial sector. In fact, the service sector represented 75% of the economy in 2015; followed by far by the industry and energy (15.6%), construction (10.1%) and agriculture and fishing (2.7%) sectors.

The main destinations for Spanish exports are all European countries, mainly France, Germany, the United Kingdom and Italy, accounting for 16.09%, 11.29%, 7.60% and 7.57% of the country's total exports, respectively.

The main products exported from Spain are cars, parts and accessories of vehicles, delivery trucks, medicines, oil and its derivatives and horticultural products.

7. The geographical situation and the vicissitudes of the history have made Spain a place of meeting for the most diverse cultures. It therefore owns a rich and heterogeneous cultural legacy. Spanish culture encompasses all forms of expression from literature to painting, from music to architecture, from theatre to cinema. In fact, Spain is one of the richest countries in the world in terms of monumental heritage, being the second country with the largest number of UNESCO World Heritage declarations.

§5. General Introduction Relating to Transportation

8. Transport in its different modes represents a 5.5% of the Spanish GDP.

Spain, due to its geographic location and cultural influences, is a meeting point between Europe, Africa, the Middle East and Latin America. On the one hand, it is a peninsula almost in its entirety surrounded by sea with an outlet to the Atlantic Ocean and another one to the Mediterranean Sea with nearly 7,800 kilometres of coast, including the islands, so that international maritime transport plays an important role. On the other hand, the historical influence of Spain in Latin America (nowadays, about 500 million people in the world speak Spanish) has turned the country into a bridge between the two continents, so that international air transport has great relevance too.

With regard to transport by land, road is the primary mode of inland transport of persons and goods, although the improvement and development of carriage by rail is a priority for the Spanish Government. From 2012 on, 619 kilometres of high-speed lines have been put into service. The objectives of the actions that have been developed or that are still in the planning stage are to complete the main strategic axes and achieve significant reductions in travel time between major cities.

§6. Inland Waterways and Ports

9. Inland navigation is of little importance, since there are only 89 kilometres of navigable inland waterways. The Port of Seville is the only inland port that exists in the country.

§7. Railroads

10. In the Spanish railway system, different networks can be distinguished. The most extensive one, that supports the highest traffic density, corresponds to the Rail Network of General Interest (*Red Ferroviaria de Interés General*), that is managed by the publicly-owned Administrador de Infraestructuras Ferroviarias (ADIF) and covers the whole Peninsula. On a second level, we find the regional rail networks, which are run entirely by the relevant Autonomous Community (Railways of the Catalonian Regional Government; Railways of the Valencian Regional Government; Railway Infrastructure of the Basque Country and Majorca Services Railway).

Spain's active railway network comprises over 15,500 kilometres of track, the vast majority of which is managed by ADIF. More than 3,200 kilometres are designed for high-speed trains.

Hence, Spain is the country with the longest high-speed rail network in Europe, and the second largest in the world, only behind China. Some 400 high-speed trains travel on the network every day, carrying almost 96,000 passengers daily and arriving at over 132 Spanish cities. Spain currently has 47 high-speed stations in 27 provinces.

§8. Road Systems

11. Spain's State Road Network is over 166,000 kilometres long, making it the longest network of highways and motorways in Europe (15,000 kilometres).

Roads represent the main means of transport chosen by people in Spain to travel around the country – accounting for 90% of all transport – and the main means of freight transport, too, accounting for 84% of all carriage of freight.

§9. Airports

12. Air transport is a strategic sector for Spain, due to its socio-economic impact and its contribution in terms of connectivity, accessibility and territorial cohesion and structure.

Spain has 52 airports, 48 of which are classified as of general interest and are managed by AENA (the public entity ENAIRE owns 51% of its shares). It is estimated that the 46 airports and two heliports managed by AENA, where more than 6,000 companies provide their services, generate 146,500 direct jobs and 440,000 jobs in total, equivalent to a 2% of the country's labour force.

A total of 230.2 million passengers passed through the Spanish airports of the AENA network in 2016, enabling AENA to consolidate itself as the leading airport manager in the world in terms of passenger numbers.

§10. Seaports

13. Spain has the longest coastline of all EU countries, with nearly 7,800 kilometres of coast, including the islands. Over 90% of Spanish frontiers are maritime borders. The Strait of Gibraltar in the south is the second-busiest stretch of water in the world (after the English Channel). Over 198,000 ships passed through it in 2014. Including merchant ships and ferries, this is almost 300 boats per day. In the north, 60,000 ships sail around the Finisterre Cape every year, situated on the northwestern edge of Spain.

The forty-six Spanish ports of general interest are managed by twenty-eight port authorities, under the coordination of the public entity Ports of the State (*Puertos del Estado*). Furthermore, Spain is the third-largest European country (behind Germany and the Netherlands) in terms of container port movements and eleventh in the world. Three Spanish ports (Algeciras, Valencia and Barcelona) are among the twenty most important ports in Europe in terms of container freight traffic.

14. The Spanish ports have become references in Europe in cruise traffic in recent years, too. The figures (around 8 million cruise passengers) represent the consolidation of this type of tourism. In particular, with 2.5 million cruise passengers in 2015, Barcelona was the leading European port and ranked fourth in the world as a home port. The Balearic Islands were visited by 1.7 million passengers and the Canary Islands by over 2.1 million.

§11. Pipelines

15. At present, the oil and gas pipelines sum in total several thousand kilometres. The oil pipeline network is branched, entirely national and limited to Peninsular Spain. The gas pipeline network is meshed with international connections:

France, Portugal and North Africa. At the end of 2010, the length of these two networks was 4,365 kilometres and 8,981 kilometres, respectively.[2]

§12. Ministry or Department Responsible for Transport Policy

16. Pursuant to the Spanish Constitution, the State holds exclusive competence over merchant navy and the registering of ships; lighting of coasts and signals at sea; ports and airports of general interest; control of air space, air traffic and transport; meteorological services and registration of aircraft (Article 149 (1) (20)); and railways and land transport passing through the territory of more than one Autonomous Community; general system of communications; motor vehicle traffic; Postal services and telecommunications; air and underwater cables and radio communications (Article 149.1.21).

In this respect, the Ministry of Public Works and Transport (*Ministerio de Fomento*) in Madrid is the main department in charge of transport policy in Spain.

17. Nonetheless, pursuant to Article 148 of the Constitution, Autonomous Communities may assume competences over rail and road infrastructures situated exclusively within their territory, as well as those transport services by rail, road or cable which fulfil the same conditions (paragraph 1.5); over ports of refuge, recreational ports and airports and, in general, those which are not engaged in commercial activities (paragraph 1.6). In fact, most Autonomous Communities have assumed these competences in their own internal legislation.

2. CEGARRA PLANÉ, M., *Consumo de energía y emisiones asociadas al transporte por tubería*, Fundación Agustín de Betancourt, Monografías EnerTrans 17, 2008, pp. 3 y ss.; http://www.fomento.es.

Part I. Introduction

Chapter 1. Definitions and Notions

by Maria-Victoria Petit-Lavall

§1. Maritime Law and Transport Law

18. Spain is a country with an important maritime legal tradition. In fact, one of the first compilations of commercial maritime usages and customs can be found in the so-called Book of the Consulate of the Sea (*Llibre del Consolat del Mar*), from the fourteenth century. Until recently, maritime law has been contained in the Commercial Code of 1885 (Articles 573 et seq.) and has thus historically been linked to commercial navigation.

However, Act 14/2014, of 24 July, on Maritime Navigation (MNA), actually in force, has somewhat shifted the perspective and, according to the authors who commented the act, configures maritime law as an autonomous and special field of law. According to Article 1 (1) MNA, the purpose of the Act is the regulation of situations and legal relationships that arise on the occasion of maritime navigation. Thus, the MNA carries out an important and broad reform of Spanish maritime law in all its aspects, both public and private law, and opts for a broad concept of maritime law, although the ports regulation remains apart.

On the one hand, the Act exceeds the commercial aspects of the subject, as the sea is not only analysed from the perspective of the commercial activity of trade or of transport for commercial purposes, but as a medium that serves as the basis for many types of activities, whether profitable or not. All institutions included in the Act share a common feature: their existence responds to the effective exposure of people and properties to the risks of the sea. In this sense, the MNA is articulated around the risks of maritime navigation.

On the other, the Act takes into account the uniformity and internationality of the subject. It adjusts the maritime law to the current practice of maritime transport and, at the same time, coordinates domestic law with international maritime law, that is, with the regulation contained in international treaties in force in Spain.

19. The Act establishes a new branch of law, maritime navigation law, which intends to be complete and self-sufficient in its regulation, inspired by its own principles and endowed with organic and legislative autonomy. In fact, this derives from

Article 2 MNA, when it establishes the autonomy of sources and of the interpretation criteria.

Pursuant to this provision, the Act shall apply when it is not contrary to international treaties in force in Spain and to the rules of the European Union governing the same subject matter. Subsidiarily, the acts and complementary regulations, as well as the usages and customs relating to maritime navigation shall apply. Only absent any specific regulation or usage, and when it is impossible to resort to analogy, general civil law shall apply. In any case, the interpretation of the provisions of the Act will have to take into account the regulation contained in international treaties in force in Spain and the desirability of promoting uniformity in the matters contained in it.

As a result, from now on the application of international treaties and EU Law will take precedence in the field of maritime navigation.

20. It should be noted that the Act also applies to navigation by inland waterways, but only in two cases: (*a*) when they are accessible for vessels from the sea, as far as the effect of the tides is felt; and (*b*) where it is carried out on navigable sections of rivers, as far as where there are ports of general interest (Article 1 (2) MNA). Thus, the Act is applicable to the navigation on the Guadalquivir River until the Port of Seville, as well as on the Galician estuaries.

In all other cases, navigation on inland waterways shall be governed by public water legislation and Act No 15/2009, of 11 November, on the Contract of Carriage of Goods by Land, that extends its scope of application to inland navigation (First Additional Provision).

21. Historically, it should be noted that some authors have denied the autonomy of maritime law. According to them, the core of maritime law is the operation of the ship for the purpose of transportation, which is also present in other forms of navigation, in particular, in air law. In this sense, it has been considered that there is a set of common principles in navigation law and in navigation by other means, the contract of carriage. Transport law would then be the branch of the legal system that regulates the contractual relationships by virtue of which one of the parties assumes the transportation of persons or goods, regardless of the medium the vehicle moves in (sea, air, land or even space). In this regard, the objective that should be pursued is a unified legal regulation of all modes of transport. In fact, the obligations of the parties, the liability regime, the documents, or even the agents involved in contracts of carriage in the different modes are becoming more and more similar.

Nonetheless, in Spain, as well as in international transport, such a unified regulation is far from becoming a reality in the short or medium term. In the recent years, the Spanish legislator has passed different Acts regulating each mode of transport, at least with respect to road, rail or maritime transport. Surprisingly, the ancient Air Navigation Act, dating back to 1960, has not yet been amended. Even more, the project of a new Commercial Code, presented in 2014, does not contain a regulation of the contract of carriage nor its definition in Title VI of Book V, but refers to the special Acts governing each mode of transport.

§2. LAW OF THE SEA

22. The Law of the Sea is a branch of international public law that counts on an own international legal instrument, the United Nations Convention on the Law of the Sea (UNCLOS), of 10 December 1982 (Montego Bay Convention). Traditionally, Law of the Sea, which regulates the relationships between States, has been distinguished from Maritime Law, which envisages relationships *inter privatus*.

However, as of today, public and private law converge in the legal regime of maritime navigation, both on a domestic and on an international level. This reality is present in the MNA, since it contains not only provisions on private maritime law, but also on administrative and even public international law. As stated in the Preamble, the Act carries out a comprehensive reform of the Spanish maritime law, contemplating all its aspects.

As a matter of fact, its first title is inspired mainly by the Montego Bay Convention and contains a basic and systematic regulation of waterway police, which has to be completed with the (public law) regulation on state ports and merchant navy. Moreover, the MNA has been given birth with the aim of reforming the pre-existent regulation. Its ninth final provision enables the Government to recast, within a period of three years, in one single text entitled 'Code of Maritime Navigation', the laws regulating all maritime institutions, regularizing, clarifying and harmonizing the Maritime Navigation Act with the consolidated text of the Act on State Ports and the Merchant Navy, approved by Royal Legislative Decree 2/2011, of 5 September.

Nonetheless, the analysis of most of these public law provisions exceeds the objective of the present treatise that, as has been said, remains limited mainly to the description of private law issued related to maritime and transport Law.

Chapter 2. Main Sources of Transport Law (Treaties and National Legislation)

by Maria-Victoria Petit-Lavall

§1. Introduction

23. Spain has duly ratified and published in the Official Gazette (*Boletín Oficial del Estado*) most International Treaties and Conventions dealing with transport, both on public and private law issues. By way of their ratification or acceptance, they become a part of the Spanish legal system. Pursuant to Article 96 (1) of the Spanish Constitution, '(v)alidly concluded international treaties, once officially published in Spain, shall form part of the internal legal order. Their provisions may only be repealed, amended or suspended in the manner provided in the treaties themselves or in accordance with the general rules of international law'.

At the same time, since 1 January 1986, when Spain acceded to the then called European Economic Community (nowadays EU), Spain is required to provide all conditions for the effective implementation of EU law (the *acquis communautaire*). As a result, EU regulations, directives and decisions are directly applicable in Spain or have to be implemented into national law.

Naturally, Spain has its own national legislation on this subject, too. This could not be otherwise since, on the one hand, International Treaties and Conventions do not fully regulate transportation but leave many questions to internal law; on the other hand, EU directives have to be transposed to domestic law.

§2. Maritime Law

24. International Treaties:

- Convention for the Unification of Certain Rules of Law respecting Assistance and Salvage at Sea (Brussels, 23 September 1910) (Madrid Gazette of 13 December 1923).
- International Convention for the Unification of Certain Rules of Law Relating to Bills of Lading, 1924 ('Hague Rules'), as amended by the 1968 Protocol to Amend the International Convention for the Unification of Certain Rules of Law Relating to Bills of Lading, 1924 ('Visby Amendments') and the 1979 Protocol Amending the International Convention for the Unification of Certain Rules of Law Relating to Bills of Lading, 1924 ('SDR Protocol') (Hague-Visby-Rules 1968) ratified on 11 February 1984 (*B.O.E.* No 36, of 11 February 1984).
- International Convention on Civil Liability for Oil Pollution Damage (CLC), adopted on 29 November 1969 (entry into force on 19 June 1975) replaced by Protocol of 27 November 1992; entry into force: 30 May 1996.
- International Convention for the Prevention of Pollution from Ships (MARPOL), adopted on 2 November 1973, as amended in 1978.

- Convention on Limitation of Liability for Maritime Claims (LLMC),London, 19 November 1976, as amended by Protocol of 1996 to amend the Convention on Limitation of Liability for Maritime Claims of 19 November 1976, London, 2 May 1996, entered into force on 10 April 2005 (*B.O.E.* No 50, of 28 February 2005).
- United Nations Convention on the Carriage of Goods by Sea (Hamburg, 1978) (the 'Hamburg Rules'), entered into force on 1 November 1992 (*neither signed nor accessed by Spain*).
- United Nations Convention on the Law of the Sea of 10 December 1982 (Montego Bay Convention) which entered into force in Spain on 14 February 1997 (*B.O.E.* No 39, of 14 February 1997).
- International Convention on Salvage, London, 28 April 1989, entered into force on 27 January 2006 (*B.O.E.* No 57, of 8 March 2005).
- United Nations Convention on the Liability of Operators of Transport Terminals in International Trade (Vienna, 19 April 1991) signed on 19 April 1991 (*not in force*).
- International Convention on Standards of Training, Certification and Watchkeeping for Seafarers (STCW), adopted on 7 July 1978.
- International Convention on Maritime Liens and Mortgages, done at Geneva on 6 May 1993.
- International Convention on Arrest of Ships, Geneva, 12 March 1999, entered into force on 14 September 2011 (*B.O.E.* No 104, of 2 May 2011).
- International Convention on Civil Liability for Bunker Oil Pollution Damage, London 23 March 2001(BUNKERS, 2001), entered into force on 21 November 2008 (*B.O.E.* No 43, of 19 February 2008).
- Maritime Labour Convention, 2006, as amended.
- United Nations Convention on Contracts for the International Carriage of Goods Wholly or Partly by Sea (New York, 2008) (the 'Rotterdam Rules'), signed on 19 January 2011 (*ratified by Spain, but not yet in force*).
- York-Antwerp Rules (YAR) 2016, adopted by the Comité Maritime International (CMI).

25. EU Regulations:

- Regulation (EC) No 392/2009 of the European Parliament and of the Council of 23 April 2009 on the liability of carriers of passengers by sea in the event of accidents (*OJ* L 131, of 28 May 2009).
- Regulation (EU) No 1177/2010 of the European Parliament and of the Council of 24 November 2010 concerning the rights of passengers when travelling by sea and inland waterway and amending Regulation (EC) No 2006/2004 (*OJ* L 334, of 17 December 2010).

26. National Legislation:

- Act No 14/2014, of 24 July, on Maritime Navigation (*B.O.E.* No 180, of 25 July 2014).

– Consolidated Text of the Act on State Ports and Merchant Navy, approved by Royal Legislative Decree 2/2011, of 5 September (*B.O.E.* No 253, of 20 October 2011).

§3. Inland Navigation

27. EU Regulations:

– Regulation (EU) No 1177/2010 of the European Parliament and of the Council of 24 November 2010 concerning the rights of passengers when travelling by sea and inland waterway and amending Regulation (EC) No 2006/2004 (OJ L 334, of 17 December 2010).

28. National Legislation:

– Act No 15/2009, of 11 November, on the contract of carriage of goods by land (first additional provision) (*B.O.E.* No 273, of 12 November 2009).
– Act No 14/2014, of 24 July, on Maritime Navigation (*B.O.E.* No 180, of 25 July 2014).

§4. Rail Transport

29. International *Treaties:*

– Convention concerning International Carriage by Rail (COTIF) of 9 May 1980, as amended by the Vilnius Protocol of 3 June 1999 (in force from 1 January 2006) together with its Appendices, in particular: Uniform Rules concerning the Contract of International Carriage of Passengers by Rail (CIV – Appendix A); Uniform Rules Concerning the Contract of International Carriage of Goods by Rail (CIM – Appendix B); Regulation concerning the International Carriage of Dangerous Goods by Rail (RID – Appendix C).

30. EU Regulations:

– Regulation (EC) No 1371/2007 of the European Parliament and of the Council of 23 October 2007 on rail passengers' rights and obligations (*OJ* L 315, of 3 December 2007).

31. National Legislation:

– Rail Sector Regulation, approved by Royal Decree 2387/2004, of 30 December (*B.O.E.* No 315, of 31 December 2004).
– Act No 15/2009, of 11 November, on the contract of carriage of goods by land (*B.O.E.* No 273, of 12 November 2009).

- Act No 38/2015, of 29 September, on the Rail Sector (*B.O.E.* No 234, of 30 September 2015).

§5. ROAD TRANSPORT

32. International Treaties:

- Convention on the Contract for the International Carriage of Goods by Road, signed in Geneva on 19 May 1956 (CMR), which entered into force in July 1961.
- Protocol to the Convention on the Contract for the International Carriage of Goods by Road (CMR), signed in Geneva on 5 July 1978.
- Additional Protocol to the Convention on the Contract for the International Carriage of Goods by Road (CMR) concerning the Electronic Consignment Note, Geneva, 27 May 2008.

33. EU Regulations:

- Regulation (EU) No 181/2011 of the European Parliament and of the Council of 16 February 2011 concerning the rights of passengers in bus and coach transport and amending Regulation (EC) No 2006/2004 (*OJ* L 55, of 28 February 2011).

34. National Legislation:

- Act No 16/1987, of 30 July, on the Administrative Organisation of Land Transport (*B.O.E.* No 182, of 31 July 1987). It has been amended by: Act No 13/1996, of 30 December; Act No 66/1997, of 30 December; Royal Decree-Law 6/1998, of 5 June; Royal Decree-Law 4/2000, of 23 June; Act No 14/2000, of 29 December; Act No 24/2001, of 27 December; Act No 29/2003, of 8 October; Act No 25/2009, of 22 December; Act No 2/2011, of 4 March; and Act No 9/2013, of 4 July.
- Regulation implementing the Administrative Organisation of Land Transport Act, approved by Royal Decree 1211/90, of 28 September (*B.O.E.* No 241, of 8 October 1990). It has been modified by: Royal Decree 858/1994, of 29 April; Royal Decree 1136/97, of 11 July; Royal Decree 927/98, of 14 May; Royal Decree 1830/99, of 3 December; Royal Decree 1225/2006, of 27 October; Article 21 of Act No 25/2009, of 22 December; Royal Decree 919/2010, of 16 July; Act 9/2013, of 4 July; Royal Decree 1057/2015, of 20 November; and it has been partially repealed by Act No 13/1996, of 30 December. Titles VII and VIII have been substantially affected by Act No 39/2003, of 17 November, on the Railway Sector and its implementing rules.
- Act No 15/2009, of 11 November, on the contract of carriage of goods by land (*B.O.E.* No273, of 12 November 2009).
- Order of the Ministry of Public Works and Transport FOM/1882/2012, of 1 August, establishing general conditions of contracts for the carriage of goods by road.

§6. Air Transport

35. Air transport has a marked international or globalized character, with a high degree of coherence between the internal rules of each State and international standards. In fact, it is one of the few disciplines in which international law has preceded domestic law and in which the rules of public law have been replaced by rules of private law. Nonetheless, one cannot lose sight of the influence of States on the regulation of the exercise of traffic rights and market access, although increasingly subject to free competition.

At the same time, air transport has a strong European character. The liberalization of the sector, on the one hand, and the configuration of the passenger as a consumer – and, therefore, the weak part of the contract – on the other, have highlighted the special attention paid by the European Union to his or her protection with the adoption of different legislative measures.

36. Spain has ratified most of the International Treaties governing international air transport and, as a Member State of the EU, all European Regulations are directly applicable. In particular:

International Treaties:

1) The so-called Warsaw System integrated by:
   - Convention for the Unification of Certain Rules of Law on International Transport by Air, signed in Warsaw, 1929 (The Warsaw Convention 1929) (Instrument of Ratification of 31 January 1930 (*Madrid Gazette* No 233, of 21 August 1931)).
   - Protocol to Amend the Convention for the Unification of Certain Rules Relating to International Carriage by Air, signed on 28 September 1955 in The Hague (The Hague Protocol 1955) (Instrument of Ratification of 6 December 1965 (*B.O.E.* No 133, of 4 June 1973)).
   - Montreal Additional Protocols Number 1, 2 and 4 to amend the said Convention, of 25 September 1975 (*B.O.E.* No 147, of 20 June 1997, and *B.O.E.* No 34, of 9 February 1999).
2) Convention for the Unification of Certain Rules for International Carriage by Air (the Montreal Convention) of 28 May 1999, which entered into force on 4 November 2003 (Instrument of Ratification of 11 May 2004 (*B.O.E.* No 122, of 20 May 2004)).

EU Regulations:

- Regulation (EC) No 889/2002 of the European Parliament and of the Council of 13 May 2002 amending Council Regulation (EC) No 2027/97 on air carrier liability in the event of accidents (*OJ* L 140, of 30 May 2002).
- Regulation (EC) No 261/2004 of the European Parliament and of the Council of 11 February 2004 establishing common rules on compensation and assistance to passengers in the event of denied boarding and of cancellation or long delay of

flights, and repealing Regulation (EEC) No 295/91 (*OJ* L 46, of 17 February 2004).

- Regulation (EC) No 1107/2006 of the European Parliament and of the Council of 5 July 2006 concerning the rights of disabled persons and persons with reduced mobility when travelling by air (*OJ* L 204, of 26 July 2006).

National Legislation:

- Act No 48/1960, of 21 June, on Air Navigation (*B.O.E.* No 176, of 23 July 1960).

§7. Multimodal Transportation

37. By the moment there is no International Treaty or EU Regulation on multimodal transport in force (the United Nations Convention on International Multimodal Transport of Goods, Geneva, 24 May 1980 has never come to enter into force).

Spain has no global domestic regulation, either.

Chapter 3. Jurisdiction and Courts

by Maria-Victoria Petit-Lavall and Achim Puetz

38. Most international conventions on transport contain rules on international jurisdiction. Naturally, such rules are to be applied by Spanish state courts since, with the ratification of or the accession to the international instrument, it becomes a part of the domestic legal system. However, the relationship between such conventions on particular matters and Regulation No 1215/2015 of the European Parliament and of the Council of 12 December 2012 on jurisdiction and the recognition and enforcement of judgments in civil and commercial matters (Brussels Ia) is not yet clear. In a first judgment, still referred to the 1968 Brussels Convention, the European Court of Justice (ECJ) found that the existence of a convention on particular matters only precludes the application of the 1968 Brussels Convention (and, as of today, the Brussels Ia Regulation) to the extent to which the case is governed by the specialized convention, while in all other cases the Brussels Convention (today, Brussels Ia Regulation) shall apply. With respect to the *lis pendens* rule in Article 21 of the 1968 Brussels Convention, it further stated that 'an action seeking to have the defendant held liable for causing loss and ordered to pay damages has the same cause of action and the same object as earlier proceedings brought by the defendant seeking a declaration that he is not liable for that loss' (a so-called negative declaratory action).[3]

Other conflictive issues related to Brussels Ia Regulation have also been decided by the ECJ, with respect to conventions that have been adopted before Regulation No 44/2001 (Brussels I) came into force. Pursuant to Article 71 Brussels Ia Regulation, in such cases, the Regulation 'shall not affect any conventions to which the Member States are parties and which, in relation to particular matters, govern jurisdiction or the recognition and enforcement of judgments'. However, in its *TNT*-judgment of 4 May 2010 (C-533/08), the ECJ held that the rules on jurisdiction, *lis pendens* and enforcement laid down in such conventions on particular matters shall only apply if they are highly predictable; facilitate the sound administration of justice; enable the risk of concurrent proceedings to be minimized; and ensure, under conditions at least as favourable as those in Brussels Ia Regulation, the free movement of judgments in civil and commercial matters and mutual trust in the administration of justice in the European Union (*favor executionis*). Finally, with respect to *lis pendens*, the Court had the occasion to once more rule on a 'negative declaratory action': in its 2013 *Nipponkoa*-judgment,[4] it declared that Article 71 Brussels Ia Regulation precludes an international convention form being interpreted in a way that does not guarantee the objectives and principles that underlie the Regulation, so that rules on *lis pendens* in conventions on particular matters may not be interpreted in the sense that an action for a negative declaration does not have the same ground of action as an action for indemnity between the same parties. Thus, once a negative declaratory action has been filed, no fresh action can be brought between

3. ECJ, judgment of 6 Dec. 1994, case C-406/92, *The Tatry*.
4. ECJ, judgment of 19 Dec. 2013, case C-452/12, *Nipponkoa*.

the same parties and the court seized in the second place has to stay the proceedings until a judgment is delivered by the court seized in the first place.

Be that as it may, the disconnection clause in Article 71 Brussels Ia Regulation (pursuant to which the Regulation shall not affect jurisdiction rules in conventions on particular matters) does not apply to conventions that have come into force after Regulation No 44/2001 (Brussels I) did so on 1 March 2002. This is the case, for example, for the amended version of the COTIF convention on international carriage by rail. However, as regards the jurisdiction and *lis pendens* rules in this particular convention, it seems that they apply directly in all EU Member States, since the European Union itself declared its accession to the convention in 2011 (2013/103/EU), which is binding upon both its institutions and its Member States (Article 67 Brussels Ia Regulation).[5] In cases not covered by the reference to 'conventions on particular matters' (e.g., passenger rights established in European Regulations), Brussels Ia Regulation applies directly.[6]

39. Where international jurisdiction lies with the Spanish courts and tribunals, Organic Act No 6/1985, of 1 July, on the Judiciary, establishes a three-tiered judicial system and assigns the competence to hear claims based on both national and international transport regulations and those relating to the application of maritime law to the Commercial Courts as courts of first instance (Article 86*ter* (2)). Commercial Courts are specialized courts within the civil jurisdiction that, apart from issues related to transport, also deal with other areas of commercial law, such as insolvency law, antitrust law and unfair competition, industrial and intellectual property, company law, as well as collective actions based on general conditions of contracts.

As a general rule, within each province there shall be one or several Commercial Courts, based in the capital of the province and with jurisdiction in all its territory. Their judgments are susceptible of appeal before the Provincial Court of the same circumscription, with the exception of verdicts handed down in oral proceedings when the litigious amount does not exceed EUR 3,000 (Article 455 Act No 1/2000, of 7 January, on Civil Procedure). Appeal in cassation before the Civil Chamber of the Spanish Supreme Court is also possible, at least when the litigious amount exceeds EUR 600,000 or, otherwise, when the revision is of 'cassational interest'. An appeal has such 'cassational interest' where the judgment conflicts with the jurisprudence of the Supreme Court, resolves points and issues on which there is contradictory doctrine of the Provincial Courts or applies rules that have not yet been in force for more than five years. In the latter case, no case law doctrine of the Supreme Court concerning previous rules of the same or similar content is required (Article 477 Act No 1/2000, of 7 January, on Civil Procedure).

40. Arbitration as an alternative means of dispute resolution is envisaged by Act No 60/2003, of 23 December, on Arbitration. It is particularly relevant for road and

5. *See*, however, the judgment of the French *Cour de Cassation* of 29 Nov. 2016: due to the 'disconnection clause' in Art. 2 of the accession agreement between the EU and the OTIF, Brussels I(a) Regulation and not COTIF applies in the mutual relations between EU Member States.
6. *See*, in particular, the ECJ judgment of 9 Jul. 2009, case C-204/08, *Rehder*.

rail transport, both on a domestic and an international level, since Act No 16/1987, of 30 July, on the Administrative Organisation of Land Transport (Articles 37 and 38), created the so-called Arbitral Boards of Transportation, the legal regime of which is contained in Articles 6–12 of the Regulation developing the Act on Administrative Organisation of Land Transport, approved by Royal Decree 1211/90, of 28 September. They hear all commercial disputes relating to the performance of contracts of carriage by land and other contracts on ancillary and complementary activities thereto, whenever the parties have mutually agreed to submit their controversies to the arbitration of the Boards. The remarkable success of the Arbitral Boards of Transportation in Spain is partly due to the fact that a decision is quickly obtained and that the procedure is gratuitous and no lawyer or *procurator litis* is required. However, it could not be explained without reference to the fact that the existence of an arbitration agreement shall be presumed, provided that the amount of the dispute does not exceed EUR 15,000 and none of the parties involved in the contract had expressly stated to the other party his or her will to the contrary before the performance of the transport activity began or should have begun.

Any transport user, carrier, shipper or intermediary who is a contracting party to a contract for the carriage by land, can seize the Arbitration Board. The claim can be filed, at the option of the claimant, at the Arbitral Board of the place of origin of the transport, the place of destination or the place of conclusion of the contract, unless a specific Board has been agreed in the contract.

There are Arbitral Boards of Transportation in all Autonomous Communities and in the cities of Ceuta and Melilla.[7]

7. *https://www.fomento.gob.es/MFOM/LANG_CASTELLANO/DIRECCIONES_GENERALES/TRANSPORTE_TERRESTRE/SERVICIOS_TRANSPORTISTA/JUNTAS_ARBITRALES/.*

Chapter 4. State Immunity and Transport Law

by Maria-Victoria Petit-Lavall

41. The Spanish Constitution contains a clear requirement of compliance with the legal obligations arising from international law (Articles 93–96). This includes the obligations contained in international treaties concluded by Spain on immunities, as well as other types of obligations deriving from customary international law or mandatory decisions of international courts.

Organic Act No 6/1985, of 1 July, on the Judiciary, provides in Article 21 (1) that 'Spanish courts shall hear claims arising in Spanish territory between Spaniards, between foreigners and Spaniards and foreigners pursuant to the provisions of this Act and the treaties and international conventions to which Spain is a party.' Nonetheless, and with regard to immunity, its second paragraph declares that they shall not hear claims with respect to persons or assets that benefit from 'immunity from jurisdiction and execution established by the rules of public international law'. In a similar sense, Act 1/2000, of 7 January, of Civil Procedure also refers to international conventions when it declares that the extent and limits of the jurisdiction of Spanish civil courts shall be determined by the provisions of the Organic Act of the Judiciary and by those of the treaties and international conventions to which Spain is a party. In any case, Spanish civil courts will refrain from hearing a claim submitted to them in the following circumstances:

1) When a claim or a request for execution is submitted with regard to subjects or goods benefitting from immunity from jurisdiction or execution in accordance with the Spanish legislation and the rules of international law; and
2) When, pursuant to a treaty or International Convention to which Spain is a party, the issue is attributed with exclusive character to the jurisdiction of another State.

42. On its part, Organic Act No 16/2015, of 27 October, on privileges and immunities of foreign States, International Organizations with headquarters or office in Spain and Conferences and International Meetings held in Spain contains a complete legal regime of the matter. In particular, it regulates the immunities before the Spanish courts and, where appropriate, the privileges applicable to war and State vessels and aircrafts. Such regulatory provisions are, in short, consistent with international law.

43. Moreover, it is important to mention that, on the one hand, Spain is a party to the United Nations Convention on Law of the Sea of 10 December 1982 (*B.O.E.* No 39, of 14 February 1997), whose Articles 32, 95 and 96 refer to the warships belonging to a State. On the other hand, the legal regime of State aircrafts is expressly excluded from the Chicago Convention of 7 December 1944 on International Civil Aviation, ratified by Spain on 5 March 1947, by virtue of its Article 3 (a).

44. With respect to private law conventions, different approaches are to be found. In the field of air transport, regarding the status of State aircrafts and vessels, it is important to mention that State aircrafts, which include military aircrafts (whose mission is the national defence or are sent by a military Commissioner), and non-military aircrafts intended exclusively for non-commercial government services, fall outside the scope of application of the Montreal Convention MC (Article 14). To the contrary, Article 1 (3) CMR includes international carriages of goods that are carried out by States or by governmental institutions or organizations.

Chapter 5. Transport Intermediaries

by Maria-Victoria Petit-Lavall and Achim Puetz

§1. FREIGHT FORWARDERS AND OTHER INTERMEDIARIES IN THE CARRIAGE OF GOODS

45. Intermediation activities in the field of land transport are governed by Act No 16/1987, on the Administrative Organisation of Land Transport (AOLTA). Pursuant to the Act, only duly authorized undertakings may engage in such activities. The offering of transport services to the public lacking such authorization is considered a serious infringement (Article 141 (7) AOLTA). On its part, the actual celebration of contracts of carriage by non-authorized intermediaries is considered a very serious infringement (Article 140 (2)), and the same is true for the performance of intermediation activities without fulfilling the requirements established in the Act and for the subcontracting of transport services with a carrier that is not duly authorized (Article 140 (16) and (17)).

The relevant authorization is that of a 'transport operator', which entitles its holder to intermediate in both international and domestic transport services (Article 119 AOLTA), regulated as of today in a Ministerial Decree of 21 July 2000,[8] concerning the implementation of the rules contained in the Regulation that develops the Administrative Organisation of Land Transport Act in the areas of freight agencies, freight forwarders and warehousing companies. The 'transport operator' can be defined as 'any natural or legal person who is legally qualified to act as an intermediary in the hiring of freight transport, acting as an organization interposed between shippers and carriers'.

46. Act No 16/1987 expressly refers to four groups of intermediaries, although it is an open list (Article 119 (1)). In the first place, freight agencies (*agencias de transporte*) are the proper and traditional intermediaries in the hiring of transport services. They are undertakings that have specialized in intermediation between shippers and carriers, although they may also perform certain activities that precede the transport operation (e.g., administrative or information tasks). In the second place, freight forwarders (*transitarios*) are companies specialized in arranging, on behalf of a third person, international transport operations. By doing so, they may: (*a*) receive goods as consignees, or undertake to hand them over to the carrier; (*b*) carry out administrative, tax, customs and logistic operations; and (*c*) intermediate in the hiring of transport services. Prior to the amendment of the AOLTA by Act No 9/2013, they were only entitled to perform such services with respect to domestic transport when it was the continuation of an international carriage. In the third place, logistic operators (*operadores logísticos*) are undertakings specialized in the organization and control, on behalf of a third person, of the operations of provisioning, transport, storage or distribution of goods that are needed by their clients for

8. *B.O.E.* No 185, of 3 Aug. 2000.

the development of their business activity. Finally, warehousing companies (*almacenistas-distribuidores*) specialize in acting as depositaries of third parties' goods that are in charge of distributing (or organizing the distribution of) such goods, according to the instructions received from the depositor.

47. The note that is common to all these actors is the fact that, in the development of their activity, they are likely to hire transport services, with more or less frequency, and this is the reason why Act No 16/1987 requires a specific authorization. However, what differentiates transport intermediaries in Spain from those in other countries is the fact that the 'transport operator', whatever his legal form, is obliged to celebrate the contract of carriage in his own name (Article 119 (3) AOLTA and Article 5 of the 2009 Carriage of Goods by Land Act (COGLA)). The contravention of this mandatory rule involves two types of consequences. On the one hand, the intermediary who refuses to celebrate the contract in his own name (but in that of the carrier or the sender) commits an administrative infraction, considered a very serious infringement (Article 140 (31) AOLTA). On the other hand, Article 5 (1) COGLA establishes that such contracts of carriage are 'supposed' to be celebrated in the contractor's (i.e., the intermediary's) own name. The exact meaning of the verb is unclear, but it seems that such contracts are presumed to be celebrated in the contractor's own name (and proof to the contrary is impossible when a professional intermediary is involved). As a consequence, regardless of whether he contracted in his own name or in that of his client, the intermediary shall always be liable for the correct performance of the contract of carriage, i.e., he is normally considered a contracting carrier. The purpose of this rule is not very clear, but it probably seeks to ensure that the shipper knows at any time who is the counterpart in the contract of carriage and to whom he can address his claim.

§2. Intermediaries in the Carriage of Passengers by Road and Rail

48. It should be pointed out, in the first place, that Article 22 (2), paragraph 3 AOLTA refers the regulation of intermediation in passenger's transport by road and rail to the legislation in the field of tourism, providing that 'the intervention of travel agencies and other intermediaries in the hiring of any modes of passenger transport shall be governed by specific tourism legislation'. Consequently, its legal regime is contained in the different regional Acts enacted in this respect, since in accordance with Article 148 (1) (18) of the Spanish Constitution, Autonomous Regions can assume this competence, and they have done so in matters of promotion and management of tourism within their territory.

In the second place, pursuant to the 1987 Administrative Organisation of Land Transport Act and its Regulation, approved by Royal Decree 1211/90, of 28 September, different subjects are entitled to carry out the activity of public passenger transport by road. The requirements are different for each category. In fact, the Act distinguishes between: (*a*) contractual carriers; and (*b*) intermediaries in the hiring of transport services. Nonetheless, it should be noted that the intermediation activity in passenger transport is not regulated in the Act itself, but its 1990 Regulation still refers thereto, reserving such activity to travel agencies (Article 165 (1)), who must celebrate the corresponding contract of carriage in their own name with both the carrier and the passenger, whenever tourist tours or occasional services are involved (Article 165 (2)); *a contrario sensu*, the hiring of regular services in the name of the passenger is not prohibited (e.g., by selling train or bus tickets). However, the Regulation has not yet been adapted to the latest amendment of the AOLTA by virtue of Act No 9/2013, the Memorandum of which establishes that, among other objectives, its aim is to reduce operative barriers, 'completely liberalizing intermediation activities in the contracting of passenger transport services, without prejudice to the regulation of travel agencies in the field of tourism'.

Finally, it should be borne in mind that the ECJ has recently handed down its judgment in the *Uber*-case[9], pursuant to which the virtual platform Uber Pop, 'the purpose of which is to connect, by means of a smartphone application and for remuneration, non-professional drivers using their own vehicle with persons who wish to make urban journeys, must be regarded as being inherently linked to a transport service and, accordingly, must be classified as "a service in the field of transport"' and not an information society service. Accordingly, in the absence of any EU rules on the intermediation service at issue, 'it is for the Member States to regulate the conditions under which intermediation services such as (Uber Pop) are to be provided'. Although the Uber Pop service has not been offered in Spain since 2014, the findings of the Court should probably also apply to the current version of the application, which only collaborates with professional drivers that are in possession of a car-hire with driver (*vehículo de transporte con conductor* or VTC) licence, as well as to other initiatives (like Cabify) the functioning of which is similar to that of Uber. This does not mean, of course, that such platforms are illegal per se, but – since arguably they are not information society services, either – it is for the Member States to regulate the conditions under which the intermediation services may be offered.

§3. Shipping Agents

49. The stay of a ship in port requires carrying out a series of administrative and commercial activities, both with regard to the ship itself and to the cargo or the passengers it carries. For the execution of these tasks, shipowners throughout the history have been counting on several collaborators. Among them, the most significant one is the shipping agent, who despite its importance in current maritime trade, appeared only relatively recently.

The ship agent is an autonomous and independent collaborator of the shipowner on land, generally located in one or more ports of a certain geographical area. He is, therefore, an independent entrepreneur, not subject to any dependency relation to the shipowner, although his activity consists of managing other people's business on their behalf. The concept of 'shipping agent' is contained in Article 319 of Act No 14/2014, of 24 July, on Maritime Navigation (MNA). Pursuant to this provision, the shipping agent is a person who, on behalf of the shipowner or the carrier, takes

9. Judgment of 20 Dec. 2017, case C-434/15, *Uber Systems Spain*.

care of the material and legal activities that are necessary for the dispatch and other attentions to the ship in port.

Two elements should be highlighted from this definition. On the one hand, it specifies the material scope of the ship agent's operations, i.e., the performance of the necessary steps for the ship's quick dispatch. On the other hand, it expressly states that the consignee does not act on his own behalf, but on that of the ship-owner.

50. The Maritime Navigation Act then contains a succinct legal regime of the contract between the shipowner and the shipping agent. Pursuant to Article 320 MNA, in the case of an occasional consignment, the internal relations between the agent and the shipowner or carrier shall be governed by the legal regime applicable to commission agents (i.e., the commercial mandate contract (*comisión mercantil*), contained in Articles 244 et seq. of the Commercial Code). On the contrary, continuous or stable agency relationships shall be governed by the legal regime applicable to the commercial agency contract. Thus, Act No 12/1992, of 27 May, on the contract of commercial agency shall apply when the parties establish a lasting legal relationship and the ship agent acts repeatedly on behalf of the shipowner whenever the ships operated by the latter visit his port.

In addition to the aforementioned regulations, it is necessary to consider the existence of standard contracts in maritime commercial practice. The most important one is FONASBA (Standard Liner Agency Agreement), approved by BIMCO in 1993, the most recent edition of which, the Standard Liner & General Agency Agreement, was adopted in 2001.

51. Article 319 MNA does not specify in a precise and detailed manner the exact content of the duties of the agent. Nonetheless, these can be extracted from the Act itself and from the operations to which it refers (mandate and agency contracts). At present, shipping agents perform a wide range of heterogeneous functions, both on a material and a legal, and on an administrative and a commercial level, but they are all related to the entry into, the stay in and the departure of the ship of a port. In fact, a progressive expansion of these tasks has taken place during history, depending on the needs of the traffic. The functions of the ship agent can be grouped into several categories: shipment, shipment and warehousing procedures, implementation of the land phases of the contract of carriage by sea and promotion of transport services. However, the tasks are not always the same, nor do ship agents carry them out in the same way in all ports. Moreover, some of these functions are now often performed by other intermediaries or collaborators (e.g., freight forwarders, chartering agents, or customs agents). In this sense, Article 323 MNA correctly points out that, when the ship agent carries out tasks of port handling of goods, the rules that govern such activities shall apply. In the same way, when in addition to his agency functions the ship agent carries out actions that are characteristic of freight forwarders or other intermediaries, the obligations specifically assumed shall be added to those established for ship agents.

52. Where the ship agent signs the bill of lading as agent only, on behalf of the shipowner or the carrier, Article 321 MNA requires him to state the name and address of the person on whose behalf he is signing (i.e., the shipowner or the carrier). Where he conceals the name and address of the shipowner and the carrier, he shall be jointly and severally liable with the shipowner or the carrier vis-à-vis the consignee of the goods for damages caused to the cargo. *A contrario*, although the MNA does not even mention this issue, it can be concluded that, where the ship agent indicates the name and the address of his clients, he shall not be liable in case such damages occur.

Correspondingly, Article 322 states that the ship agent shall not be liable vis-à-vis the consignees for damage or loss of the cargo or for delay in its delivery. However, he shall be liable to the shipowner or the carrier for any damage caused by his fault. The MNA correctly reserves a certain role to the ship agent with respect to the handling of claims. Pursuant to Article 322, he shall receive the claims and reservations for loss or damage to the goods made by the consignee, and he is bound to communicate them immediately to the shipowner or the carrier. The claims and reservations communicated to the ship agent will have the same effects as those made to the shipowner or carrier itself.

Consequently, as a general rule, the ship agent is not liable vis-à-vis third parties for the tasks performed in the name and on behalf of his principal (shipowner or carrier). And this is so regardless of whether he acts in the framework of an agency contract (Articles 1 and 2 of the 1992 Commercial Agency Contract Act) or a mandate contract (Article 247 Commercial Code). Obviously, for this to happen he has to clearly indicate the name of the person on whose behalf he was acting and he shall not exceed his power of representation (authority).

Finally, like any other contracting party, the ship agent is liable against the shipowner or the carrier in case of negligent or intentional breach of his obligations, whether committed by himself or by his dependents or by a subcontracted third party (Articles 252, 253 and 255 Commercial Code; Article 9 Commercial Agency Contract Act of 1992).

§4. Ship Managers

53. Under a ship management agreement, the ship manager undertakes vis-à-vis the owner to perform, on behalf of the latter, the legal and material acts that are deemed necessary to adequately administer all or some of the aspects involved in the operation of the ship. The law of ship management has traditionally been form-based, and those that are most frequently used in practice are BIMCO's Shipman and Crewman forms. Until the entry into force of the 2014 Maritime Navigation Act, the ship management contract did not count on a legal regulation in Spain. Today, Articles 214–318 MNA include a short definition of the ship manager, define his standard of care, envisage two specific questions as regards liability and determine the rules to apply in case the parties do not agree on a specific issue. However, the importance of forms is still undisputed.

The reasons that may lead to outsourcing the management of ships are mainly: (*a*) the lack of skills on the part of the owner (e.g., oil companies acquiring ships, foreclosure by a financing bank that holds a security interest in the ship, K/S companies); (*b*) the complexity of the fleet owner's corporate structure: it is common that all ships owned by one ship companies that belong to the same group of companies are managed by a single ship manager (which may itself belong to the group); (*c*) flags of convenience: when the ships owned by one ship companies fly a flag of convenience, it is common for the management of the whole fleet to be entrusted to a manager established in a country with a long maritime tradition; and (*d*) economies of scale and experience in management (young or small shipping companies, compliance with increasingly complex regulations, benchmarking, etc.).

54. There are two fundamental classification criteria of ship managers. The first one is based on the relationship, corporate or not, between the owner and the manager, so that in-house ship management is distinguished from third-party ship management. The second criterion is based on the scope of the services entrusted to the manager, who may assume all or only some of the aspects involved in the operation of the ship. In particular, he may assume: (*a*) the technical or nautical management, which involves, *inter alia*, to ensure that the ship complies with the legislation of the flag state and international codes (ISM and ISPS), or to guarantee the supply of provisions, spare parts and lubricants; (*b*) the crew management, i.e., the manager (then also called manning agent) has to ensure the management of the crew, either in exchange for reimbursement of expenses plus a commission (Crewman A), or in exchange for a lump sum (Crewman B); (*c*) the commercial management, i.e., to seek employment for the ship; and (*d*) the insurance management: the manager undertakes to provide for insurance, e.g., for the hull and liability *vis-à-vis* third parties.

55. As a general rule, the manager assumes one or more best effort obligations. However, even though the manager's activity sometimes exceeds the mere accomplishment of acts with legal significance for the owner and his remuneration is not subject to the achievement of a result, the contract does not seem to be a service contract. Quite the opposite, the fact that the manager always acts on behalf of the owner, even if exceptionally he does so in his own name, should lead to the conclusion that the ship management agreement belongs to the so-called contracts of collaboration between businessmen. As a consequence, the decision of the Spanish legislator to subject the contract to the rules that apply to commission and commercial agents (Article 317 MNA), similarly to what happens with the shipping agent, should be considered to be adequate.

56. The basic rule as regards liability of the manager *vis-à-vis* the owner is Article 252 of the Spanish Commercial Code: 'The agent [i.e., the manager] who, without legal cause, does not comply with the commission he accepted or has begun to evacuate will be liable for all damages incurred by the principal [i.e., the owner]'. Thus, with respect to the best effort obligations assumed by the manager, there is a breach when he does not observe due diligence, which is that of an orderly businessman (Article 315 MNA). Additionally, the BIMCO forms envisage some special cases of force majeure, limit the maximum amount of compensation due by the manager and provide a Himalaya clause in favour of the manager's agents and servants.

The limit of the shipowner's liability *vis-à-vis* the manager, on its part, is also force majeure. To this respect, the BIMCO forms include an indemnity clause: in the event that the manager is held liable for an act made on behalf of the shipowner, he can recover the amounts paid from the latter; a rule that, in Spain, can also be based on Article 246 *in fine* of the Commercial Code, which safeguards the manager's action against the principal where he has acted in his own name.

57. Finally, as regards the liability of the manager *vis-à-vis* third parties, liability in contract and liability in tort have to be distinguished. With respect to liability in contract, similarly to what happens with the shipping agent, Article 316 (1) MNA obliges the manager to act on behalf and in the name of the shipowner (although it does not seem to be an obligation in a technical legal sense, but rather a burden). The provision does not, however, specify the consequences in case he acts in the name of the owner. So, arguably, Article 247 (2) of the Commercial Code shall then apply, pursuant to which, if the manager acts in the name of the owner, the third party is bound to the latter and has no action against the former. To the contrary, if the manager acts in his own name, he will be held joint and severally liable with the shipowner for the obligations assumed on behalf of the latter (Article 316 (2) MNA); the same applies if the manager makes it clear that he acts *alieno nomine* (as agent only), but does not indicate the person in whose name he does so.

With respect to the manager's liability in tort, Article 318 MNA declares the joint and several liabilities of the manager and the owner for damages caused 'extra contractually' (i.e., in tort) to third parties. The provision can be considered a specific legal regulation of the liability for another person's acts, that is, the liability of the manager is 'attributed' to the owner, so that the latter shall not be held liable when the harmful event is not attributable to the ship manager in the first place; a solution that is shared, e.g., by Article 3 (2) in conjunction with Article 1 (3) of the 2001 BUNKER Convention. Furthermore, although Article 318 MNA does not say so, it seems that the shipowner shall not be liable when the manager acts completely outside the functions assigned to him by the owner (by way of a teleological reduction of Article 318 MNA).

Be that as it may, Article 318 MNA also admits a second reading: the manager is jointly liable with the shipowner when the rule invoked holds the owner liable in the first place (e.g., in case of collision or pollution of the marine environment). However, for this to happen, the direct liability of the shipowner has to be based on an act or omission of the manager or his agents and servants (e.g., where liability is focussed on the owner, regardless of who caused the damage). And even then, it seems difficult to declare the liability of the manager in case of pollution, since Article III (4) (c) of the CLC Convention excludes this possibility, except for fraud or wilful misconduct, in which case the action would have to be based on national law, because the CLC Convention does not envisage claims different from those against the shipowner. In any case, the rights of both the owner and the manager to limit their liability according to Title VII of the Maritime Navigation Act, which refers to the 1976 London Convention, are not affected (Article 318 *in fine* MNA).

Part II. Maritime Law

by Juan L. Pulido-Begines

Chapter 1. The Vessel

§1. Definition and Legal Status of Vessels

58. In general, Spanish law gives a very broad definition of ship but not an exhaustive one. Artefacts that do not fall under the category of *ship* are referred in the law as *vessels*, *naval devices* or *fixed platforms*.

The MNA provides the following definitions of various naval crafts:

1. *Ship* (Article 56) is any kind of craft with the structure and capacity to sail on the sea to transport individuals or things, having a continuous bulkhead deck and a length equal to or greater than twenty-four metres. A structure is only regarded as a ship if it is capable of movement and intended to navigate at sea, by its own means of propulsion or with other pushing or pulling force. Barges can fall under the description of ship. The fact that a ship has no rudder, or boilers, or is without crew, does not mean that it ceases to be a ship within the ambit of the statutory definition.
2. *Vessel* (Article 57) is any craft not having a continuous bulkhead deck and not exceeding twenty-four metres in length, as long as, in one case and another, it is not classified by the implementing regulations as a *minor unit* according to its characteristics of propulsion or use.
3. *Naval device* (Article 58) is any floating structure, regardless of its size, capable of sheltering people or things, the specific purpose hereof is not navigation, but rather to remain in a fixed place on the waters. Naval artefact status shall also be given to a ship that has lost its condition as such due to having been moored, beached or anchored at a fixed place and assigned, permanently, to activities other than navigation.
4. *Fixed platform* (Article 59)is any building or structure able to carry out the economic exploitation of the marine resources or any other activities, laid or anchored on the seabed or resting thereon. Due to it being permanently attached to the bottom of the waters, the fixed platform is considered as an immoveable asset pursuant to the Spanish Civil Code.

It is a question of fact as to whether any particular craft comes within the scope of the statutory definitions. Moreover, to fall within the statutory definition, a ship must be used in navigable maritime waters. Artefacts intended to navigate at inland waters are not regarded as ships for the purposes of MNA, since navigation within inland waters shall be governed by the regulatory legislation for the public water domain and by the other applicable provisions, with the exception of navigation which takes place on the waters of rivers, canals, lakes or natural or artificial reservoirs when these are accessible by ship from the sea, but only within tidal waters, as well as the navigable reaches of rivers up to where ports of general interest exist (Article 1.3).

59. Regarding the legal nature of ships, they are *recordable, complex and moveable assets* (Article 60 MNA).

First of all, they are considered as *assets* or *objects* (Articles 333–334 Civil Code), although in many ways they have the characteristics of persons: they have a name, an address, a nationality, etc.

Secondly, ships are *moveable assets* but equivalent to immoveable things: many provisions regarding the real property are applicable to them.

Ships are also *complex things*. They are composed of constituent or integral components and fittings.

1) *Integral components* are the elements that constitute the structure of the ship, so they cannot be separated from it without detracting from the entity itself (hull, helm, motor, rudders, etc.). In other words, the integral components are those things that cannot be removed from the ship without damage to it.
2) *Fittings* refer to the elements assigned to serve the ship permanently, but that are not integrated in its structure (navigational aids, radar, anchors, and shipping documents, life boats, compasses, etc.). Fittings are not a constituent part of the main object, the ship: they have been designed to be placed in a particular position on the main object, and contribute to its use.

A ship conserves its identity even when its integral components or fittings are successively substituted.

Accessories are according to Article 61 of the MNA the consumable elements assigned to the ship on a temporary basis (fuel).

Finally, ships are *recordable* assets.

§2. Registration and Nationality of Ocean-Going Ships

I. Obtaining of Nationality by Registration

60. Under Spanish law, a ship acquires Spanish nationality by registration in the *Register of Ships and Shipping Companies* (Article 88 MNA). Registration means the entering of the ship in the public records. The nationality of the ship correlates with the ship's registry and the ship's flag, since the ship's link to a certain jurisdiction is confirmed by the award of that state's nationality to the ship. All ships registered in the Spanish Register of Ships shall fly the Spanish flag. The flying of the national flag is visual evidence of a ship's nationality and the assumption of exclusive jurisdiction and control by Spain over the vessel.

A provisional permit may be issued for the time required for the ship acquired abroad to be able to complete the necessary voyages to reach a Spanish port (Article 89 MNA).

Spanish ships leased by a resident outside of Spain may be authorized to temporarily register in the State of residence of the lessee for the term of the lease agreement. Reciprocally, foreign ships taken on lease by residents in Spain may be authorized to fly the Spanish flag for the time the agreement remains in force. The regime of temporary change of registration shall also be applicable to agreements other than those of lease that entail temporary possession of the ship (Article 94 MNA).

If registered in the Spanish shipping registry, the ship must bear a name and the indication of its port of registry (Articles 20–33 of the Royal Decree 1027/1989, of 28 July, on the Flagging and Registry of Ships, as well as on the Maritime Register (RAMB)).

II. Ship Registration

61. The ships need to be registered in the national shipping registry. Registration involves the public recognition and protection of the ship owner's title to the vessel as well as the conferment of nationality.

Registration procedure of ships in Spain is laid down in MNA 2014 and in the *State Ports and Merchant Navy Act* 1992 (SPMNA). In order to register a ship, the owner must select a name for the ship and a port of choice. The proposed named must be approved by the Register.

Without registration, no ship is entitled to sail at sea. The public law functions of registration include the allocation of a vessel to a specific State and its subjection to a single jurisdiction for most purposes and the right to naval protection by the flag State.

62. Seagoing ships, vessels naval artefacts under the Spanish flag must be registered in two different registers:

1. The *Register of Ships and Shipping Companies*, designed to maintain identification and administrative control of Spanish ships and vessels. This registration enables, for example, ships to be traced in the event that they have caused loss or damage for which their owners are exposed to liability.
2. It is also mandatory for ships, vessels and naval artefacts under the Spanish flag to be registered at the *Register of Moveable Assets* (Ships Section), in order to provide security in their legal relations, since it allows for information relating to the ship to be gathered and made available to those who need to know, as well as for registering of mortgages. In this case, registration of recreational or sports ships and vessels is discretional. Ships under construction may be registered in any case, but their inscription is mandatory when they are to be mortgaged. In this register, ownership and encumbrance of ships, vessels and naval

artefacts shall be registered. In all matters not foreseen in the MNA, the *Mortgage Act* shall govern everything applicable thereto under supplementary terms.

The entries performed at the Ships Section at the Register of Moveable Assets must be coordinated with annotations that are made on the entry sheet of the Register of Ships and Shipping Companies by notifications that must be issued directly in the manner determined by the provisions of the Merchant Navy.

63. There is also a *Special Register of Ships and Shipping Companies*, based in the Canary Islands, which is the second registry of Spain. It permits benefits in fiscal and social taxations. For the registry of vessels in the Canary Islands, under Spanish Flag, shipping companies must have the control centre of shipping operations based in the Canaries or in the case of mainland Spain or abroad, have a permanent establishment or legal representation in the Canaries, authorized by Public Deed. It is also necessary to establish an international business company in the Canary Islands.

III. Registration Procedure

64. Ship registration in the *Register of Ships and Shipping Companies* is carried out by the *Maritime Captaincy*'s offices (*Capitanía Marítima*), and takes the form of an administrative procedure. The conditions to grant this registration are governed by the terms set forth in the provisions of the Merchant Navy (RAMB).

The documents necessary for permanent registration are as follows:

1. Proof of ownership of the ship (bill of sale).
2. Deletion certificate issued by a foreign register (where applicable).
3. Proposal of the ship's name (three names must be proposed).

The period of validity of a regular certificate of registry is unlimited.

65. Ship registration in the *Register of Moveable Assets* is carried out by the Public Registry dependent of the Ministry of Justice. Entries in this register may only be done on the basis of valid official deeds or notarized private deeds. A Spanish Notary Public or Consul of Spain abroad who authorizes a public deed or intervenes in a policy regarding ships, vessels or naval artefacts must obtain the appropriate information from the Ships Section at the Register of Moveable Assets on the status of ownership and charges. This registration is a strong evidence of title in the event of a dispute developing about ownership.

IV. Documentation of Spanish Ships

66. Generally, registration and documentation of a vessel go hand in hand, but these two concepts must not be confused. Documentation of ships is mainly concerned with granting and evidencing the entitlement of the shipowner to use that ship in navigation.

In addition to certificates and documents related to safety of navigation, combating maritime pollution, exterior health, customs regime and others that are relevant to Spanish laws and the international conventions to which Spain is a party, all Spanish ships must carry on board:

1. The *Certificate of Registration,* document that must literally record the content of the entry recorded on the relevant sheet. It must be renewed every time any amendment takes place. The Registration Certificate proves that the ship is legally registered in Spain and it shall be produced at the request of the competent authorities of the Spanish Maritime Authorities, of the coastal State or the Port State.
2. The *Certificate of Seaworthiness* (Patente de Navegación). It certifies that the ship has been authorized to sail the seas flying the Spanish flag, and the identity of the master, or the person to which command of the ship has been granted.
3. Dispatch and Crew List.
4. Captain's Log and Engine Room Log, and, where appropriate, the Ship's Log and the Insurance Certificates.

V. Classification

67. Classification societies perform a dual role in the present situation, and have both a public and a private scope, although both of them aim at the same goal of enhancing the safety of ships and their equipment. The main feature of the statutory role of classification societies is that their activity is compulsory, whereas the classification services are, at least in theory, voluntary.

The Maritime Navigation Act includes a very relevant provision on classification societies (Article 106). But it refers only to what are usually named *classification services*: a private task which consists of the issuing of rules for safe shipping and performing surveys to ensure that those rules are being applied. This activity is mainly developed in private interest, but indirectly it is also beneficial for maritime safety, because it helps to prevent accidents. Over the years, the maritime industry has grown to depend heavily on these services, since classification societies provide a vital function with respect to the insurability and the marketability of a vessel.

First of all, a kind of definition of the classification contract is provided: by means of a classification contract, the classification company certifies that a ship or any of its components or fittings complies with the terms established in the relevant class rules.

Secondly, it is stated that classification companies shall be held liable for damages and losses caused to those who contract with them and that are a consequence of lack of diligence by them in inspecting the ship and in issuing the certificate.

Finally, a very innovative rule is laid down, regarding liability to third parties: the liability of classification companies to third parties shall be determined pursuant to Spanish Civil Law, without prejudice to the applicable International and Community Law provisions.

68. MNA does not include any regulation regarding the *certification* or *statutory services*, through which classification societies, under powers delegated by flag States and other national authorities, enforce the maritime safety regulations contained in international conventions, carrying out surveys and inspections on behalf of the flag State, and issuing the official certificates of conformity to such regulations. This matter is found in the EU legislation, in the general framework of the Maritime Safety Policy (Directive 2009/15/EC of the European Parliament and of the Council, of 23 April 2009, *on common rules and standards for ship inspection and survey organizations and for the relevant activities of maritime administrations*). The Spanish implementation of that Directive can be found in the *Real Decreto 877/2011, de 24 de junio, sobre reglas y estándares comunes para las organizaciones de inspección y reconocimiento de buques y para las actividades correspondientes de la Administración marítima.*

§3. Acquisition and Ownership

I. Acquisition

69. The modes of acquisition of property under Spanish civil law apply to ships (Article 609 Civil Code). Therefore, a ship can be acquired by way of contract (purchase from her original owners, shipbuilding, donation, etc.), inheritance or incorporation. Ownership includes complete dominion over the ship and all property rights: possession, enjoyment, control and disposal thereof.

As a general rule, Spanish law does not require contracts to be made in writing in order to ensure that they become legally binding. However, acquisition of the ship, vessel or naval artefact must be recorded in a *written document*. This bill of sale is the ordinary evidence of title to a ship. But otherwise the contract will have legal effect between the contracting parties anyway, since this requisite works only as a matter of proof.

Anyway, in maritime practice, agreements to sell ships are invariably inscribed on a recognized and approved form. In Spain, the most commonly used standard form is the *Norwegian Sale Form* (NSF), whose current version is of 2012.

No acquisition, transfer or extinction of ship ownership shall act against a third party, unless registered in the corresponding Ships Section at the Register of Moveable Assets, by virtue of a public deed, policy under notarial intervention, definitive judicial resolution or administrative document issued by an officer with sufficient powers by virtue of his office (Articles 63 and 73 MNA).

70. Ownership of the ship can also be acquired by *possession in good faith*, continued over three years, with a duly registered and just title. When any of these requisites are missing, ten years of continued possession shall be required.

71. The sale (or any other legal transactions) of a ship shall include its integral components and fittings, but not the accessories thereof, except if otherwise agreed.

II. Ordinary Co-ownership

72. Ships can be owned by either one person or co-owners.

Ordinary co-ownership of a ship, vessel, naval artefact or fixed platform is governed by general provisions of civil law (Articles 392–406 Civil Code).Unless otherwise proved, co-ownership shall be divided into equal indivisible parts among the co-owners (Article 393 Civil Code).The part owners shall enjoy rights and bear obligations relating to their ship in accordance with their respective shares. The right to control and use the ship is reserved for the majority interest.

III. Special Ship Co-ownership

73. When the *purpose* of the co-ownership of a ship is a business operation, it is deemed as *co-ownership of a ship or vessel*, and it shall be governed by the provisions set forth in Articles 150–155 MNA.

In this case, in order to perform any act or legal transaction of administration, disposal or encumbrance of the ship under co-ownership regime, an agreement by co-owners who represent the majority of the ownership stakes shall suffice. A sole co-owner may hold such a majority. But all co-owners who have not participated, or who have opposed the decision to sell the ship are entitled to demand that it be sold at a public auction.

Chapter 2. Maritime Liens and Mortgages

§1. Maritime Liens

I. General Concepts: Introduction

74. The Spanish legislation on maritime liens is laid down in Articles 122–125 of the MNA. It is a very short regulation, because the MNA refers directly to the terms set forth in the *International Convention on Maritime Liens and Mortgages*, done at Geneva on 6 May 1993 (Article 122 MNA).This regime is applicable to ships, vessels and naval artefacts.

Under the MNA and the Convention of 1993, special status is granted to the claims against the shipowner if certain requirements are met.

75. Maritime liens are in nature *statutory proprietary rights*: they arise automatically and there is no need to register or declare them.

According to International and Spanish Law, Maritime liens have the following characteristics:

1. They contain the right of maritime claimants to take *priority in compensation* against shipowners: a *substantive right over maritime property* which entitles the claimant to subject that property to a judicial sale, and to have the claim satisfied out of the proceeds in priority to non-lien creditors.
2. They are *rights of real nature* on a ship. They encumber the ship itself, following it wherever it goes in spite of change of ownership, registration or flag (Article 8 Convention). The lien remains indelible notwithstanding sale of the ship.
3. They are not based on possession. The lien may attach irrespective of personal fault of the owner.
4. They are *statutory rights:* they arise automatically, unlike a mortgage, without the need for registry publicity, having the nature of a *secret encumbrance*. It attaches to property automatically by operation of law, upon the occurrence of the relevant events, irrespective of grant or consent.

Maritime liens shall cover neither insurance compensation for losses and damages caused to the ship, nor other substitute credits such as those arising from collision, contribution to the general average or any other cause (Article 125 MNA).

Maritime liens do not presuppose personal liability on the part of the shipowner. A lien can arise in connection with a vessel under the control of persons who do not own the ship.

II. Categories of Maritime Liens

76. Maritime liens give the claimants of the specified maritime claims set forth in the applicable law the right to secure compensation for these claims against the owner, demise charterer, manager or operator of the ship.

Different legal systems identify different claims that give rise to a lien. In uniform maritime law, as statutory proprietary rights on ships the categories of claims secured by maritime liens are those stipulated in the *International Convention on Maritime Liens and Mortgages* 1993:

(a) Claims for wages and other sums due to the master, officers and other members of the vessel's complement in respect of their employment on the vessel, including costs of repatriation and social insurance contributions payable on their behalf;
(b) Claims in respect of loss of life or personal injury occurring, whether on land or on water, in direct connection with the operation of the vessel;
(c) Claims for reward for the salvage of the vessel;
(d) Claims for port, canal, and other waterway dues and pilotage dues;
(e) Claims based on tort arising out of physical loss or damage caused by the operation of the vessel other than loss of or damage to cargo, containers and passengers' effects carried on the vessel.

Maritime liens secure specific maritime claims for which shipowners or operators are responsible. The claim is given rise to by the ship.

III. Enforcement of Maritime Liens

77. In order to enforce the maritime lien, the persons entitled must apply to the Commercial court to have their rights and legal interests protected. It is a charge on property, enforceable only by proceedings against the property.

Maritime liens are enforced by courts, through an ordinary judicial process, by arresting and selling by auction the ship that gave rise to the maritime claim.

Arrest and sale by auction of the ship shall be executed by a Commercial court upon application by a claimant, in accordance with:

1. International Convention on Maritime Liens and Mortgages 1993.
2. Civil Procedure Act (Ley de Enjuiciamiento civil).
3. The administrative regulations that may be applicable for auction of moveable assets subject to public registration.
4. MNA (Articles 480–486).

The persons entitled to enforce Maritime liens are any maritime claimant whose claim is secured by Maritime lien by virtue of Articles 4 of the *International Convention on Maritime Liens and Mortgages* and 123–124 of the MNA.

78. Regarding the properties subject to enforcement, according to Article 122 of the MNA, maritime liens can only be enforced on *ships*, *vessels* and *naval artefacts*, in the sense of Articles 56–58 of the same Act. The claim secured by the maritime lien follows the ship, notwithstanding any change of ownership or of registration.

79. The enforcement procedure is that laid down in the *Civil Procedure Act* 2000 and in the *Insolvency Act* of 2003. The persons entitled have the right to apply to the court requesting the arrest of the ship.

IV. Concurrent Liens

80. In addition to the liens listed in the *International Convention on Maritime Liens and Mortgages*, a ship may also be subject to other liens recognized pursuant to the Spanish *Civil Law* or special laws, although such liens, whatever the rank of pre-emption they are granted pursuant to the laws that recognize them, shall be classified after mortgages and other registered charges and encumbrances.

Likewise, pursuant to the terms envisaged in the European Union provisions, or in the applicable treaties and, failing that, subject to the principle of reciprocity, other liens apart from those established in Article 4 of the *International Convention on Maritime Liens and Mortgages* may be recognized, encumbering foreign ships pursuant to the law of the country where they are registered. They shall also be classified after mortgages and other registered charges and encumbrances.

V. Ranking

81. Different legal systems have different priorities in respect of competing liens.

In Spain, as maritime liens are statutory rights, the categories of claims secured by maritime liens are established in the MNA.

However, the list and ranking of the maritime liens is referred by the MNA directly to the terms laid down in the *International Convention on Maritime Liens and Mortgages* 1993. The Spanish legislation only sets forth some special rules to complete that convention.

As a consequence of maritime liens, the claimants of the specified maritime claims have priority over the other claimants whose claims are not secured by maritime liens according with the rule established in Article 5.1 of the *International Convention on Maritime Liens and Mortgages* 1993: *the maritime liens shall take priority over registered mortgages, 'hypothèques' and charges, and no other claim shall take priority over such maritime liens or over such mortgages, 'hypothèques' or charges.*

82. Those claims enjoy preference over mortgages and other registered charges and encumbrances, whatever their date of inscription, without any other credit being able to be placed before such liens. With two exceptions laid down in Article 122 (2) of the MNA:

(a) *Assignment of the sum obtained from the auction or direct sale of the ship.* The proceeds of the sale shall first be used to pay the procedural costs and expenses arising from the arrest, or for the enforcement and subsequent sale of the ship. Such costs and expenses include, among others, the expenses of conserving the ship and maintaining the crew, as well as the wages and other sums, and the expenses to which Article 4 (1) (a) of the *International Convention on Maritime Liens and Mortgages* refers, accrued from the moment of the arrest, or from commencement of the enforcement. The remainder shall be distributed according to the terms set forth in the International Convention on Maritime Liens and Mortgages. Once all the credits are settled, the balance, if any, shall be delivered to the owner and shall be freely transferable.

(b) The fees that are to be paid to the Maritime Authorities for removal of shipwrecked or sunken ships.

Maritime liens can only be enforced on the ship giving rise to the maritime claims secured by maritime lien.

83. However, the Spanish legislation also establishes a special rule for *liens binding the fleet* in Article 123 of the MNA. Although maritime liens may only be enforced against the vessel in question and not against sister ships, when it is not possible to determine the ship on board which a lien has arisen regarding wages and other sums owned to the master and other members of the ship's crew arising from the ship's shipment contract and from Article 4 (1) (a) of the *International Convention on Maritime Liens and Mortgages*, due to having generated the credits on different ships operated by the same company or same corporate group, the privilege shall cover them all. This maritime lien shall be extinguished with the credit guaranteed and also by the lapse of one year (the term beginning to elapse from the moment when the ship's shipment contract is terminated between the creditor and the company or corporate group) unless, prior to expiry of that term, judicial enforcement proceedings have been initiated against any of the ships on board which the lien credit has arisen, or if these become subject to arrest.

84. Maritime liens shall be enforced in the proceeds of the sale by auction of ship concerned in the order specified in the MNA and the *International Convention on Maritime Liens and Mortgages* 1993 (Article 5):

1. Claims for wages and other sums due to the master, officers and other members of the vessel's complement in respect of their employment on the vessel, including costs of repatriation and social insurance contributions payable on their behalf;
2. Claims in respect of loss of life or personal injury occurring, whether on land or on water, in direct connection with the operation of the vessel;
3. Claims for reward for the salvage of the vessel (however, maritime liens securing claims for reward for the salvage of the vessel shall take priority over all other maritime liens which have attached to the vessel prior to the time when the operations giving rise to the said liens were performed);
4. Claims for port, canal, and other waterway dues and pilotage dues;
5. Claims based on tort arising out of physical loss or damage caused by the operation of the vessel other than loss of or damage to cargo, containers and passengers' effects carried on the vessel.

These maritime liens take priority over registered mortgages, '*hypothèques*' and charges.

The maritime liens securing claims for reward for the salvage of the vessel shall rank in the inverse order of the time when the claims secured thereby accrued. Such claims shall be deemed to have accrued on the date on which each salvage operation was terminated.

VI. Choice of Law

85. Maritime liens are rights of real nature on a ship and hence are governed by the law of the flag. Their ranking depends on the seizure against the ship and is therefore governed by the *lex fori*.

VII. Extinction of Maritime Liens

86. Since maritime liens on ships are in nature proprietary rights in rem on ships, to secure the payment or compensation of specified claims, they are so subordinated to the claims.

As subordinate rights, their existence is conditional upon the survival of the claims they secure. Therefore, where a claim secured by maritime lien is extinguished, the maritime lien securing this claim shall be extinguished, too.

87. Maritime liens shall be extinguished after a period of one year unless, prior to the expiry of such period, the vessel has been arrested or seized, such arrest or seizure leading to a forced sale (Article 9 *International Convention on Maritime Liens and Mortgages* 1993).

In the event of the forced sale of the vessel all liens and other encumbrances of whatsoever nature, shall cease to attach to the vessel, provided that at the time of the sale, the vessel is in the area of the jurisdiction of Spain and that the sale has been conducted in accordance with the Spanish law.

§2. Ship Mortgages

I. General Concepts

88. Spanish civil law, as other early civil codes, did not recognize mortgages over a ship, mortgages being limited to immoveable property. Only in 1893 the institution of the ship mortgage was introduced, with the *Ley de Hipoteca Naval*, in force until September 2014.

According to Spanish current law, *ship mortgage* is a special kind of mortgage, regulated in the provisions of the MNA (Articles 126–144) and the *International Convention on Maritime Liens and Mortgages* 1993. In all matters not envisaged by those regulations, the terms set forth in the *Mortgage Act* 1946 (updated by Act No 13/2015, of 24 June, *on Reform of the Mortgage Act*) shall apply as basic law.

89. In Spain, to ensure the payment of debts, all ships, vessels and naval artefacts, even those being built, may be subject to a ship mortgage without transferring the possession of the property.

A ship mortgage *directly* and *immediately* encumbers the ship upon which it is imposed, whoever its owner may be, to the fulfilment of the obligations for guarantee of which it is constituted. The principal right of a mortgagee is to prosecute the ship or ships encumbered if there is default of the security.

The action to demand payment of debts guaranteed by a ship mortgage, as well as other issues related to the procedure to be followed and competence to hear such claims shall be subject to the terms set forth in the *Civil Procedure Act* (Articles 681–698), notwithstanding the special features established in the Maritime Navigation Act. These rules shall only apply when enforcement is directed exclusively against pledged or mortgaged assets guaranteeing the debt on which they are based. Action intended to demand the payment of debt guaranteed by a pledge or mortgage may be exercised directly against the assets pledged. The enforcement claim must be made against the debtor and, possibly, against the non-debtor party which has taken on the mortgage or against the third party which owns the assets mortgaged on condition that the last mentioned had accredited the acquisition of these assets to the creditor.

90. The ship mortgage creditor may exercise its right against the ship or ships encumbered to its satisfaction in the following cases:

a) On expiry of the term to return the capital or pay interest, in the manner that may have been agreed.
b) In case the debtor is declared bankrupt.
c) In case the ship mortgaged suffers deterioration that makes it definitively not seaworthy.
d) When there are two or more ships assigned to fulfil a same obligation and loss or deterioration arises that makes either of them definitively not seaworthy, unless otherwise agreed.
e) On fulfilment of the conditions agreed to terminate the obligation guaranteed, and all those that take the effect of making the capital or interest callable.

II. Creation of the Ship Mortgage

A. Persons Entitled to Grant Ship Mortgage

91. The right to establish mortgage on a ship is in nature a reflection of ownership of the ship. Consequently, only the shipowners or persons so authorized by the shipowners may establish mortgage on a ship. A mortgage can only be constituted by owners who have free disposal of their assets or, if they do not have such, by those who are authorized for that purpose pursuant to the law. Those who have the power to establish a mortgage, may do so themselves or through a proxy who holds a special power of attorney (Article 130 MNA).

The mortgage may be constituted in favour of one or several specific persons, or in favour of whoever is the holder of the credit if constituted to guarantee securities issued nominatively, to the order or to the bearer.

A ship mortgage may also be constituted to guarantee current accounts for credit or bills of exchange or other instruments, as established in the *Mortgage Act* 1946.

B. Ships Subject to Mortgage

92. A mortgage can only be established on *ships*, *vessels* or *naval artefacts*, as defined in Articles 56–58 of the MNA.

Although a ship under construction is not *stricto sensu* a ship before she fulfils the requisites of Article 56 of the MNA (basically, structure and capacity to sail on the sea to transport individuals or things), a mortgage on ships under construction may also be established by the principal if it has specifically been granted that power. In this case, it is indispensable for a third of the budgeted amount of the total hull value to have been invested in it and for the ownership of the ship to be registered on the Register of Moveable Assets.

93. Where a mortgage is established on a ship, it shall cover both the *component parts* (Article 60 (2) MNA) of the ship as well as its *fittings* (Article 60 (3) MNA) but not its *accessories* (Article 61 MNA), neither the fuel, oil or cargo that belongs to the shipowner or to another person. Notwithstanding this, it does not include fittings registered at the Register of Moveable Assets, on behalf of a third party, or the property of which has been acquired by the latter on a prior date to that of the relevant legal transaction or act that generates the encumbrance.

Regarding the *insurance money* due to the owner under the ship's policy of insurance and other *ships earnings*, the MNA establishes that, except if otherwise agreed specifically, the mortgage also covers the compensations for material damage caused to the ship and not repaired due to collision or other accidents, as well as the contribution to the general average and that of the insurance, both for not repaired damage suffered by the ship, as well as its total loss.

At any time, the mortgage creditor may provide certifiable notification of the existence of the mortgage to the insurer of the ship. When such notification is received, the insurer may not pay out any sum whatsoever to the insured in compensation for loss of the ship or not repaired damage without the specific consent of the mortgage creditor (Article 135 MNA).

III. Formalities Relating to the Creation of Mortgage

94. Two requisites must be fulfilled in order for ship mortgage to be validly constituted:

a) It must be granted in a public deed or in a private document.
b) It must be registered on the Register of Moveable Assets.

A. *Mortgage Deed*

95. All agreements constituting a ship mortgage shall record:

a) Creditor, debtor and, where appropriate, non-debtor mortgagor, specifying all the personal particulars required by the mortgage legislation;
b) The amount of the loan guaranteed by mortgage and of the sums that, if appropriate, shall cover the encumbrance for enforcement costs and expenses, and of the remuneration and delay interest and other expenses;
c) Maturity date of the capital and payment of the interest;
d) Description of the ship and all the identifying data envisaged by the MNA (name, licence, International Maritime Organization number, flag, gauge), that may be recorded, stating, where appropriate, that the ship is under construction;
e) The value or appraisal made of the ship and, where appropriate, that may be taken as the auction rate; and the addresses that the debtor and, where appropriate, the non-debtor mortgagor, provide for demands and notifications;
f) Sums assigned to each ship, in the event of two or more being mortgaged to guarantee a sole loan;
g) The regulatory circumstances determined in the case of a mortgage to guarantee titles, whatever their denomination;
h) Other clauses that are established by the parties to the contract on interest, insurance, early maturity, extension and any others deemed convenient.

B. *Recording or Registration*

96. As most ship registers, Spanish Register provides for the registration of mortgages.

The inscription of the mortgage shall record the circumstances stated in the mortgaged deed that have transcendence in rem, as well as the others required by the mortgage laws (Article 133 MNA).

IV. Ranking

97. Where the debtor fails to pay due debt, the creditor has the right to seek preferred payments from the property, the ship or vessel.

The ship mortgage shall enjoy preference from the moment of inscription at the Register of Moveable Assets. The date of inscription for all effects shall be considered that of the presentation entry, which shall be recorded in the actual inscription. In order to determine preference between two or more inscriptions on a same date related to a same ship, the time of the respective titles being lodged at the Registry shall be taken into account (Article 137 MNA).

V. Validity Period and Extinction of Mortgage

98. A ship mortgage is in nature a proprietary right in rem on ship to secure the payment of specified claims and it is *subordinate* to the credit it secures. Therefore, its extinction is linked to the extinction of that credit: where a claim secured by ship mortgage is extinguished, the ship mortgage securing this claim shall be extinguished at the same time.

Another cause of extinction is limitation of actions: a ship mortgage action becomes time-barred in three years, from the moment when it may be exercised, pursuant to the specifications of the MNA.

The ship mortgage shall subsist while not cancelled with regard to each ship, on the total amount thereof, even though the guaranteed obligation is reduced, and on any part thereof that is conserved, even when the remainder has disappeared (Article 134 (4) MNA).

Furthermore, the registry holder of a ship may request cancellation due to expiry of the inscription of mortgage, when six years have elapsed from maturity, if there is no record of renewal, interruption of limitation period or exercise of the mortgage action.

VI. Ship Mortgage and International Law

99. Under Spanish conflict-of-laws rules, the law applicable to ship mortgage is the law of the vessel's flag. Nevertheless, the Spanish courts could uphold and enforce a mortgage on a foreign ship if it is valid according to the law of the ship's flag. Recognition and enforcement by the Spanish courts of the mortgages and in rem encumbrances constituted on foreign ships are subject to fulfilment of the following requisites:

a) For them to have been constituted and registered on a public register pursuant to the laws of the State in which the ship has been registered.
b) For such registration, pursuant to the laws of the State of registration of the ship, to be freely available for consultation by the public and it being possible to apply for and obtain statements and copies of the entries or documents recording such from the registry.
c) For the registration or some of the documents aforementioned to specify at least the name and address of the person in favour of whom the mortgage or encumbrance has been constituted, or the fact that the guarantee has been constituted to the bearer, the maximum amount guaranteed, if the laws of the State of registration establish that requisite, or whether that amount were to be specified in the document of establishment of the mortgage or encumbrance, and the date and other circumstances that, pursuant to the laws of the State of registration, determine their specific rank with regard to other registered mortgages and encumbrances.

Chapter 3. Master and Crew

§1. Master

100. The master is the sole person who has the command of the ship. From being appointed as such, the master shall command and direct the ship, as well as lead its crew and represent the public authority on board. He has legal and moral responsibility for the safety of the ship and for the well-being of every person on board.

I. Appointment of the Master

101. The master can be appointed, and discharged from his office, by the ship operator, the shipowner or his representative, without prejudice to the appropriate compensations pursuant to Labour Law. In the case of bareboat charter, the master shall be appointed by the ship charterer, because both of them are the counterparts of the contract of employment.

In order to qualify for this function on board of a ship flying the Spanish flag, the Master must fulfil the following requirements:

1. The master must hold a professional qualification that evidences his skill, capacity and the necessary conditions to command and direct a ship, as established by the specific laws or regulations (Article 173 MNA).
2. The master (and the first deck officer) must possess a Spanish or a Member State of the European Economic Area citizenship, except in cases when the Maritime Authorities specify that such posts shall be covered by Spanish citizens due to such post usually involving the effective exercise of the prerogatives of a public authority, such exercise not representing a very small part of the holder's activities. To these ends, nationals of third States who are relatives of a citizen of the European Union or a national of a Member State of the European Economic Area shall have the same status as these, as long as they comply with the requisites established by in the implementing regulations(Article 162 MNA, sixteenth additional provision SPMNA).

In the event of death, absence, illness or other impediment that the master may suffer during navigation, the MNA contains an express provision regarding his replacement: the command of the ship shall be taken over by the highest-ranking deck officer who, in turn, shall be replaced by the officers from the same department following him in category. In the last instance, command of the ship shall be taken by the officers from the engine department, consecutively by rank.

102. The contract between the master and the owner is a *special* employment contract: a *senior management contract* in accordance with Royal Decree 1382/85. Should any disputes occur, labour courts are competent. The master may freely cancel his contract by serving at least three months' advance notice. The ship operator may also freely cancel his contract serving the same advance notice. In this case, the master has the right of compensation equal to seven days' pay per year worked, up to a maximum of six months' pay.

Termination of the *senior management contract* can be made at any time, but ship operators may not dismiss the master or adopt other measures of a penalizing kind against him, due to having been forced to disregard instructions in view of the need to act in the most adequate way to safeguard safety, according to the professional criterion inherent to a competent mariner (Article 184 (2) MNA).

103. The Master has his own powers and functions established by law and by the employment contract. His functions are divided between *public*, *private* (representative functions and duties of financial nature) and *technical* functions. The different functions of the master entail public as well as private powers and duties, as he represents different interests of public and private law.

II. Public Functions of the Master

104. The master is responsible for the safety of the ship, as well as the law and order on board. He shall ensure that the ship and the crew carry the certificates and documents required by the law.

Because of this great responsibility, the maritime law affords unique authority to the ship master: he is in the supreme command of the expedition. This authority is not derived from land-based concepts of employment law, but rather in public law and in ancient commercial practices.

105. The master is the representative of public authority on board; for that reason, he has *public authority status on board* and shall fulfil and enforce all obligations that the law or regulations impose on him by virtue of his office, especially that of maintaining order and safety on board (Article 176 (1) MNA).Due to their nature of public law, these functions of the master may not be altered or modified by the terms of the contract of employment concluded with his employer.

Since the master has *public authority status on board*, he must also act accordingly.

First of all, the master has power to give orders which shall be carried out by anyone on board. The master's orders are obligatory to all those present on board. The members of the crew and other individuals on board the ship have to obey the orders given by the master, without prejudice to their right to make the claims that they may deem appropriate before the competent administrative or judicial authority once the ship reaches port. The disobedience to the orders of the master may give rise to administrative sanctions (Articles 306 (3), 307 (2) and 308 (3) SPMNA).

Secondly, the master may adopt as many restrictions of freedom measures as deemed necessary to *maintain order on the ship*, as well as to *guarantee the safety* of those who are on board. Within the master's competence during a voyage is the restriction of freedom of any person on board seriously endangering the ship, life and property on board, or the environment by pollution. But such a measure may be applied only if necessary and shall not endure longer than the ship's arrival at the first port of call (Article 300 SPMNA). Therefore, he has the power to confine or take other necessary measures against any person who has committed a crime or violated the law or the regulations on board.

He is also competent, when an individual dies on board and no doctor is enrolled, to issue the death certificate, but he may not do so until twenty-four hours have elapsed from the moment at which, in his reasonable opinion, unequivocal signs of death have appeared. In all cases, the master shall keep an inventory of his papers and belongings, aided by two of the ship's officers and two witnesses, who shall preferably be passengers.

Besides, the master of the ship shall be bound to record the incidents involving individuals on board during navigation, which he deems may constitute a criminal or administrative offence, in the Captain's Log.

106. He also has, when on board, the same duties and powers as a *Civil Registry officer* with regard to recordable facts and acts that arise during a voyage at sea and that affect the civil status of the individuals on board. So the master may draft and issue civil *registry certificates*, when necessary (of births or deaths that occur on board during navigation, as well as the marriages held in danger of death). Those certificates must be recorded by the master in the Captain's Log, adjusting their content to the terms set forth in the Civil Registry Act. In the case of individuals disappearing during navigation, he shall record the relevant summary information, and the Captain's Log shall record the main circumstances of the disappearance and the search and rescue measures adopted.

107. Finally, the master can act as a *public notary*: he has to authorize maritime last wills and testaments and receive closed testaments in the cases and with the formalities set forth on this matter in the Spanish Civil Code, leaving a record of this in the Captain's Log. Delivery of a holographic last will and testament shall also be recorded in the same book.

Spanish Civil Code regulates a special category of will: *the maritime will* (Articles 722–731), that is, open or closed wills made by persons on board in a maritime journey. On merchant ships, they shall be authorized by the Captain, or the person acting in his stead, with the attendance of two suitable witnesses. The witnesses shall be chosen among the passengers, if any; but one of them, at least, must be able to sign, and shall do so for himself and for the testator, if the latter does not know how to or is unable to do so.

If the vessel should arrive at a foreign port where there is a Diplomatic or consular agent of Spain, the Captain of the merchant ship shall deliver to such Agent a copy of the open will, or the deed of execution of the closed will, and the note taken in the Logbook. The copy of the will or the deed must include the same signatures as the original, if the persons who signed it are alive and on board; otherwise, it shall be authorized by the Paymaster or Captain who received the will, or the person acting in their stead, and shall also be signed by those of the persons who took part in the will who are currently on board. The Diplomatic or consular agent shall procure that the formality of delivery is laid down in writing and, having closed and sealed the copy of the will or that of the deed of execution in the event of a closed will, shall forward it, together with the note taken in the Logbook, to the Minister of Justice by the corresponding channels, and the Minister shall order its deposit in the

Files of his Ministry. The Commander or Captain who delivers the copy shall receive from the Diplomatic or consular agent a certificate of having performed such delivery, and shall make a note thereof in the Logbook.

When the vessel arrives to the first port in the Kingdom of Spain, the Commander or Captain shall deliver the original will, closed and sealed, to the local naval Authority, with a copy of the note taken in the Logbook; and, if the testator should have died, a certificate evidencing the death. Delivery shall be evidenced in the manner provided in the preceding article, and the naval Authority shall forward it all without delay to the Minister of Justice.

If there should be *danger of shipwreck*, the will of the crew and passengers may be executed orally before two witnesses. However, this will shall become ineffective if the testator should be saved from the danger in consideration of which he made the will.

III. Private Functions of the Master

108. The times when the master was deemed as the decision-maker of the ship and cargo under commercial law, more like shipowners than like seafarers, ended in Spain with the abrogation of the Commercial Code of 1885.

Anyway, in the scope of the new Maritime Navigation Act, the master still holds the representation of the ship operator to contract all obligations related to the ordinary needs of the ship on the latter's behalf (Article 185 MNA): he may conclude salvage agreements and all legal transactions essential for the completion of the voyage.

The ship operator is bound to fulfil those obligations without it being possible to allege abuse of trust or transgression of the powers granted. If the ship operator places any restriction on the legal authority of the shipmaster, these restrictions shall have no legal effect upon third parties who are unaware of them.

This is notwithstanding the liability of the master to the ship operator for the acts and contracts performed in breach of the specific legitimate instructions the latter has given.

109. In his capacity as the ship operator's representative, the master is entitled to take actions and institute proceedings before foreign judicial and administrative bodies, for the purpose of protecting the ship operator's rights and interests. The master has active and passive legitimation to appear as representative of the ship operator in all judicial or administrative proceedings related to the ship under his command.

IV. Main Duties of the Master

110. The main duty of the master is technical: he shall provide the *technical direction for navigation* of the ship: the master governs the ships and is responsible for her safety. He is authorized and obliged to issue orders intended to make the ship and its navigation safe. The master shall also be responsible for the care and management of the ship, its cargo and crew.

He must undertake the effective command of the vessel when he sees fit. He must be present on the bridge and undertake direct command of the ship during landings, port arrival and departure manoeuvres and, in general, in all circumstances in which the risks of navigation are notably increased, without prejudice to the necessary rest to maintain his physical faculties.

The MNA expressly lays down the *Primacy of the professional criterion* of the master: neither the ship operator, nor the fleet operator or any other person with an interest in the ship or its cargo may hinder or restrict the master of the ship from adopting or implementing any decision that, in his professional judgment, may be necessary for the safety of human life at sea and protection of the marine environment (Article 184 MNA). So the master has the right of independent action and shall bear the final responsibility with respect to securing the safety of life and property on board, ship's security and prevention of pollution.

111. In addition, except in cases of duly justified force majeure, the masters of Spanish ships have to obey all orders or instructions given by a Spanish State ship. That duty shall subsist even when the ships are not in the Spanish maritime areas, without prejudice to the powers that, according to International Law, are held by the coastal State or the port State (Article 174 MNA).

112. In the event of bad weather or risk of shipwreck, the master must adopt as many measures as he may believe necessary to ensure the safety of the ship and to save individuals and property, seeking shelter, by forced docking or resorting without delay to issuing a call for rescue, being able to hire one if necessary.

The master shall not abandon a ship in danger before having lost all hope of saving it and, once the appropriate measures have been adopted to save individuals, assets and official documents that may be on board.

113. Finally, the master is bound to take measures to save human lives in danger at sea, as long as he may do so without severe danger to the ship, its crew or passengers, and in all cases shall leave a record of the proceedings in the Captain's Log. Therefore, he must make the best efforts to run the rescue of lives at sea.

V. Liability of the Master

114. The infringement of the master's duties can have consequences in private and in public law.

First of all, regarding the *civil liability*, the master's liability towards the owner and the operator of the ship is subject to general principles of private law and those specifically stated in Maritime Navigation Act.

Persons who, in the performance of their obligations, should incur in wilful misconduct, negligence or default, and those who in any way should contravene the content of the obligation shall be subject to compensation of any damages caused (Article 1101 Civil Code).

The debtor's fault or negligence consists of the omission of the diligence required by the nature of the obligation that corresponds to the circumstances of the persons, the time and the place. In performing his technical duties, the master must act with the diligence required from a competent mariner at all times (Article 182 (3) MNA).

According to the general rule as defined in Article 1104 of the Civil Code, the master is subject to civil liability arising from breach of the obligations of his post, notwithstanding criminal liability, should this arise. He is liable for any personal fault. Liability arising from wilful misconduct is enforceable for all obligations. Waiver of the action to enforce it shall be null and void. Liability arising from negligence is equally enforceable in the performance of all kinds of obligations; but may be moderated by the Courts on a case-by-case basis.

When the act of God or force majeure is justified, he shall be exonerated of all liability (Article 1105 Civil Code: *no one shall be liable for events which cannot be foreseen or which, being foreseen, should be inevitable*).

115. In the scope of the contract of employment, contractual liability of the master shall be determined by the contract and by Labour law.

116. On the other hand, regarding *public and disciplinary liability*, the infringement of the master's duties is treated as an administrative offence, and sanctions are provided for in Part III of the SPMNA (Articles 295–320).

With regard to his responsibility and authority, the provisions envisaged by international regulations on management of operational safety of the ship and preventing pollution shall apply.

§2. Crew

117. The Kingdom of Spain has ratified the *Standards of Training, Certification and Watchkeeping Convention* of 1978 (STCW Convention 1978), including its amendments of 1995.

Spain is also a party to a large number of the ILO conventions and recommendations dealing with labour and living standards on ships, aiming at protecting the rights of seafarers while serving on board. These regulations regard seafarers as a special category of workers requiring exceptional consideration and treatment, in order to avoid exploitation, abuse and discrimination. In February 2006 Spain ratified the *Maritime Labour Convention* 2006 (MLC), and harmonized the national legislation with the requirements of that convention as well as with the EU Council Directive 2009/13/EC of 16 February 2009, *implementing the Agreement concluded by the European Community Shipowners' Association (ECSA) and the European Transport Workers' Federation (ETF) on the MLC, and amending Directive 1999/63/EC*. MLC 2006 can be considered the most significant development in the history of seafarer's labour law: it includes standards for conditions of employment, hours of work and rest, accommodation, food and catering, health protection, medical care, welfare and social security protection. But the main innovation of MLC 2006 is that it includes maritime labour laws in the framework of Port State Control: consequentially, MLC's standards are enforced on ratifying nation's ships and on foreign ship, irrespective of whether their flag State has ratified the Convention, calling at ratifying nation's ports.

118. Concept of crew. The crew includes, according to Spanish law, the set of individuals *employed on board* a ship in any of its departments or services, hired either directly by the ship operator or by third parties (Article 161 MNA). The concept of crew does not include individuals whose work does not form part of the *daily activity* of the ship, or who only work briefly on it, and whose *main place of work* is not on it but ashore (like shipyards repairs technicians or pilots).

This concept, as that include in MLC 2006, is very broad. The crew entails not only those who offer maritime labour or navigation services *stricto sensu* (sailors, engineers, etc.) but also those who perform general or supplementary services on board (doctors, cookers, waiters, musicians, hairdressers, etc.). The MNA laid down a classification of the personnel on board. The basic categories of maritime personnel are as follows:

a) Captain,
b) Officers,
c) Subalterns.

The persons forming those categories must hold the relevant professional qualifications or specialization certificates to be able to act as members of the crew of merchant ships as determined by the implementing regulations (STCW/95).

119. To perform work of any relevance to the safety of navigation, the ship must have an adequate number of crew members with proper qualifications: the number of members of the crew of ships and their conditions of skills and professional training shall be adequate to guarantee the safety of the ship and navigation at all times, as well as to protect the marine environment. The Maritime Authorities must establish the standard quota to ensure the safety for each Spanish ship according to its technical circumstances, navigation and traffic, as well as the regime and organization of work on board. The Maritime Authorities issue a '*Minimum Safety Crew Certificate*' that must be carried on board and shown to the authorities of the port the ship visits and when so required (Article 161 MNA).

I. Contract of Employment for Crew Members

120. In Spain, the contract of employment for crew members is a labour contract: a legal relationship witnessed by the contract of maritime employment into which they have entered with the shipping company employing them, submitted to the special labour laws.

The Spanish legislation on the maritime employment contract is laid down in the Statute of Workers Rights (*Estatuto de los Trabajadores*), which contains general provisions and those of conclusion of employment contracts, performance and termination. In the absence of specific provisions in the MNA or in the SPMNA, a crew member's contract of employment shall be governed by the general provisions dealing with the matter, contained in the Statute of Workers Rights.

121. Another important source of rights and obligations of employers and employees may be found in the collective bargaining agreements, negotiated between shipowners and trade unions. They usually determine wages and conditions for all of the seafarers affected by the agreement (its scope can be a ship, a company or the whole sector).

122. The contract of maritime employment can be written (Article 8 *Statute of Workers Rights*), but is still valid if it is not in writing.

The contract links the sailor to the shipowner. It can be signed between the seaman and the master (as representative of the shipowner).

The contract of employment is recorded by the port or consular authority in the *Crew List.* Crew members should be in the *List* on board a particular ship and boarding or landing personnel of Spanish ships have to be performed with intervention by the Maritime Authorities, performed by the master of the ship at foreign ports, who shall proceed to record the enrolment and release proceedings on the *Dispatch and Crew List* and in the *Seaman's Certificates* (Article 159 MNA).

To be employed on board a ship flying the Spanish flag, a seafarer should meet the requirement established by IMO. No Spaniard may be a member of the crew of ships and vessels in the Spanish merchant navy if he has not obtained a Merchant Mariner's Document (MMD) or Seaman's Certificate, except in duly justified cases of urgency (Article 158 MNA).

With regard to foreigners, in order for them to board, they shall hold the national identity card of the mariner that shall be issued by the country of his nationality, or they shall board with a special permit granted to them by the master of the ship.

II. Recruiting

123. The crew can be selected by the shipowner, the ship operator or the master (as representative of the shipowner). More commonly nowadays, they rely on manning agencies to recruit reliable and skilled seafarers.

No operation to hire ships' crews may give rise to the mariners having to pay any remuneration, directly or indirectly, to any natural or legal person (Article 164 (1) MNA).

124. The agents or representatives of foreign ship operators who hire national or resident mariners in Spain *to serve on foreign ships* are jointly and severally liable with that ship operator for fulfilment of the contract entered into. They shall also be bound to arrange a mercantile insurance contract to grant compensation of a similar amount to those established in the Spanish Social Security regime in cases of death, disability due to accident and repatriation. The emigration authorities shall not approve contracts entered into that do not fulfil that requisite.

Moreover, MLC 2006 contains standards for seafarer's recruiting designed to protect them from abuses. States that have ratified the Convention must require the shipowners flying their flag to use only recruitment services that conform to those standards.

III. Duties of the Employer and Employee

125. The duties of the crew are established in the MNA and in the Statute of Workers Rights. The main obligations are:

a) The members of the crew are obliged to obey to their superiors (Article 176 (2) MNA). They must follow the orders given by the master, without prejudice to their right to make the claims that they may deem appropriate before the competent administrative or judicial authority once the ship reaches port.
b) To be on board on time and perform their duties on time. Unjustified delays can be a good reason for termination of the contract (Article 54 (2) (a) Statute of Workers Rights).
c) Comply with all duties and disciplinary rules of the Merchant Navy set forth in the SPMNA.

IV. Termination

126. The duration of a seafarer employment contract is generally regulated by the individual contract and by the collective bargaining agreement. As a rule, the agreement terminates when the vessel is shipwrecked, lost or becomes unseaworthy. In these cases, seafarers are usually entitled to repatriation and compensation for loss of personal effects at the shipowners' expense (MLC 2006, Guideline B2.5.1, paragraph 1).

Spanish labour law provides all employees with protection against being unfairly dismissed (*despidoimprocedente*). Seafarers who are improperly terminated from employment are entitled to repatriation and earned wages plus damages. Damages can vary from twenty to forty-five days wages per year of duration of the contract.

Shipowners are prohibited from requiring seafarers to make an advance payment of their repatriation expense. Seafarers can be required to pay their own repatriation expenses only when they are in serious default of their employment contract, such as quitting their job without a cause.

Since the agreement between the master or the crew and the owner is an employment contract, if any disputes occur regarding the termination of the contract, the competent courts are the labour courts.

127. According to the general rules of labour law (Article 49 *Statute of Workers Rights*), a contract of employment may terminate due to:

a) an agreement between the employer and employee;
b) a reason validly stated in the contract;
c) the expiry of the contractual period, if the contract was of a fixed-duration;
d) death of the employee;

e) the employee reaching retirement age;
f) retirement due to disability;
g) dismissal of the worker.

If the contract expires while the ship is at sea, generally the employment continues under the same conditions and terms as the expired contract until the vessel arrives in port.

Chapter 4. Liability and Limitation of Liability in Maritime Law

§1. Liability of the Ship Owner and the Crew

128. As a rule, the general provisions of civil law contained in the Spanish Civil Code, covering liability for breach of contract and tort liability, shall apply in the determination of the liability of the shipowners, their servants or agents.

Regarding contractual liability, persons who, in the performance of their obligations, should incur in wilful misconduct, negligence or default, and those who in any way should contravene the content of the obligation shall be subject to compensation of any damages caused (Article 1101 Civil Code).Liability arising from wilful misconduct is enforceable for all obligations. Waiver of the action to enforce it shall be null and void. Liability arising from negligence is equally enforceable in the performance of all kinds of obligations, but may be moderated by the Courts on a case-by-case basis. The debtor's fault or negligence consists of the omission of the diligence required by the nature of the obligation that corresponds to the circumstances of the persons, the time and the place.

As for tort liability, the basic rule is stated in Article 1902 of the Civil Code: the person who, as a result of an action or omission, causes damage to another by his fault or negligence shall be obliged to repair the damages caused.

According to the principle of *vicarious liability*, the ship operator shall be liable for the damages caused by their employees, in the service in which they are employed or in the performance of their duties, as for its own acts or omissions (Article 1903 Civil Code).

Outside the cases expressly mentioned in the law, and those in which the obligation should require it, no one shall be liable for events which cannot be foreseen or which, being foreseen, should be inevitable (Article 1105 Civil Code).

129. The MNA only establishes a basic principle on this subject in Article 149: the *ship operator* shall be held liable to third parties for acts and omissions by the master and crew of the ship, as well as the obligations contracted by the master pursuant to his power of representation of the ship operator, without prejudice to his right to limit its liability in the cases established in the MNA.

Therefore, the person liable for the obligations that outcome in connection with navigation and exploitation of a ship shall be the ship operator. Besides the liability for his own acts and negligence, he is also liable for the master's, crew's or pilot's acts committed in the course of their employment.

A ship operator is the party that, whether or not it is the owner, has the *possession* of a ship or vessel, directly, or through its servants, and uses it for navigation in its own name and under its responsibility.

§2. Limitation of Liability

130. The general principle in law provides for the unlimited liability of the liable person. According to Article 1911 of the Spanish Civil Code the debtor is liable for the performance of his obligations with all present and future property. Therefore, each debtor is liable with all his assets for damages from tortious actions conducted by him or his representatives or agents.

131. However, in maritime law, according to a very old principle rooted back in the Antiquity, under some conditions the person liable enjoys the benefit to limit his financial exposure for maritime claims up to a maximum sum regardless of the actual amount of the claims being brought against him.

Throughout history, several systems of limitation of liability have been applied in the different jurisdictions. In order to provide international uniformity, the *International Maritime Committee* (CMI) introduced the *Convention on Limitation of Liability for Maritime Claims*, done at London on 19 November 1976 (LLMC), which is currently the most widely accepted treaty on global limitation of liability. Previously, the Conventions of 1924 and 1957 had been adopted, on the same subject.

I. Sources of Law

132. The Kingdom of Spain traditionally regulated the limitation of liability via the provisions of the Commercial Codes of 1829 and 1885. But in 2014, the MNA simplified the previous – domestic and international – regimes, which were fairly confusing. It did so based on LLMC, amended by the Protocol of 1996 (Title VII, *On limitation of liability,* Articles 392–405).

According to Article 392 of the MNA, the right to limit liability in claims arising from a same accident shall be governed by the terms set forth in the *Protocol of 1996* that amends the *Convention on Limitation of Liability for Maritime Claims*, done at London on 19 November 1976, with the reservations made by Spain in the Instrument of Adhesion, and in the MNA. Therefore, LLMC has been given domestic effect in the Kingdom of Spain.

133. The LLMC and the MNA (Articles 392–405) regulate what can be called the *general* or *global* regime of limitation of liability, the so-called *limitation of liability for maritime claims*. But in the same MNA there are also other special regimes of limitation applicable to the sea carrier of goods or passengers within the framework of claims for breaches of the relevant transport contracts. Shipping companies may opt for the overall amount or the specific ones to which they may be entitled due to contracts to use the ship (as a carrier of merchandise or to transport passengers) or due to other specific clauses (Article 395 MNA).

Limitation of liability is a right that may be invoked in any proceedings. The general regime of limitation of liability shall apply independently of whether the liability is demanded in a judicial procedure of a civil, labour or criminal nature, or by administrative means (Article 393 MNA).

Concerning the scope of application of the general regime of limitation of liability, it shall be applied always if any of the holders of the right to limit his or her liability invokes that right before the competent Spanish judicial or administrative bodies. To that end, the nationality or domicile of the creditors or debtors shall be irrelevant, as well as the flag of the ship with regard to which the right of limitation is invoked (Article 394 MNA).

II. Ships for Which Limitation of Liability Can Be Invoked

134. Limitation of liability may be invoked for all sea-borne craft with the exception of naval artefacts and fixed platforms built to explore or exploit natural resources on the seabed or subsoil (Article 394 (2) MNA).

In the field of towage, limitation of liability raises some particular questions that are not solved in Spanish national legislation. For example, can limitation be invoked at all in respect of the tug and tow, considering both of them the *seagoing ship* within Article 1 (2) LLMC?

III. Claims Subject to Limitation

135. Credits liable to cover the general limitation regimen are defined positively and negatively in the LLMC and the MNA.

Article 396 of the MNA lists the types of claims in respect of which the right of limitation is available:

a) Claims for death or bodily injuries, or for losses or damage to property, including damage to port works, navigable channels, aids to navigation and other property of the maritime or port domain, that may take place on board or be directly linked to operation of the ship or to the salvage operations, as well as damages arising from any such causes;
b) Claims related to damages arising from delay in transporting cargo, passengers and their luggage;
c) Claims related to damages arising from breach of non-contractual rights, arising directly from operation of the ship or from salvage operations;
d) Claims promoted by a person other than the one responsible, related to the measures taken in order to avoid or lessen damage with regard to which the party responsible may limit its liability and those subsequently caused by those measures, except when those have been adopted by virtue of a contract arranged by the person responsible.

These claims are subject to limitation of liability regardless of the basis of liability, notwithstanding the action exercised having a contractual or tortious nature.

IV. Claims Excluded from Limitation

136. The following claims are expressly excluded from the general limitation regime (Article 397 MNA):

1. claims for salvage or contribution in general average;

2. claims for oil pollution damage within the meaning of the International Convention on Civil Liability for Oil Pollution Damage, dated 29 November 1969 or of any amendment or Protocol thereto which is in force;
3. claims subject to any international convention or national legislation governing or prohibiting limitation of liability for nuclear damage;
4. claims against the shipowner of a nuclear ship for nuclear damage;
5. claims by servants of the ship operator or salvor whose duties are connected with the ship or the salvage operations, including claims of their heirs, dependents or other persons entitled to make such claims.
6. claims by the Maritime Authorities or a Port Authority that are envisaged by the provisions on removal of ships of the MNA and of the SPMNA.

V. Counterclaims

137. As expressly provided for in Article 5 of the LLMC, where a person entitled to limitation of liability has a claim against the claimant arising out of the same occurrence, their respective claims shall be set off against each other and the balance, if any, shall be subject to limitation.

To be able to implement this provision, it is necessary first to establish that the parties involved are persons entitled to limitation of liability under the LLMC and that their claims arose out of the same event.

VI. Conduct Barring Limitation

138. A person liable shall not be entitled to limit his liability if it is proved that the loss resulted from his personal act or omission, committed with the intent to cause such loss, or recklessly and with knowledge that such loss would probably result (Article 4 LLMC).

VII. Persons Entitled to Limit Their Liability

139. The grounds of the limitation of liability regime are objective (as it refers to certain credits alone) and it does not generate presumption of liability when claiming (the act of invoking limitation of liability shall not constitute an admission of liability).

Persons entitled to limit liability are those stated in Article 1 of the LLMC:

1. *Shipowners.* The term *shipowner* shall mean the owner, charterer, manager and operator of a seagoing ship. In the framework of the LLMC, the liability of a shipowner shall include liability in an action brought against the vessel itself. Since the concept of shipowner in LLMC has not been defined clearly enough, the question must be solved according to national law (in the Spanish jurisdiction, according to Articles 145, 203, 207 and 314 MNA).

2. *Salvors.* For limitation purposes, the term salvor means any person rendering services in direct connection with salvage operations. Salvage operations shall also include the raising, removal, destruction or the rendering harmless of a ship which is sunk, wrecked, stranded or abandoned, including anything that is or has been on board such ship, and the operations taken in order to avert or minimize loss for which the person liable may limit his liability in accordance with the LLMC, and further loss caused by such measures.
3. *Servants and Agents.* Any person for whose act the shipowner or salvor is responsible. If a claim subject to limitation of liability is made against the master or a crew member, or against any other person for whose act, neglect, or default the ship operator or salvor is responsible, such person shall have the right to limit his liability to the same extent as his principal.
4. *The insurer of liability* for claims subject to limitation in accordance with the rules of the LLMC shall be entitled to the benefits of this Convention to the same extent as the insured himself. Consequently, if the insured is denied the right to limit, then the insurer will also be prevented from limiting his liability.

VIII. Maximum Sums of Compensation

140. The *general limits of liability* are stated in Article 398 of the MNA: the maximum sum of compensation payable on limitable claims shall be calculated for each accident, progressively, according to the gross tonnage of the ship with regard to which the credits have arisen, pursuant to the terms set forth in Articles 6–9 of the Convention on Limitation of Liability for Maritime Claims.

141. Article 399 establishes the *special limits of liability:*

1. With regard to *claims related to death or bodily injuries of passengers* on a ship arising out of a same accident and notwithstanding its gross tonnage, the limit to liability shall be the sum established in the international conventions and the provisions of the European Union multiplied by the number of passengers the ship is authorized to transport, pursuant to its certificate. To these ends, the concept of passenger shall be deemed to include individuals who, with the consent of the carrier, are travelling on board accompanied by a vehicle or live animals, by virtue of a goods transport contract.
2. The limits on liability applicable to ships and vessels with a tonnage under 300 tonnes are:
    a) One million special drawing rights for claims related to death or bodily injury;
    b) Five hundred thousand special drawing rights for other limitable claims.

142. In case of concurrence of creditors, Article 400 of the MNA rules that the sums obtained pursuant to the terms set forth in the preceding rules shall form the relevant fund, which shall be distributed among the creditors arising from the same accident, in proportion to the amount of their recognized claims. Notwithstanding this, if the amount dedicated to claims for death or injury does not suffice to settle their full amount, the creditors shall compete for the remainder with the other limitable creditors for collection, with equal rank, from the fund assigned to settle the material credits.

In all cases, the Maritime and Port Authorities shall have preference in collection over all the creditors whose claims are not due to death or bodily injury, in the case of claims for damage caused to port works, navigation channels, aids to navigation and, in general, the maritime or port property.

The person responsible, its insurer or any third party that has paid out a claim assignable to a limitation fund prior to its distribution, shall subrogate itself in the rights the person compensated would have had to that fund (Article 401 MNA).

143. The MNA (Article 402) also establishes a rule on the conversion to Spanish currency of the sums referred to in the LLMC and the MNA: they shall be converted to euros at the current exchange rate on the date when the relevant limitation fund is constituted. That exchange rate shall be calculated according to the evaluation method effectively applied by the International Monetary Fund to its operations and transactions on the date concerned.

IX. Limitation Fund

144. According to Spanish Law, as a condition of the right to limitation, a person intending to limit its liability should set up a limitation fund. The effect of such limitation is that the creditors may enforce their respective claims against any assets of the liable party, but only up to the limitation amounts.

For valid allegation of the right to limitation before the Spanish jurisdictional bodies, the holder must constitute the relevant limitation fund, formed by the sums established in the MNA, along with the legal interest accrued from the date of the accident that gave rise to the liability (Article 403 LNM).

A fund may be constituted by depositing the relevant sum or providing a sufficient guarantee in the opinion of the Court.

The duly endowed fund may only be used to settle claims with regard to which limitation of liability may be invoked, even in the case of bankruptcy of the holder of the right to be limited.

Once the limitation fund is constituted, the holders of limitable credits shall lack action to pursue any other assets of the debtor, as well as against other debtors related to the same credit.

Where a limitation fund has been properly constituted, the ships or any other assets belonging to the holder of the right to be limited, that have been arrested or seized to respond for a claim that may be brought against the fund constituted, shall be released by order by the Court that oversaw the constitution thereof (Article 404 MNA).

To constitute a limitation fund, as well as to distribute it among the different creditors, the procedure regulated in Articles 487–500 of the MNA, as described further below, shall apply.

The right to constitute a limitation fund shall expire within the term of two years, from the day of lodging the first judicial claim arising from the accident that gives rise to invocation of the right to limit.

X. Procedure

145. The procedure to limit liability for maritime credits is established in Articles 487–500 of the MNA. It is a non-contentious procedure. Its provisions apply when a person entitled to limitation of liability pursues such limitation before a court.

The shipowners, charterer, operator, salvor or liability insurer against whom claims are made and who applies for limitation of liability in accordance with law after occurrence of a marine accident may constitute a limitation fund with a maritime court having jurisdiction.

The limitation fund should be set up with the competent commercial court. The commercial court hearing any limitable claim that has been filed against the holder of the right to limit shall be competent to hear the constitution of the liability limitation fund. In the event of intending to invoke the right to limit before Spanish judicial bodies with regard to claims filed before foreign judicial bodies, the terms foreseen in the European Union provisions and relevant treaties shall apply (Article 487 MNA).

A. Invocation and Term of Constitution

146. An application for limitation of liability may be submitted by any person entitled by law to limit his liability.

All persons who invoke the right to limit the liability claimed in civil proceedings must commence formalities to constitute a limitation fund within the maximum term of *ten days* from the invocation.

To that end, they should file an application to constitute the fund, in the manner determined in the MNA, before the same Court that hears the claim, which shall be processed in a separate Section to the main suit (Article 488 MNA).

B. Invocation in Other Proceedings

147. When the limitations are alleged in criminal, contentious-administrative or labour court proceedings, or in administrative proceedings, the application to constitute a fund must be filed before the commercial court of the same place, being proven by testimonial to the Criminal Court, the Contentious-Administrative or Labour Court or administrative body within the term of ten days.

In these cases, the final judgments or resolutions handed down in those proceedings shall not be enforceable other than against the fund regularly constituted.

The competent commercial court shall process the application according to the terms provided in the MNA and, in all matters not foreseen herein, by the oral trial proceedings, regulated in Articles 437–447 of the *Civil Procedure Act*. The oral trial shall commence with a concise claim indicating the identification particulars and circumstances of the claimant and the defendant and the address or addresses where they can be summoned and specifying the claim with clarity and precision.

C. *Content of the Application*

148. As provided for in Article 490 of the MNA, the application to constitute a limitation fund must be filed in writing signed by a barrister and a solicitor. It has to record the relevant facts regarding the limitation invoked, accompanied by the following documents:

a) Document that evidences deposit in the account of the Court of the amount of the maximum sum of compensation, according to the nature of the claims formulated, increased by their legal interest from the date of the accident until that of constitution. The deposit may be substituted by a sufficient guarantee in favour of the Court granted by a financial institution authorized to operate in Spain;
b) Certified copy of the tonnage certificate;
c) Crew list of the ship at the moment of the accident;
d) In the case of the limitation stated referring to claims for death or injury of passengers, certificate of the maximum number of passengers the ship is authorized to carry;
e) Certified copy of the certificate of seaworthiness of the ship;
f) Certificate by the monetary authority on the euro conversion rate of the Special Drawing Right (SDR) at the moment of constituting the fund;
g) Document that records calculation of the amount of the limitation;
h) List of creditors subject to limitation, stating their address, if known, the title claimed and the estimated amount.

D. *Admission and Correction*

149. If the court decides that the applicant is entitled to limit its liability in the case under consideration, it will issue an order admitting the application.

The Court shall hand down that order if the above requisites are fulfilled, granting the applicant, in the contrary case, a term of five days to correct the omissions appreciated.

150. The Court may reject the application if he considers the amount of the fund is wrongly calculated according to the data stated, in which case it shall specify the adequate amount and also grant a term of five days to correct this (Article 491 MNA).

E. Order of Admission or Refusal

151. In the order on admission to consideration, the Court shall *declare constitution of the limitation fund,* without prejudice to the motions to challenge that may subsequently be filed.

The testimonial of that order shall be a sufficient title to obtain, in any other judicial or administrative proceedings arising from the same accident, the removal of any arrests or other injunctive measures on the ship or other assets owned by the person who holds the right to limit. The same loss of actions shall take place before other debtors with the same credit, on behalf of whom the fund may have been established.

Such proceedings shall continue until a judgment is handed down, although their enforcement against the persons who benefit from the limitation shall forcibly be accumulated in the file on integration and distribution of the fund.

152. The order refusing constitution of the fund may be contested on appeal by the applicant.

F. Appointment of a Commissioner-Liquidator

153. In the order of admission, the Court shall order appointment of a commissioner-liquidator.

The parties concerned may object to the commissioner-liquidator invoking the causes established regarding experts in the Civil Procedure Act (Articles 120–123).

The expert appointed has to accept office within the term of three days by appearing before the Court. He shall be entitled, in fees and expenses, to remuneration equal to 1% of the fund finally distributed among the creditors, and may request a provision of funds for immediate expenses, which shall be borne by the applicant.

G. Forming Sections and Provisional Distribution

154. The commissioner-liquidator shall form the separate sections. The first shall be dedicated to regulating the statement of liabilities of the fund, the second shall contain everything related to the statement of assets and the third shall be the section on distribution.

155. The commissioner-liquidator may submit a proposal to the Court, when deemed convenient, for provisional distribution of part of the fund. If the Court were to approve this, the commissioner-liquidator may advance payments, within the limits established in each case, which shall always be to the account of what shall be deemed appropriate according to the definitive distribution.

H. Publicity in Establishing the Statements

156. Once the order constituting the fund is final, the commissioner-liquidator shall notify all the creditors stated in the writ by the applicant, as well as all those who subsequently appear, of commencement of the proceedings and of their right to declare their credit and to be a party to the proceedings.

The order shall be advertised in the *Official Journal of the Business Registry* and, if the commissioner-liquidator sees it fit, in other media.

The notifications and other incidents regarding creditors, their claims and titles, their respective amount and their integration in the block assets shall be ordered in the first section.

The creditors shall be granted a term of thirty days to present their titles and receipts of credit. That term shall be doubled for those residents abroad. The commissioner-liquidator may demand the documentation he considers necessary from each creditor to duly evidence credit.

I. Order Drawing up the Statement of Liabilities

157. The party constituting the fund or the creditors may submit the allegations to the commissioner-liquidator leading to challenging the appropriateness or amount of the credits. They may also allege the inappropriateness of their inclusion in the statement of liabilities.

The commissioner-liquidator shall submit a report to the Court with the list of credits admitted in the statement of liabilities and their provisional or final amount, as well as the motions to challenge or allegations received and the reasons to justify his decision. Considering that report, the Court shall decide by order on the composition of the statement of liabilities.

A reconsideration request may be filed against the order by the parties concerned, and a remedy of appeal may be filed against the decision thereon before the Provincial Court of Appeal (*Audiencia Provincial*).

J. Order Forming the Statement of Assets

158. The section on the statement of assets of the fund must record the motions to challenge that, where appropriate, the creditors may make regarding the appropriateness of the right to limit the liability or amount and type of fund. Notification of such motions to challenge shall be given to the applicant so allegations may be submitted within the term of twenty days.

The motions to challenge must be filed within the maximum term of three months once each creditor is notified of the proceedings, not being admissible thereafter.

Once the latter term has elapsed, whether or not motions to challenge have been filed, the commissioner-liquidator shall submit his report to the Court on the validity and amount of the limitation fund, as well as the motions to challenge filed and the reasons that justify his opinion.

Finally, the Court shall issue an order on the appropriateness and amount of the fund, and a remedy of appeal may be filed against the decision thereon before the Provincial Court of Appeal.

K. Complement to the Statement of Assets

159. Should the proceedings to which the above article refers establish a different amount of the fund to that already deposited or constituted, the applicant shall make up the latter within the term of ten days, even if that order is appealed. If it does not do so, it shall forfeit its right to limit its liability with the effects foreseen below.

L. Termination Due to Inappropriateness of the Limitation

160. If a final resolution were to establish that limitation of liability is inappropriate, the Court shall declare conclusion of the proceedings. Notwithstanding, the bank guarantee or sum deposited shall be withheld for sixty days to assure the claims that are submitted to the competent Court and also to guarantee enforcement of those that have already been filed.

M. Section and Order on Distribution

161. The fund shall be distributed amongst the creditors whose claims qualify for settlement out of the fund in proportion to their established claims against it.

When the orders approving the statements of assets and liabilities of the fund are final, the commissioner-liquidator shall prepare a proposal for distribution according to the terms discussed above. The creditors shall be notified of the proposal, having a term of twenty days to challenge.

Considering the definitive report by the commissioner-liquidator, the Court shall resolve, by order that may be challenged by a request for reconsideration and by appeal.

Chapter 5. Charter Parties

§1. Definition and Varieties of Charter Parties

I. Definitions of Charter Party

162. In maritime business, the term *charter party* (derived from the Latin *carta partita*) is used to designate the *document* in which are set forth the contractual engagements entered into when one person (charterer) takes over the use of the whole (or part) of a ship belonging to another (owner). Charter parties contracts differ from bill of lading contracts: they are classified as contracts for the use of the vessel, as opposed to bill of lading contracts, which are classified as contracts for the carriage of goods.

However, for Spanish Law, in general, a charter party is mainly used for the purpose of carriage of goods by sea. Therefore, charter parties are generally deemed as contracts of carriage of goods by sea. In fact, this charter is merely a special kind of contract of carriage.

163. A contract of carriage of goods by ship may be concluded for the carriage of goods in the whole ship, in a proportional part of the ship, or in a specified space thereof (*Charter Party*, in strict sense or *voyage charter party*), or for the carriage of specific goods (*Contract of Carriage by bill of lading*).

Article 203 of the MNA provides a concept of charter party: *the contract for carriage of goods by sea, also called charter party, binds the carrier, in exchange for a freight, to transport goods by sea and deliver them to the consignee at the port or place of destination.* Therefore, the legal nature of a voyage charter as a contract of carriage of goods by sea does not mean that it is not a charter party.

164. Notwithstanding this, sometimes it may be used for other purposes, e.g., for the employment of a ship as a floating hotel under a bareboat charter party. In cases where the availability of a ship is contracted for purposes other than carriage of goods, the provisions established for charter parties that refer to availability and use of the ship, as well as to its charter and early termination, shall apply, to the extent that such provisions are compatible with the purpose of the contract entered into (Article 210 MNA).

165. As a rule, in commercial practice these are two different kinds of contracts, documented in different kinds of documents: charter parties and bill of ladings, respectively. Charter parties are normally used in tramp trade, and bill of ladings in liner trade. However, a bill of lading can also be used in the framework of a charter party: the charterer by time or voyage may also enter into charter parties on its own behalf for carriage of specific goods under bill of lading regime with third parties. In that case, the carrier and the charterer shall be held jointly and severally liable to third parties for damages and breakage of the merchandise transported, pursuant to the rules of transport under bill of lading, without prejudice to the right to reimbursement amongst them as set forth in the charter party (Article 207 MNA).

II. Varieties of Charter Parties

166. The MNA laid down a specific systematization of the *contracts for the employment of ships* used in shipping industry and maritime trade, in Title IV.

First of all, contracts for the employment of ships may take the form of *demise charters* (Articles 188–202: *On ship lease contracts*). This contract (known in practice as *bareboat charter party*, or *bareboat charter* or *charter party by demise*) is defined in Article 188 MNA as a contract under which the shipowners provide with an unmanned ship which the charterers shall possess, employ and operate during the contractual period against payment of hire. The bareboat charter party is not deemed as contract of carriage of goods by sea. The charterer not only has the use of the vessel, but also engages its own crew, maintains and insures the ship and controls its commercial operations. In other terms, the charterers become the de facto owners of the ship for the period of lease.

The so-called *contracts of affreightment* or *charter parties* in strict sense are further divided into several categories: *contracts of carriage of goods by sea under bill of lading* and *contracts relating to other maritime transport services.*

Moreover, a charter party may be concluded for one or more voyages (*Voyage Charter*), or for a certain period of time (*Time Charter*).

167. The MNA treats each of the above contracts separately.

1. In voyage charters, the carrier undertakes to perform one or several specific voyages. The voyage charter party or *voyage charter* is defined in Article 204 (1) of the MNA as a charter party under which the shipowners charter out and the charterers charter in the whole or part of the ship's space for the carriage by sea of the intended goods from one port to another and the charterers pay the agreed amount of freight. These provisions entail the use of the entire ship and the transport of cargo. The ship is manned and navigated by the owner.
2. In time charters, the carrier undertakes to perform all the voyages the charterer has ordered during the period agreed, within the limits agreed. The time charter party or *time charter*, is defined in Article 204 (2) of the MNA as a contract under which the shipowners provide a designated manned ship to the charterers and the charterers employ the ship during the contractual period for the agreed service against payment of hire. The time charterer undertakes business management of the ship and, unless otherwise agreed, shall bear all variable operating expenses. In voyage charters, such expenses shall be borne by the carrier, except if otherwise agreed. Under Spanish Law, a time charter party is deemed as contract of carriage of goods by sea.
3. As for the charter for transport of specific merchandise under *bill of lading regime*, the MNA states that a charter party may also refer to carriage of goods determined by their weight, size or class. In that case, the conditions of the contract may be recorded in the bill of lading or other similar document (Article 205).

In the preceding cases, the parties may mutually compel each other to sign a charter party.

168. Finally, the contract may also refer to transport of a set of goods in several ships or on several voyages, *Bulk contracts*, in which case the provisions on voyage charter shall apply to each one of those agreed, unless otherwise agreed by the parties (Article 208 MNA).

§2. Applicable Laws

I. Domestic Laws

169. In Spanish Law, charter parties are dealt in the MNA (Articles 203–286).

II. Standard Forms of Charter Parties

170. Under Spanish Law, the parties to a charter party have a wide freedom to negotiate the terms of the contract that suit their particular business; they may freely negotiate their contractual relationship except with regard to those issues which have been regulated by an express mandatory rule of the MNA.

As a matter of general principle, the provisions of the MNA dealing with charter parties are of an optional nature and non-compulsory, with the exception of some special rules regarding the seaworthiness of the ship (the carrier's obligation to exercise due diligence to make the ship seaworthy) and the liability of the carrier.

In consequence, in Spain, charter parties are on most occasions formed and concluded on the basis of a standard form. Charter parties are highly standardized. The rights and obligations of the shipowners and the charterers are mainly determined by the terms and conditions of the charter party. The regulations set forth in the MNA shall be applicable if the agreement between the parties (the charter party) does not provide otherwise.

Charter parties are on most occasions formed and concluded on the basis of a chosen standard form applicable to the particular trade, and then amending its provisions and including typewritten addenda to reflect the particular agreement made between the parties. There are various standard forms of charter parties of worldwide use, also employed in Spain, such as those produced by the BIMCO. For example: *Gencon* (for voyage charters of dry cargos), *Asbantankvoy* (voyage charters of oil trades), *Baltime* (for time charters) and *Barecon* (for bareboat charters). Other relevant standard form is NYPE 93 (for time charters). There are also other standard forms of charters for specific trades: *Graincon* (for grains trade) or *Cementvoy* 2006 (for cargos of bulk cement).

§3. Charter That Refers to the Whole or Part of the Ship's Cargo Space: Voyage Charter Party

171. The voyage charter contract is a contract whereby the ship manager undertakes to provide the charterer the entire ship, or its part, to carry out a particular voyage with a particular cargo. This is the charter contract *in the strict sense*, and the oldest form of charter, whereby the ship, as an element of the agreement, is at the disposal of the charterer. Under Spanish Law, a voyage charter party is deemed as a contract of carriage of goods by sea. The legal nature of a voyage charter as a contract of carriage of goods by sea does not mean that it is not a charter party.

The ship *constitutes an element of the contract.* The charter contract is a contract whereby the ship owner undertakes to provide the charterer the ship to carry the goods by sea, whereas the carrier or charterer undertakes to use it according to the contract and to redeliver the ship upon the termination of the contract.

In this sense, a charter party is a bilateral agreement concluded between two parties: the *shipowners* (who provide the ship) and the *charterers* (who hire the ship for either a certain voyage or voyages against a fixed remuneration, called freight or hire). The owners retain the possession of the vessel and responsibility for the full cost of running it (capital, operation, insurance, maintenance and repair). The risk of the duration of the voyage is on the owners.

This charter party entails the usual terms of a contract such as the name of the contracting parties, the name of the ship, the duration of the voyage and the loaded cargo and the remuneration, the freight or hire.

172. As a general rule, the provisions in the MNA governing charter parties are mainly non-compulsory. However, since Spanish Law puts the shipowners under a voyage charter party basically in the same position as a carrier under a contract of carriage of goods by sea, some of the rules regarding carriage of goods by sea shall compulsorily apply to the shipowners.

I. Duties of the Shipowner

A. *To Make the Ship Available to the Charterer or Stevedore in the Port and on the Date Agreed*

173. The basic obligation of the shipowners is to provide the agreed ship to the charterers, in a seaworthy condition, within the period of time fixed in the charter, when the ship is expected ready to load.

The ship shall be made available to the charterer or stevedore at the *port agreed* in the contract, presuming, except for proof to the contrary, that both parties knew its characteristics on entering into the agreement. If the port agreed is impossible to enter or unsafe for the ship, either of the parties may terminate the contract, except if the impossibility or lack of safety is only temporary, in which case they shall be bound to wait a reasonable time to overcome the obstacle (Article 215 MNA).

174. The MNA also contemplates the *right to assign the port*, in Article 216. Should the charterer have reserved the power to assign the port where the ship is to be made available in the contract, it shall choose a safe port that is accessible to the ship within the appropriate term. Should the port not fulfil those conditions, the carrier may demand assignment of another port within the same area in order to fulfil the contract and, if the charterer does not do so, it may terminate the contract, without prejudice to claiming damages for losses. The carrier will have the same right if the charterer does not assign the chosen port in a timely manner.

In the case of damage suffered by the ship as a consequence of lack of safety of the dock or loading place assigned by the charterer, it shall be held liable for such, except if it is proven that the master did not act with the required nautical diligence of a competent commander. In time charters, this provision is applicable in relation to all the ports the charterer has assigned during the term of the contract.

Regarding the *dock or loading place*, according to Article 217 of the MNA, two different rules shall apply.

1) In voyage charter parties, unless otherwise agreed, the charterer may assign the dock or loading place the ship shall head for within the port where it is made available, as long as this is safe and accessible for the ship before, during and after loading. Should such assignment not have been established within a reasonable term, the carrier may keep the ship at anchor while awaiting orders, or head for the usual dock or loading place for the goods concerned, charging the charterer for the time elapsed.
2) In charters to carry goods under bill of lading regime, the power to choose the loading place lies with the carrier, who shall report his choice to the consignor with enough time in advance.

175. The charterer may terminate the contract if the ship is not available on the date agreed. It may also claim compensation for the damage suffered if breach thereof is due to the carrier (Article 214 MNA).

B. To Carry the Cargo in the Ship Expressly Stipulated

176. It is the shipowner's basic duty to carry the cargo in the ship expressly stipulated in the contract, or in one having the specified features.

The ship must have the conditions set forth in the contract regarding nationality, classification, speed, consumption, capacity and other characteristics. Should the ship not fulfil any of these, the charterer may demand compensation for the damages caused, except if the breach hinders the intended purpose of the contract, in which case the latter may also terminate the contract(Article 213 MNA).

Should the contract refer to a specific ship, it may not be replaced by another, except for an explicit agreement authorizing this.

If the parties did not expressly agree upon a particular ship or its features, the carrier is bound to carry the cargo by a ship having features customary for the stipulated carriage.

C. To Make the Ship Seaworthy

177. The shipowner must deliver the ship to the charterer in the condition that makes her suitable for the purposes identified in the contract. According to Article

212 of the MNA, the carrier shall ensure that the ship is in an adequate seaworthy state to receive the cargo on board and to transport it safely to its destination, taking into account the foreseeable circumstances of the voyage planned, its phases and the nature of the cargo contracted.

This is a *compulsory non-delegable statutory obligation*; contractual provisions to the contrary will not have any legal effect. This *ius cogens* provision renders the *Owners' Responsibility Clauses* of standard voyages charter parties, totally or partly invalid.

However, the MNA regulates differently the scope of the obligation at the diverse stages of the voyage:

1) The state of seaworthiness *shall exist at the moment the voyage commences*, or on each one of the voyages included in the contract. At the moment of receiving cargo on board, the ship shall be at least in a state that makes it able to preserve the goods safely.
2) The carrier shall exercise *reasonable diligence* to *maintain* the ship in an adequate state of seaworthiness during the whole time the contract remains in force.

Therefore, the shipowners shall be bound, during the whole time the contract remains in force, to exercise due diligence to make the ship seaworthy. But in the previous stages of the trip, the obligation is not an obligation of means, but of result: the ship owner guarantees the seaworthiness of the ship.

178. The consequences of the lack of seaworthiness are stated in Article 224 (1) of the MNA: If, due to failure of the ship or another cause that disables it to sail, the voyage is interrupted at a port other than that of destination, the carrier shall provide custody for the merchandise while correcting the causes of having to put in. Should the ship be definitively incapacitated or if the delay might severely damage the cargo, the carrier has to provide transport at its expense to the agreed destination. Should the carrier not do so, the goods shall not accrue any freight whatsoever.

D. To Undertake the Voyage Without Undue Delay

179. An essential arrangement in every voyage charter is the obligation of the shipowner to proceed with reasonable dispatch, not only on the voyage itself, but also on the approach trip. That means that the owners are obliged, once the cargo is loaded, to carry it to the port of destination with *reasonable dispatch*.

The carrier must undertake the voyage and complete it as far as the destination port without undue delay (Article 220 MNA).

The carrier shall be liable for damages and losses caused due to unjustified delay in commencing the voyage (Article 221 MNA).

E. To Carry the Goods to the Port of Discharge on the Agreed or Customary or Geographically Direct Route Except for Reasonable Deviation

180. As a consequence of the obligation of *reasonable dispatch*, the carrier shall undertake the voyage and complete it as far as the destination port without undue delay and using the route agreed or, failing that, by the most appropriate route according to the circumstances (Article 220 MNA). Therefore, the owners must perform the voyage without departing intentionally from the agreed or usual route.

The carrier shall be liable for damages and losses caused by diversion of the ship from the agreed route or, failing that, from the most appropriate route according to the circumstances, should *such a diversion not be performed to save human lives or for any other reasonable, justified cause* that does not arise from an initial state of the ship not being seaworthy (Article 222 MNA).This compulsory statutory obligation renders *deviation clauses* of standard voyages charter parties, totally or partly invalid

F. Duty of Custody and Deliver

181. As we have already seen, the MNA puts the shipowners under a voyage charter party basically in the same position as a carrier under a contract of carriage of goods by sea.

The carrier must provide custody of the goods carried during all the phases of the voyage in an adequate manner according to their nature and circumstances, and must deliver them to the recipient at the final destination place (Article 220 MNA).

Consequently, the carrier shall be responsible for loss or damages suffered by the merchandise as a consequence of breach of the duty of custody pursuant to the terms set forth in the MNA for transport under bill of lading (Article 223 MNA): the carrier is liable for all damage or loss of goods, as well as delay in their delivery, caused while they are under custody.

182. Contractual clauses that aim directly or indirectly to attenuate or annul such liability to the detriment of the person entitled to receive the goods shall not take effect. However, such clauses, when agreed in the charter policy and if they do not involve exoneration for wilful misconduct or gross negligence by the carrier, shall be valid exclusively in the relations between it and the charterer, without those parties being able to oppose them to the consignor if he is a person other than the charterer in any case (Article 277 MNA).

183. The carrier must deliver the goods carried to the recipient authorized to receive them without delay and pursuant to the terms agreed. If the recipient does not appear or refuses delivery, the carrier may store the goods until their delivery, at the expense of the consignee, or resort to their judicial deposit (Article 228 MNA).

The *destination port* must be safe. Should the destination port assigned in the contract not be accessible under safe conditions for the ship, the carrier may head for the nearest convenient port and demand that delivery of the goods be accepted there. It may not make use of this faculty if the obstacle for access is only temporary, in which case it shall wait until correction within a reasonable time (Article 225 MNA).The carrier shall notify the consignee without delay and, in all cases, the charterer, of the diversion to the nearest port.

Should the cause of lack of safety exist at the moment of contracting, the carrier shall bear the expenses arising from unloading at a port other than that agreed, except if the circumstances lead to believe that it did not know the unsafe factors of the port at the moment of entering into the contract.

The same provisions shall be applicable to determining the *dock or unloading place* (Article 226 MNA).

II. Duties of the Charterer

A. *The Charterer Is Obliged to Pay the Shipowner the Agreed Freight*

184. The basic duty of the charterer is to pay the owners a sum of money known as *freight*. Freight is a fixed price for a particular voyage carrying a particular cargo. In commercial practice, the freight is normally calculated on the amount of shipping (the quantity of goods carried at a given rate per tonne).

Sometimes, the freight is fixed on a lump sum basis, irrespective of the actual quantity of goods supplied and loaded on board.

185. The MNA provides some rules for the calculation and accrual of the freight, in Article 233. The freight shall be calculated in the manner agreed in the contract and, failing that, according to the following rules:

a) If the freight is calculated by weight or volume of goods, it shall be set according to the weight or volume declared on the bill of lading, except for wilful misconduct or error;
b) In time charters, the freight shall be accrued on a daily basis during the whole time the ship is available to the charterer under conditions that allow its effective use.

186. Unless otherwise agreed, freight shall not accrue on goods lost during the voyage, except if the loss is due to their nature, inherent vice or defective packaging. If the loss is partial and the freight has been agreed according to the weight or size of the goods, the freight for the lost part shall not be accrued. Damaged goods shall accrue the freight agreed, without their abandonment to the carrier as a means of payment being valid (Article 234 MNA).

187. The charterer is bound to pay the freight under the conditions settled. Notwithstanding this, it may be agreed that the freight be payable by the recipient of the merchandise, this being recorded on the bill of lading or consignment note. In this case, the recipient shall be bound to pay the freight if it accepts or withdraws the merchandise at destination. Should the consignee refuse or not withdraw the goods, the freight shall be paid by the party that contracted the carriage (Article 235 MNA).

188. If the charterers fail to pay the freight and other expenses as agreed, the shipowner may exercise *lien* on the goods belonging to the charterers, according to Article 236 of the MNA. The goods transported shall be assigned preferentially to payment of the freight, delays and other expenses arising from their carriage until their delivery and during fifteen days thereafter, except if conveyed to a third party in good faith within the latter term.

The carrier shall be entitled to withhold the goods carried in its possession until it receives the freight, delays and other expenses arising from such carriage. It may not exercise that right against a consignee other than the charterer, except if the bill of lading or consignment note records the mention that the freight is payable at destination. It may also resort to deposit proceedings and sale of goods and luggage, requesting a Notary Public to sell the goods, with the same limitation with regard to a non-charterer consignee (Article 237 MNA), according to the procedure established in Articles 512 et seq. of the MNA.

The application for deposit and sale shall clearly state the following particulars:

a) Carriage concerned, with a copy of the bill of lading or title of passage;
b) Identity of the consignee if known;
c) Charter, passage or expenses claimed;
d) Description of the kind or quantity of goods for which deposit is requested, with their approximate appraisal;
e) Grounds for the application, whether for non-payment or failure to withdraw the goods.

The party applying for such a deposit shall propose the individuals or entities referred to in Article 626 of the Civil Procedure Act, on *Deposit in court and appointment of custodian*. The party subject to enforcement shall be appointed as the custodian should he have been using the attached assets for a productive activity or should they be difficult or costly to transport or store. Where it may be deemed more suitable, the Court Clerk may appoint the party seeking enforcement as the custodian or, after hearing such party, a third party by means of an order to move the proceedings forward. The appointment may be made to the Professional Association of Court Representatives of the location where the enforcement is being carried out, as long as it has a suitable service to undertake the legal responsibilities laid down for custodians. Should this be the case, the Association shall be empowered to proceed with the location, management and deposit of the assets and it shall be issued with the necessary credentials for such purposes.

Should the impediment to conclude the carriage be due to a fortuitous circumstance arising during the journey, which makes its continuation impossible, illegal or prohibited, indisputable evidence of the relevant event shall be provided.

189. When the application is admitted to consideration, the Notary Public shall require immediate payment to the consignee of the goods or luggage recorded in the title submitted. If it is not nominative, the demand shall not be made, except if so requested in the application, appointing a specific person for the purpose.

Should the consignee not be found, or the party required does not pay or grant a sufficient guarantee of payment in the act of demand or within forty-eight hours thereafter, the Notary Public shall order deposit of the goods or luggage.

Once the deposit is performed and the custodian named, the Notary Public shall order the appraisal and sale by a specialized individual or firm or at public auction, to the ends stated.

Sale of the items deposited shall also be appropriate when a risk of deterioration arises, or when, due to their conditions or other circumstances, the conservation or custody expenses are disproportionate.

The proceeds of the sale shall first be used to pay the expenses of deposit and the auction, and the remainder shall be delivered to the applicant to pay for the charter or expenses claimed, and up to that limit.

B. The Charterers Shall Properly and Carefully Carry the Loading and Stevedore Operations Within the Laytime

190. As noted above, the shipowners must provide the agreed ship to the charterers within the time or period of time fixed in the charter when or during which the ship is expected ready to load (*laytime*).

Accordingly, unless the charter party provides otherwise, the charterer or stevedore shall place the goods alongside the ship and shall perform the loading and stacking thereof at its expense and risk, with the adequate diligence required by the nature of the merchandise and the voyage planned (Article 218 MNA).

However, even when it is agreed that the loading and stacking be performed at the expense and risk of the charterer or consignor, the carrier shall be liable for the consequences arising from defective stacking that compromises the safety of the voyage. Therefore, if bad stowage constitutes unseaworthiness of the ship, the shipowners obligation to exercise due diligence to make the ship seaworthy stated in Article 194 of the MNA is not discharged and they shall be liable for loss of or damage or delay in delivery of goods resulting from it. It must be underlined that, according to SPMNA, loading and stacking is a *harbour service*, regulated in Articles 108 and 130 and following of the SPMNA, which incorporates the regulation of the economic regime and provision of services in ports of general interest. The provision of this service corresponds to private individuals, after obtaining a licence which can be acquired by competitive bidding in accordance with the specifications approved by the respective Port Authority. As all harbour services, loading and unloading is provided under a competitive system, and only in cases where there is a lack of private initiative does the SPMNA allow these services to be directly provided by the Port Authority.

The carrier may board goods on deck as long as the charterer specifically accepts this, or when it is in keeping with the practices or regulations in force (Article 219 MNA).

191. The charterer or recipient shall also unstack and unload the goods without delay at its cost and risk, as well as withdraw them from alongside the ship. The parties may establish diverse specific clauses regarding such operations (Article 227 MNA).

C. The Charterer Is Obliged to Pay the Expenses Made Due to the over Delay

192. In return for the payment of freight, the owners will allow an agreed period of time for the cargo to be loaded and a further period for its discharge in the port of destination. This time is called *laytime.*

The MNA contains some rules for the *calculation of laytime* in Articles 239 and 240:

1. If the contract were to establish a laytime for loading or unloading the goods, this shall be calculated excluding holidays according to the official calendar or practices in the port concerned, except if otherwise agreed. If a set term is not established, the laytime shall be the usual term according to the conditions of the ship, port and goods.
2. Nor shall the laytime be calculated, except if otherwise agreed, during periods when it is impossible to work, due to fortuitous causes, on the respective loading or unloading operation.
3. Laytime calculation shall commence, except if otherwise agreed, when the ship has reached the dock or loading or unloading place assigned, is ready to perform such operations and when the charterer or person assigned in the contract has received the relevant notification.

193. Once the laytime has ended, without having concluded the loading or unloading operations, the *delay time* (or *demurrage*) shall automatically begin to be counted. The charterer shall pay the amount set in the contract for the delay time arising. If its amount has not been agreed, a sum shall be paid equal to that which may have been set according to the business practice for ships of similar characteristics, with a similar cargo and voyage (Article 241 MNA). In this field, as an agreed reference for dispute resolution, *the Laytime Definitions for Charter Parties* 2013 could be applicable, adopted by BIMCO at the Documentary Committee in Paris in May 2013. These rules were developed to provide practitioners with a set of meanings of commonly-used words and phrases. The objective is to help reduce disputes about party intentions in a market where fixtures are often concluded on the basis of a recap message and listed amendments, without the exchange or return of draft contracts.

The duration of the delay term shall be set in the charter party and, failing that, shall last as many days as the working ones in the laytime. Calculation of the delay shall be by consecutive hours and days, being suspended only when it is impossible to load or unload due to causes arising from operation of the ship (Article 242 MNA).

Once the delay period has expired without the loading or unloading having concluded, the carrier may demand compensation of the losses caused due to *subsequent detention of the ship* without this being subject to the contractual or legal amount set for delays. Notwithstanding this, the carrier may also set sail with the goods loaded up to that moment, or unload them on its account in the most adequate manner, depending on whether the expiry of the delay period took place in the port of loading or unloading. In the first case, it may claim the freight on the relevant empty carriage; in the second, the expenses arising from unloading not due to it pursuant to the contract (Article 243 MNA).

Unless otherwise agreed, the laytime rules established in the charter party for loading or unloading shall be calculated independently one from the other.

D. The Charterer Shall Provide the Agreed Goods for Loading

194. The charterer is also responsible for bringing the goods for loading to the agreed place, and for giving the appropriate certificate for loading and receipt for unloading.

He must also hold the necessary documents in order to clarify possible controls from the Port National Authorities on port legislation, safety, customs, borders and immigration, police, health, the environment and fishing, as well as the operating conditions established. As stated in Article 7 (3) of the MNA, authorization to enter port shall be granted by the Port Authorities, at the request of the ship operators, shipping companies, masters or shipping agents, and it shall also be subject to compliance with the Spanish legislation.

Regarding the delivery of the goods for loading, Article 229 of the MNA states that the charterer must place the merchandise alongside the ship for loading, except if another means of delivering the goods for transport has been agreed.

If it does not do so, the carrier may terminate the contract once the laytime has elapsed, and also claim compensation for the losses suffered.

The charterer that does not load all the goods contracted must pay the charter for the amount it has ceased to load, except if the carrier has taken another cargo to make up the capacity of the ship (Article 230 MNA).

195. The charterer may not load clandestine or hazardous goods. Should this happen, the MNA provides some remedies, on behalf of the shipowners.

Regarding clandestine loading, by virtue of Article 231, no goods of a kind other than that contracted may be loaded, except if it is possible to do so without any damage to the carrier and other consignors. In the latter case, the carrier may demand the freight that would usually be paid for the goods loaded. If different goods are loaded without notifying the carrier, the charterer shall be responsible for all damages and losses that might arise from such to the carrier or other consignors, without prejudice to the obligation to pay the relevant freight. The carrier may unload the goods if this is convenient to prevent severe damages to the ship or the cargo.

As for the loading of hazardous good, Article 232 states that these goods may not be loaded without prior declaration of their nature to the carrier, and without its consent to transport such, and in any event, they shall be marked and labelled by the consignor pursuant to the rules in force for each class of such goods. Should the charterer load hazardous goods, it shall be held liable to the carrier and before the other consignors for all damages and losses caused. Moreover, such goods may be unloaded, destroyed or transformed to make them harmless at any time, as required by the circumstances, without right to compensation.

Even in the case of correctly declared loading of hazardous goods, these may be unloaded, destroyed or transformed to make them harmless at any time if they become a real hazard to individuals or property, without right to compensation, unless the carrier is responsible for the situation of danger, or when it is appropriate to pay these in the general average.

III. Other Statutory Provisions

196. The conditions of chartering of a ship can be set forth in the charter party, but there is no legal obligation to conclude the agreement in writing. However, the parties of the voyage charter may mutually compel each other to sign a charter party (Article 204 (3) MNA).The document serves as a proof of the terms of the contract, since the charter party is only an evidence of the contract. In other terms, the charter party is not a formal contract: its conclusion can also be made orally, although in commercial practice that situation is rather uncommon.

197. Spanish Law also regulates the *subcharterer*: the charterer of the ship by time or voyage may, except for specific provision to the contrary in the policy, subrogate a third party in the rights and obligations arising therefrom, without prejudice to continuing to be responsible for fulfilment thereof before the carrier (Article 206 MNA).

198. As for the *Multimodal transport*, the MNA states that should the transport contract include the use of means of transport other than sea, the rules of MNA shall apply only to the maritime phase of the transport, the other phases being regulated by the specific regulations thereon, as long as these are imperative (Article 209). These rules are, mainly: the Carriage of Goods by Land Act (Ley 15/2009, de 15 de noviembre, *del Contrato de Transporte Terrestre de Mercancías)*, and the Air Navigation Act (Ley 48/1960, de 21 de julio, *de Navegación Aérea*).

§4. Time Charter Party

199. A charter party may be concluded for a certain period of time (*Time Charter*). In contrast with voyage charters, the time charters are defined through the fixed period of the hire of the ship. Under a time charter party, the owners undertake to place their ship at the disposal of the charterers for a defined period of time, generally for the carriage of goods in accordance with the charterers' instructions.

Most of the rules established in the MNA for charters parties, in general, and voyage charter parties, in particular, are applicable, if the nature of the obligation in case make it possible, to time charter parties. But since the arrangement in charter parties is of some permanency, it is only logical that the clauses of the contract tend to assure the charterer a good deal more about the character and particulars of the ship he is getting.

It is a consequence of the fact that according to the general definition of Article 203 of the MNA, time charters are also deemed as contracts of carriage of goods by sea: *the contract for carriage of goods by sea, also called charter party, binds the carrier, in exchange for a freight, to transport goods by sea and deliver them to the consignee at the port or place of destination.*

In time charters, the carrier undertakes to perform all the voyages the charterer has ordered during the period agreed, within the *trading limits* agreed. The charterers' right to the commercial exploitation of the vessel is usually subject to certain geographical limits and to the exclusion of certain cargoes that it may carry (of dangerous or noxious nature).

200. The main feature of time charter party is defined in Article 204 (2) of the MNA: it is a contract under which the shipowners provide a designated manned ship to the charterers and the charterers employ the ship during the contractual period for the agreed service against payment of hire. In consequence, the vessel remains in both the ownership and possession of the owner, since the crew who man it will be the employees of the owner, not the charterers.

The time charterer *undertakes business management of the ship* and, unless otherwise agreed, shall bear all the variable operating expenses. It is a contract whereby the owners put the commercial operation of the vessel at the charterer's disposal. The owner keeps the nautical management, and the charterer the commercial management. The risk of delay to the ship in its commercial operation lies on the charterers.

This implies that the owner must deliver the ship to the charterer together with the ship's crew in accordance with the contract. The charterer has the right to give orders to the master related to the use of the ship for the purposes identified in the charter contract, but the charterer shall have no right to give the master orders related to the internal order on the ship, the composition of the crew, or the operation of the vessel.

201. Other specific rules for time charters contained in the MNA are the following:

1. In time charters, the freight (remuneration in the form of hire) shall be accrued on a daily basis during the whole time the ship is available to the charterer under conditions that allow its effective use (Article 233). The charterers are obliged to pay hire continuously for the entire period of the charter, unless they are denied the use of the ship by breach of charter by the owners. The hire will run from the commencement of the charter (*delivery*), to its termination (*redelivery*). However, its running may be interrupted by the operation of an *off-hire* clause, which provides for the temporary cessation of hire if certain events occur which deprive the charterers of the full use of the vessel.
2. In time charters, the carrier may withhold or deposit the goods due to nonpayment of freight when these belong to the charterer. Should they be owned

by third parties who have hired the charterer to provide carriage, the carrier may only withhold or deposit the goods for the amount of the freight they still owe the charterer (Article 238).
3. The contract shall be terminated at any moment when the ship is lost or definitively incapacitated to sail (Article 272 (1)).
4. In actions to compensate losses, breakages or delays suffered by the goods, the term shall be counted from the day on which the freight or other fees are due under the policy (Article 286 (3)).

However, it must be underlined that most of the obligations of the shipowners and the charterers under a time charter provided for in the MNA are non-compulsory. As a rule, the parties to a time charter may freely negotiate their contractual relationship except with regard to those issues which have been regulated by an express mandatory rule of the MNA.

202. The parties of the time charter may mutually compel each other to sign a charter party (Article 204 (3) MNA). In Spain, the most used document is the *Baltime* time charter.

§5. Early Termination of the Contract

203. The MNA contains a specific section on early termination of the contract of charter party (Articles 272–276).

First of all, the law enumerates the cases of extinction in Article 272. The contract shall be terminated in the following cases:

a) If, before the chartered ship sails it were to be lost or definitively unable to sail without any of the parties being to blame. In time charters, the extinction shall take place at any moment when the ship is lost or definitively incapacitated;
b) If the charter is by voyage or related to carriage of goods under the bill of lading regime and these are lost before loading without the charterer or consignor being at fault. In time charters, extinction due to loss of the goods shall not be applicable;
c) If, prior to the ship setting sail, the contractual carriage becomes impossible due to natural events, due to decisions by the authorities or causes beyond the control of the parties;
d) If, prior to the ship setting sail, an armed conflict breaks out in which the country of the port of loading or unloading is involved.

In all those cases, the carrier shall proceed, as appropriate, to unload and return the goods loaded. The cost of the operation shall be borne by the charterer.

204. The contract shall also be terminated in cases of *temporary impediment,* at the request of any of the parties if, prior to commencement of the voyage, an impediment were to arise, beyond the will of either party, that causes such a prolonged delay that the parties could not be expected to wait for it to disappear (Article 273 MNA).

In cases of *impediments arising during the voyage*, and they make it impossible, unlawful or prohibit its continuation or an armed conflict exists making the ship or cargo subject to risks not considered on entering into the contract, the carrier may put into the most convenient port for the common interest and unload the goods there, requiring the charterer to take charge of them at that place. In that case, the carrier shall be entitled to the freight in proportion to the distance covered. The cost, time and risks the party is subject to in proportion to the total voyage shall be taken into account in order to calculate the partial freight (Article 274 MNA).

205. There could also occur a *change in destination by the charterer*, when chartering the full ship by voyage: the charterer may order it to unload at a different port to that agreed, as long as it does not so expose the ship to higher risks than those foreseen on entering into the contract, paying the total contractual freight and the increased expenses caused(Article 275 MNA).

206. Finally, in cases of *sale of the ship* before loading of the goods commences, the buyer shall not be bound with regard to contracts entered into by the seller, the charter contract being extinguished if it refers to the ship sold, without prejudice to the right of the charterer to compensation from the seller(Article 276 MNA).However, the buyer of the ship shall respect the charters for a term exceeding one year when it knows of their existence at the time of acquiring the ship.

Should the sale take place once loading has commenced, or when the ship is on a voyage, the buyer shall fulfil the contracts regarding the goods on board, subrogating itself in the rights and obligations of the carrier.

§6. Bareboat Charter Party

I. Applicable Law

207. In the Title IV of the MNA (*on contracts for use of ships*), there is a specific chapter provided for the regulation of the bareboat charter: *on ship lease contracts* (Articles 188–202 MNA).

As a matter of general principle, the provisions of the MNA dealing with bareboat charter are of an optional nature, with the exception of those which have been expressly made mandatory.

Therefore, most of the obligations of the contract are freely settled by the parties, generally using one of the standard forms. In commercial practice, the most common standard contract in use is *Barecon 2001*.

II. Concept and Form of the Contract

208. Spanish Law contains a concept of the contract: by means of a ship lease agreement, the lessor is bound, in exchange for a set price, to deliver a specific ship to the lessee in order for the latter to use it temporarily according to the terms agreed or, failing that, according to its nature and characteristics (Article 188 MNA). It is not a contract for the carriage of goods by sea, but for the rent of a thing: the ship. Therefore, as a supplementary source, the provisions of the *Civil Code* regulating *the contract of lease* shall be applicable (Articles 1543 et seq.).

Regarding the form of contract, by virtue of Article 189 of the MNA the lease contract of the ship shall be recorded in writing.

Spanish Law also provides a measure of legal certainty: in order for third parties in good faith not to be able to allege ignorance thereof, a lease contract of a ship shall be registered on the Register of Moveable Assets (Article 190 MNA).

III. Obligations of the Lessors

A. *Delivery of the Ship*

209. The lessor is bound to deliver the ship leased and its fittings under the conditions specified in the contract and, in everything not foreseen therein, the adequate ones for the agreed use (Article 191 (1) MNA). Delivery means giving up possession and control of the ship.

The delivery shall take place in the place and within the time set in the contract and in such ready berth as the hirers may direct. Hire becomes due from the date of delivery.

210. Regarding the state of seaworthiness on delivery, Article 192 of the MNA states that except if otherwise agreed, the lessor shall deliver the ship in a seaworthy condition and shall take charge of the repairs arising from flaws inherent to the ship. This means that the shipowners shall deliver her certificates to the charterers and that the ship must have that degree of fitness which an ordinary careful owner would require his ship to have at the commencement of her voyage.

The lessor shall be held liable to the lessee for damage caused by defects in seaworthiness; unless it is proven that the flaw could not have been discovered by use of a reasonable diligence. Whether the vessel is seaworthy or not is a question of fact to be determined in every case depending upon the particular circumstances of the case.

This principle shall have an *imperative nature* in lease contracts of ships and vessels whose exclusive use is recreational, to practice sports without a lucrative purpose, or non-professional fishing.

B. *To Maintain the Lessee in the Peaceful Enjoyment of the Ship*

211. According to the general principles of lease contracts (Article 1554 (2) Civil Code), the shipowner has to maintain the lessee in the peaceful enjoyment of the lease for the whole term of the contract.

Therefore, if the ship is arrested due to any dispute over its ownership or debts owed by the shipowners, they shall guarantee that the interests of the hirers are not affected, and the lessee shall be entitled to compensation for the damages and losses that are a consequence of the withholding (Article 198 (3) MNA).

In commercial practice, this obligation of the lessors includes a guarantee against the execution of maritime liens (clause 16 of Barecon 2001, that provides an indemnity to the owners if the vessel is arrested or detained).

IV. Obligations of the Hirers

A. *To Pay the Rent*

212. The lessee shall be bound to pay the price agreed at the time and in the place agreed (Article 193 MNA).

Spanish Law also regulates the effects of the *interruptions in the use of the ship leased* in Article 198 of the MNA: without prejudice to the liability of the lessor for the state of seaworthiness on delivery, if the ship could not be used during a period exceeding forty-eight hours arising from inherent flaws, the obligation to pay the price shall cease during the whole period of inactivity.

In lease agreements of the ships and vessels whose exclusive use is recreational, to practice sports without a lucrative purpose, or non-professional fishing, that impossibility to use shall entitle the lessee to opt for a price reduction or to terminate the agreement, without the possibility of agreeing otherwise and notwithstanding the compensations for damages and losses to which the lessee might be entitled.

B. *To Use the Ship Leased According to the Terms Established in the Agreement*

213. The hirer shall be bound to use the ship leased according to the terms established in the agreement and, in all matters not foreseen, according to the technical characteristics of the ship (Article 193 MNA). In this framework, the hirers may trade the ship as they see fit, without seeking the permission of the owners, unless the latter place any restriction or *trading limits* either upon the geographical area in which the ship should be free to trade, or as to the cargoes that she should be free to carry.

Under a bareboat charter the owners part with possession and control of the ship; therefore, the complete responsibility for the operation of the ship is passed by the owners to the hirers. The hirers must put their own crew on board.

C. *To Maintain the Ship in a Seaworthy State*

214. The lessee shall be bound, during the time the agreement lasts, to maintain the ship in a seaworthy state (Article 194 MNA).Therefore, the hirers shall be responsible for the repair of the ship during the bareboat charter period. The charterers generally maintain and insure the vessel.

It shall also be bound to inform the lessor of damage suffered by the ship that affects or may affect its classification. The lessor may inspect the ship at any time to check its state, without this negatively affecting its normal operation, bearing the cost of the expenses caused.

In lease agreements and vessels whose exclusive use is recreational, to practice sports without a lucrative purpose, or non-professional fishing, the lessor shall bear the expense of the necessary repairs to maintain the vessel in a seaworthy state, except those for which the lessee is to blame. Any clause that fully or partially exonerates the lessor of this obligation shall be null and void.

D. To Return the Ship on Conclusion of the Contract in the State in Which It Was Delivered

215. The hirers are bound to return the ship at the moment established in the agreement and in the same state, structure, condition and class in which it was delivered, except for the normal wear and tear arising from the agreed use.

If it is not returned within the term foreseen, it shall compensate the lessor for the damages and losses that may be caused by the delay. Notwithstanding this and unless otherwise agreed, the agreement shall be deemed to be extended for the excess period arising from the duration of the last voyage in progress reasonably ordered by the lessee (Article 195 MNA).

The lessee must return the ship at the place agreed and, if no place was agreed, at the same place where the ship was delivered.

E. Obligation of the Lessee to Indemnify the Lessor

216. The lessee is bound to maintain indemnified the lessor from any charges and rights in favour of third parties that may arise from use of the ship leased (Article 197 MNA). Consequentially, if during the charter period the hirers' possession, employment or operation of the ship has affected the interests of the shipowners or caused any loss to them, the hirers shall be liable for eliminating the consequences or compensating for the loss.

V. Other Statutory Provisions

A. Effects of Disposal of the Ship on the Lease

217. In the event of disposal of the ship, the acquirer shall be subrogated in the existing lease agreement, as long as this is registered on the Register of Moveable Assets or its existence is effectively known at the moment of the purchase. Otherwise, the contract shall be terminated notwithstanding the right of the lessee to be compensated by the lessor. In any event, the acquirer shall respect the voyage underway at the moment of the conveyance (Article 196 MNA).

B. Sublease of the Ship and Assignment of the Agreement

218. The lessee may not sublet the ship or assign the agreement to a third party without consent by the lessor (Article 199 MNA).

If appropriate, the sublease agreement shall be recorded in writing and shall be registered on the Register of Moveable Assets.

The lessee who subleases the ship shall remain bound to pay the lease price to the lessor. Should the lessor not obtain payment from the lessee, it may take action against the sub-lessee to demand the price of the sublease that has not yet been paid by the lessee (Article 200 MNA).

Regarding the effects of the lease assignment agreement, by virtue of Article 200 of the MNA, consented assignment of the lease agreement gives rise to severance of the lessee from the agreement and subrogation by the assignee in the legal position the former occupied.

C. Limitation of Actions

219. Actions arising from the ship lease agreement shall prescribe within the term of one year, from the date of termination of the agreement, or return of the ship if later.

The term shall only begin to elapse for actions arising from the obligation of the lessee to indemnify the lessor from any charges and rights in favour of third parties that may arise from use of the ship leased as from when the lessor is bound to bear the charge or right concerned (Article 202 MNA).

Chapter 6. Piloting

§1. Introduction

220. Under Spanish Law, pilotage is a technical-nautical specialized administrative port service, regulated in the SPMNA (Article 126) and in the corresponding regulations: Royal Decree 393/96 on the *General Regulation on Pilotage* (Real Decreto 393/1996, de 1 de marzo, *por el queseaprueba el Reglamento General de Practicaje*). The public interest in the existence and provision of pilotage services justifies that its regulation is administrative, in order to search for and maintain trained professionals who ensure safe navigation. It is characterized by the fact that it includes exercise of authority and is indivisible.

According to Article 126 of the SPMNA, pilotage is the advisory service, within the public domain (in Spain the ports are considered strategic and are in the public maritime domain), rendered on board, to the master of ships in order to facilitate the safe navigation of the ships or floating structures in ports, straits, shallow or other dangerous areas. Article 149 (1) (20) of the Spanish Constitution gives the State exclusive competences over ports of general interest. Therefore, the supervision and regulation of the pilotage service is a function of the Ministry of Public Works and Transport (*Ministerio de Fomento*) and of the Port Authorities. The *Particular Specifications Requirements* for each port service must be approved by each Port Authority prior binding report of the Ministry of Transport. All ships are entitled to the pilots' services under the same terms and conditions.

221. Pilotage is qualified as a private commercial activity, provided in the port environment, under the control of the Port Authorities, but without any implication for the latter on its ownership or provision. The provision of this service corresponds to private individuals, after obtaining a licence which can be acquired by competitive bidding in accordance with the specifications approved by the respective Port Authority. As all harbour services, pilotage is provided under a competitive system, and only in cases where there is a lack of private initiative does the SPMNA allow these services to be directly provided by the Port Authority.

In every major seaport (ports of general interest managed by the Spanish State), there is a pilotage administrative body (*Corporación de Prácticos*) rendering pilotage services for ships in or off their respective ports. The service must be provided on a regular continuous basis, and must be operational twenty-four hours a day for the whole year.

§2. Statutory Provisions

222. A ship's pilot is an independent skilled professional who holds an effective certificate of competency of a pilot and is employed by a pilotage administrative body (*Corporación de Prácticos*) to render his service (Article 279 SPMNA). The pilot is a person with specialized knowledge of the local navigation conditions of a port or waterway area and its navigational hazards. According to the SPMNA, the pilotage service is defined as the assistance provided to captains of vessels and floating crafts, to facilitate their entry and exit and nautical manoeuvres within the geographical limits of the pilotage zone, in conditions of safety, as established by the Law, the service regulation and the regulating code of the said service. This service shall be provided on board vessels, including instructions given by the pilots from the moment in which they leave the pilotage station to provide services.

A pilot must have adequate qualifications, including training, experience and professional examination. The whole system and performance of any given pilot service remains under the supervision of the Ministry of Public Works and Transport (*Ministerio de Fomento*). This Ministry establishes the minimum requirements and professional qualifications to be met by applicants to pilots and the conditions for lifelong learning of pilots (proficiency tests and checks of technical skills and physical fitness).

The pilot is not a member of the crew of the piloted ship, providing his services in autonomous way to the shipowner, without being a part of its organization.

223. In the framework of the administrative service of pilotage, a private contract of pilotage is concluded between the pilot and the shipowner. This contract of services is governed by the MNA (Chapter III, Title V, *On pilot contracts*, Articles 325–328). The pilot is hired by the shipping company to conduct the ship to a specific location or berth, guiding her into or out of the port, or through a particular stretch of enclosed waters, strait, channel or river.

According to Article 325 of the MNA, under a *pilotage contract*, an individual called a pilot is bound, in exchange for a price, to advise the master on performing the diverse operations and manoeuvres for safe navigation of ships in port or adjoining waters.

The pilotage service is rendered upon request of the hirer. Depending on statutory provisions and requirements, the pilotage may be compulsory or optional. In Spanish harbours pilotage is usually compulsory, for the sake of safe navigation, by decision of the harbour authorities (Article 112 (1) SPMNA). It is compulsory not only to enter it but, in most cases, there is no freedom to opt as to the pilot administered. However, some ships can be completely exempted from the compulsory pilotage.

As a general rule, in major Spanish ports pilotage service is mandatory for all ships with the exception of:

1. Vessels with a tonnage under 500 GT.
2. Warpings that do not entail the vessel casting off or the use of tugboats.
3. The exceptions set out in Article 9 of the General Regulation on Pilotage (approved by Royal Decree 1 March 1996).

§3. Duties of the Pilot

224. By virtue of the Pilotage Administration Provisions and of the MNA on pilotage contracts, a pilot has the following duties:

1. The pilot acts as a nautical adviser to the shipmaster. Therefore, the presence of the pilot on board does not exonerate the watch officer in command from his duties in relation to safety of navigation, nor substitutes the higher authority of the master in everything related to nautical steering and management, without prejudice to the advice by the pilot being embodied in direct handling instructions, or even performing these himself, with specific or tacit consent by the master (Article 327 MNA on *Pre-eminence of the master*). The pilot is under the authority of the master and the master is responsible for the conduct of the ship as he still retains that responsibility while the ship is being piloted.
2. Both the pilot and the captain of the ship have reciprocal duties. Master and pilot are bound to jointly plan the ship's manoeuvres and, to that end, to exchange the necessary information for that purpose. Likewise, master and pilot shall collaborate together during execution of the manoeuvres (Article 326 MNA).
3. The pilot shall conduct pilotage with due care. He must pilot the ship from the required place of commencement of pilotage to the required place of destination of pilotage. The pilot is under a duty to guide the ship and give the master all necessary advice and warnings with regard to navigation, berthing and anchoring of the ship, including local conditions, rules of navigation and navigational risks. It is an obligation of means not of result: the pilot does not guarantee the successful result of performing manoeuvres in safety. As will be shown immediately *infra* in §4, if the pilot correctly assists the master, he has met his contractual obligation, even if the manoeuvre is not performed for any reason out of his control.
4. The SPMNA (Article 110) states the public service obligations to be met by all providers of pilotages services: where a traffic accident occurs to the ship under pilotage, the pilot shall take effective measures to mitigate loss or damage. The pilot shall also report maritime accident, pollution accident or action in violation of regulations he has discovered.

§4. Liability of the Pilot

225. As provided for in Article 327 of the MNA, pilotage, whether compulsory or not, does not relieve the shipmaster of the duty to conduct the navigation and manoeuvres of the ship, and of all responsibilities ensuing therefrom. The master remains fully responsible for the vessel.

As stated before, the obligation of the pilot is of means not of result: the pilot does not guarantee the successful result of performing manoeuvres in safety.

Accordingly, where a maritime accident occurs due to the fault of the pilot during the pilotage causing loss of or damage to the ship under pilotage or liability of her owners to third parties, as a general rule, neither the pilot nor the pilotage body in which the faulty pilot is employed shall bear any civil liability for such loss, damage or liability to vessel or to any third parties.

Consequently, the shipowners or other persons who are responsible for the acts or omissions of the master shall be fully responsible for the vessel and for any loss, damage or liability to any third parties.

226. However, the MNA expressly stated that the pilot must bear his own responsibility in some cases: damage and accidents caused to the ship or to third parties *due to inexactness or omission in advice* that the pilot is due to provide the master shall be responsibility of the pilot, without prejudice to the concurrent fault that may be appreciated when the master has committed an error or negligence in following the instructions received (Article 328 MNA on *Liability for damage during execution of pilotage*). Thus, the pilot is only liable for damage caused to the vessel due to his negligent provision of the advice. In the same line, according to Article 24 (2) of the *General Regulation on Pilotage,* the pilot is held responsible for damage caused due to inaccuracy, error, or omission in the assistance of the navigation of a vessel, and the nautical courses or manoeuvres needed to ensure safe navigation.

Moreover, the pilot shall be held liable for damage caused due exclusively to him.

In addition, the master and ship operator shall be jointly and severally liable for damage caused with shared blame.

227. In all those cases, the rules limiting the liability of ship operators and pilots shall apply. According to Article 281 of the SPMNA, such liability is statutorily limited to the amount of EUR 20 per unit of tonnage, with a limit of EUR 1 million. Any agreement made before the damage was caused and setting forth different limits of liability of the pilotage company, shall have no legal effect.

The patrimonial liability of the Spanish Maritime Administration is directly excluded, except in cases where for a lack of offer that Administration has to support direct management of the pilotage service. Since pilots are not part of the Administration, they are not under the responsibility of the Administration. Therefore, damage caused to third parties within the scope of the service granted by the pilot is not attributed to the granting authority, but to the concession holders, except where the damage is the result of a clause imposed by the port authority on the concession holder with which it is difficult to comply.

Chapter 7. Towing and Pushing Contract

§1. Introduction

228. The Spanish legislation on towage contracts is laid down in Articles 301–306 of the MNA. It is a very short regulation, because the MNA refers directly to the freedom of contracts of the parties, with a few exceptions. A contract of towage in most cases is concluded on the basis of a standard form thereof as agreed between the two parties. Internationally standardized contracts are widely used (*UK standard conditions for Towage and Other Services*, and those produced by the BIMCO: standard towing contracts TOWCON, TOWHIRE, etc.).

The agreement of towage is a contract for services. Towage is one of the categories of *contracts for use of ships*. The towage of one ship by another as a maritime operation began with the development of the steam paddle tug in the 1820s and 1830s. At a first stage in time, tugs were assisting the sailing ships in harbours and rivers to expedite their voyages, when nothing more was needed than the accelerating of her progress. But as they grew more powerful, they were engaged to tow sailing ships or barges on longer voyages.

229. In practice, there are at present usually two categories of towage contracts.

First, *harbour* or *manoeuvres* towage, used to facilitate the ship's manoeuvres when conditions are difficult or risky (mostly in harbours and other enclosed areas, for example, the tug is under a duty to take the ship out from its berth and place it into a position to proceed safely under its own propulsion and steering). This kind of towage involves the use of one vessel to expedite the sailing of another when nothing more is required than the acceleration of her progress.

Secondly, *transport* or *offshore* towage, used to take a ship or craft without its own propulsion to the stipulated destination. In these cases, the tug operator may undertake the carriage of cargo by means of towage.

From another point of view, a division may be made between *optional* and *compulsory* towages.

§2. Statutory Provisions

I. Concept of Towage Contract

230. In maritime practice, towage arises from a contract. Therefore, the ordinary principles of the law of contract will apply to towage contracts (Civil Code, Book IV, *On obligations and contracts*).

The contract of towage is defined in Article 301 of the MNA: by means of a towing contract, the ship operator is bound, in exchange for a price, to perform the necessary manoeuvres with the ship to displace another ship, vessel or naval artefact, or to provide its collaboration for manoeuvres by the ship towed or, where appropriate, to accompany or make the ship available.

231. The parties to the towage contract are the *owner or operator of the tug* (towing party) and *the operator of the craft or ship to be towed* (towed party). But in the standard towage contracts, the parties are defined as *tug* and *hirer*: such terminology is incorrect, since the contract of towage is one for the provision of services, not a contract of hire of the tug. The possession of the tug is never passed to the towed party.

II. Transport Towing

232. According to Article 302 of the MNA, when the ship operator of the tug has undertaken to move the ship or artefact towed, the rules of affreightments contracts on making the ship available in the charter party shall be applicable, as long as those rules are consistent with the object of the contract.

In cases in which the elements towed are delivered to the towing tug, it shall be deemed that it accepts their custody, with the relevant liability. In these cases, the operator of the tug is responsible for the cargo (if any) on the towed vessel and his liability for any damage sustained by the cargo will be subject to the rules governing the carrier's liability for cargo regarding the carriage of goods by sea and the contract of affreightment.

233. The rest of the obligations of the parties under the transport towing contract shall be decided by the terms of the contract of towage and general provisions contained in private law.

Generally, the tug owner must provide a tug fit for the towage service. For large-scale operations of ocean towage, it is common to contract the services of a particular named tug. Therefore, the tug owner must provide a tug which is properly equipped and manned to perform the contractual service.

The tow must also be fit for towage service and is obliged to show proper seamanship during the towage service. The tow owner owes a duty to exercise reasonable care and diligence to put the tow in such a condition to be fit for towage (to withstand the perils which may foreseeably be encountered on the voyage in question). This is an equivalent obligation to the duty to ensure that a vessel is seaworthy applicable in contracts of affreightment.

As a rule, the obligation of the tug owner under this contract is of result: he guarantees the successful result of performing the voyage agreed in safety. Therefore, failure to achieve the intended outcome may determine the existence of contractual non-compliance.

234. The breach of contract obligations involves contractual liability, under the principles of General Law of contracts (Civil Code, Articles 1101 et seq. and 1254 et seq.).Persons who, in the performance of their obligations, should incur in wilful misconduct, negligence or default, and those who in any way should contravene the content of the obligation shall be subject to compensation of any damages caused.

Liability arising from wilful misconduct is enforceable for all obligations. Waiver of the action to enforce it shall be null and void. Liability arising from negligence is equally enforceable in the performance of all kinds of obligations; but may be moderated by the Courts on a case-by-case basis.

III. Manoeuvre Towing

235. *Harbour* or *manoeuvres* towage, must be analysed from two points of views.

In private law, according to Article 303 of the MNA, when the tug contract concerns assistance by the tugboat in manoeuvring the ship towed, it shall be deemed that, except if otherwise agreed, handling the manoeuvre befalls the commander of the ship towed.

Regarding Public Law, it must be underlined that as stated in SPMNA, towage is a *Harbour service*, regulated in Articles 108 et seq. and 127. It means that the service comes under the competence of the port authority. Harbour Towage is qualified as a private commercial activity under the control of the Port Authorities, but without any implication for the latter on its ownership or provision. The provision of this service corresponds to private individuals, after obtaining a licence which can be acquired by competitive bidding in accordance with the specifications approved by the respective Port Authority. As all harbour services, towage is provided under a competitive system (except for minimum obligations to maintain the continuity, universality and safety of the service), and only in cases where there is a lack of private initiative does the SPMNA allow these services to be directly provided by the Port Authority.

According to Article 127 of the SPMNA, ship towing is described as a broad range of services: actions carried out to help the port manoeuvres of the towed ship, as well as pushing, towing, keeping, escorting and speeding her up, following the instructions of the master of the towed ship, within the area of the harbour waters.

Enterprises providing towage services in ports are subject to authorization and certification; consequently, these companies must be certified by the Port Authorities (*Autoridades Portuarias*).

236. The obligations of the parties of the contract shall be decided by the terms of the conditions stated by the Port Authorities, in the contract of towage and in the general provisions of private law. But the provisions of the contract of towage shall only apply when there are no different provisions in the applicable Port Regulations.

237. The breach of contract obligations involves contractual liability, under the principles of General Law of contracts (Civil Code, Articles 1101 et seq. and 1254 et seq.). As a rule, the tug must exercise proper skill and diligence in performing the service (e.g., in anticipating what the tow might do or how she might navigate during towage, or exercise all reasonable care to keep clear of the tow during the port manoeuvres).It is an obligation of means not of result: although the tug owner is under the ordinary duty to exercise reasonable care and skill performing the service, he does not guarantee the successful result of performing all the manoeuvres in safety. Therefore, failure to achieve the intended outcome does not determine in itself the existence of contractual non-compliance.

IV. Towage and Salvage

238. A towage concluded for the purpose of a salvage operation is classified as a salvage contract and is not taken as a contract of towage in Law. That means that contractual nature of towage is of particular significance in considering the relationship between towage and salvage, since the significant feature of salvage is that, unlike towage, salvage exists independently of any contract.

Nevertheless, in practice it is not always easy to distinguish between towage and salvage, since the dividing line between both of them will depend upon the presence of a towage contract and upon the extent of the contractual services to be rendered under that contract. To provide solutions in those border cases, the MNA and the Salvage Convention contain special rules.

239. In the MNA, Article 305 lays down a rule for *Special towing* (*Remolque de fortuna*). This must be deemed as a kind of ordinary maritime services and thus normally not regulated by the provisions of salvage at sea. When towing services are requested in an *extraordinary situation*, that *do not amount to a case of maritime salvage*, without previously having set the conditions of service and price, the ship operator of the towing ship shall be entitled to an adequate remuneration for the services provided. That remuneration shall include the damages and losses suffered by the ship due to towing, the gains it has ceased to obtain during the towing time and an adequate price for the service.

Unlike the salvage operation, the Special towing is not based upon the principle of *no cure, no pay*. In this kind of maritime service, the remuneration shall not be subject to the success of the operation.

240. A different situation is that of the *salvage towing*: if the towed ship became imperilled by circumstances for which the tug operator is not liable, and if the tug successfully performed or participated in a salvage action, the tug operator will be entitled to a salvage reward. In these cases, salvage and the entitlement to remuneration arises irrespective of the existence of a contract between the salvor and the vessel or other property being salved. There will be no such reward if the towage contract contemplates that the towage remuneration shall include any salvage reward (Article 17 of the Salvage Convention). But where a tug is engaged by a ship under towage contract to perform some towage operation, that operation will not constitute salvage.

§3. Liability and Limitation of Liability

I. Liability Between the Contractual Parties under the Contract of Towage

241. The liability of one party under a contract of towage to the other shall be determined by the applicable law. The duties upon a vessel in relation to towage navigation arise from two sources:

First of all, from the ordinary duty to exercise reasonable care and skill performing the service. In this regard, the MNA contains an express provision containing a general rule of liability between the tug and the towed ship in Article 304 (1) (*Liability for damages*): the ship operators of each one of the ships shall be held liable for damages caused to the other as a consequence of negligence in fulfilment of the services they are due to provide. As previously mentioned, in Spanish Law, persons who, in the performance of their obligations, should incur in wilful misconduct, negligence or default, and those who in any way should contravene the content of the obligation shall be subject to compensation of any damages caused.

Secondly, liability may arise from a collision between tug and tow. On this subject, the MNA does not contain any special provision. Nevertheless, it must be underlined that other articles of the MNA on towage contracts can have an important effect on the liability regime in collision cases.

According to Article 303, when the tug contract concerns assistance by the tugboat in manoeuvring the ship towed, *it shall be deemed* that, except if otherwise agreed, handling the manoeuvre befalls the commander of the ship towed. This means that, as a matter of general principle, the operator of the towed ship will bear responsibility for any damage caused during the towage. But the operator of the towed ship has the right to prove that the liability for the damage lies with the tug. At the end, in the event that tug and tow are both to blame, the ordinary rules of apportionment and of cross-actions will apply (Article 1103 Civil Code: *liability arising from negligence is enforceable in the performance of all kinds of obligations; but may be moderated by the Courts on a case-by-case basis*). Nonetheless, if the tug is alone at fault, it will be liable.

In the cases of transport towing, the opposite rule operates. Article 302 MNA states that when the ship operator of the tug has undertaken to move the ship or artefact towed, it shall be deemed that, except if specifically agreed otherwise, management of the manoeuvre lies with the master of the tug.

242. In the event of damage caused by collision between the tug and the towed ship, the issue of liability will be governed by the provisions of the MNA dealing with collision liability (Articles 339–346).

As a second source, the liability of one party under a contract of towage to the other shall be determined by terms of the contracts. There is a great diversity of liability clauses in the various standard forms of ocean towage, but in Spain it is common to use *Knock-for-Knock clauses*: a contractual agreement stating that each party will be liable for any damage or loss to its own property or accident or injury to staff, and will not make a claim against the other party, even if that party is at fault (policies of BIMCO, Heavycon, Towhire and Towcon). Under the *knock-for-knock* principle, the basic premise is that each party bears its own risk (possible costs and compensation for any loss or damage to persons or things)whatever the cause giving rise to the potential claim. They are a way of creating certainty in respect of apportionment of risk.

Nevertheless, it must be underlined that in Spanish law such a system could find difficulties to fit with the compulsory rules on contractual and tort liability (e.g.: according to Article 1102 Civil Code, liability arising from wilful misconduct is enforceable for all obligations. *Waiver of the action to enforce it shall be null and void*).

243. Finally, a party may also incur in tort liability to the other party, due to his tortuous act or omission not covered by the contract or by the statutory provisions (Article 1902 Civil Code: *the person who, as a result of an action or omission, causes damage to another by his fault or negligence shall be obliged to repair the damaged caused*).This obligation is enforceable not only as a result of one's own actions or omissions but also of those of such persons for whom one is liable.

II. Liability Against Third Parties

244. It is very common that the damages arising from a towage operation are suffered by a third party, due to the fault of the tug or the towed party or both. In this case, the law frequently establishes that both parties of the towage contract are jointly and severally liable to that third party. The reason of this protective rule is that it is generally very difficult for a third party to prove which contracting party of the agreement of towage committed fault or what was the proportion to the extent of their respective faults.

Regarding liability against third parties, Article 304 (2) of the MNA states that both ship operators are held jointly and severally liable to third parties for the damages caused by the towing train, except to the extent that any of them may prove that such damage is not due to causes for which an element in the towing train is to blame. In any case, the right to be reimbursed shall be applicable against the ship operators with attention to the respective degree of fault.

So, if the damage was sustained by a third party, this party may arise claim against either the tug or the tow, or both of them, for full compensation for his losses, regardless of which party was at fault. Where as a result of this rule of joint and several liability a party has paid compensation to a third party in an amount exceeding the proportion for which he must be liable, he has the right of recourse against the other party to be reimbursed.

245. In cases of harbour towage, the patrimonial liability of the Port Administration is excluded, except in cases where for a lack of offer that Administration has to support direct management of the towage service. Since tug owners are not part of the Administration, they are not under the responsibility of the Administration. Therefore, damage caused to third parties within the scope of the harbour service granted by the tug owner is not attributed to the granting authority, but to the concession holders, except where the damage is the result of a clause imposed by the port authority on the concession holder with which it is difficult to comply.

III. Limitation of Liability

246. The MNA provides no special limits of liability for damages sustained or caused during towage. Thus, general limitation of liability for maritime claims determined by virtue of Articles 392–505 of the MNA will apply.

In the field of towage, limitation of liability raises some particular questions that are not solved in Spanish national legislation. For example, can limitation be invoked at all in respect of the tug and tow, considering both of them the *seagoing ship* within Article 1.2 LLMC?

IV. Limitation of Actions

247. Actions arising from a towing contract shall prescribe within the term of one year (Article 306 MNA).

Chapter 8. Salvage and Assistance

§1. Definition

248. According to the general principles of maritime law, salvage at sea can be defined as any act or activity undertaken to aid or assist a ship or any other property in danger at sea or other navigable waters, rendered on a voluntary basis, and only if it manages to carry out a beneficial effect (principle of *no cure no pay*).The person providing the service (the *salvor*) is entitled to payment (the *salvage reward*).

The MNA establishes a legal concept of salvage, in Article 358: *salvage is considered any act undertaken to aid or assist a ship, vessel or naval artefact, or to safeguard or recover any other assets that are in danger in any navigable waters, except for continental ones that are not connected the seawater and are not used by seagoing ships.* This concept is in line with the one included in the Salvage Convention 1989: *salvage operation means any act or activity undertaken to assist a vessel or any other property in danger in navigable waters or in any other waters whatsoever.*

249. Moreover, Spanish law lays down some criteria in order to clarify what cannot be considered as a salvage service:

1. Assistance provided to assets fixed permanent and intentionally to the coast.
2. Any operation whatsoever related to the underwater cultural heritage, as they shall be governed by its specific legislation and the international treaties in force to which Spain is a party.

Finding an immediate recovery of abandoned assets in the waters or their coasts shall be considered salvage, except if they are a product of the sea or the navigable waters themselves.

Under Spanish Law, there is no difference between salvage and assistance: salvage embodies assistance.

250. The service of salvage must be rendered *on a voluntary basis*, in the sense of being attributable neither to pre-existing contractual or statutory duty owed to the owner of the salved property. Therefore, if the persons rendering a salvage operation were contractually bound to look after the ship and property thereon (e.g., as master, crew, or persons acting under statutory duty), they are not entitled to any salvage award. The salvage service must necessarily be undertaken voluntarily. Therefore, so long as their contracts of employment are in force, a master and crew cannot claim a salvage reward on the grounds that they have assisted in saving their own ship. On the other hand, passengers may claim a salvage reward.

Before any entitlement to a reward arises, there must be *a real danger* to the vessel, life or object salved.

251. The authorities of the ports are bound to facilitate entry and storage of the goods salvaged, notwithstanding which they may charge the legitimate owner for the expenses incurred. In any event, goods salvaged by publicly-owned ships, fitted and equipped for salvage, shall be exempt of any expenses and charges (Article 368 (6) MNA).

§2. Statutory Provisions

I. Legal Regime

252. Salvage and assistance are internationally regulated by the *International Convention on Salvage*, done at London on 28 April 1989 and came into force on 14 July 1996. This convention shall not apply to fixed or floating platforms or to mobile offshore drilling units when such platforms or units are on location engaged in the exploration, exploitation, or production of sea-bed mineral resources (Article 3).

In order to promote uniform regulation, the MNA refers to the London International Convention on Salvage 1989, the most significant development in the international law of salvage since 1910, to regulate the same matter in national Spanish Law: *Salvage shall be governed by the International Convention on Salvage, done at London on 28 April 1989, by the Protocols that amend it to which Spain is a party and by the provisions of this Chapter* (Article 357). Therefore, the London Convention on Salvage 1989 is also Spanish national law. It takes account of changes in salvage since the 1910 Convention, in particular, increased concern for the environment.

Chapter III of Title VI of the MNA, under the name *On salvage* (Articles 357–368), contains regulation on some matters not treated in the convention.

253. Spain is also a part of the *International Convention on Maritime Search and Rescue*, known as SAR, signed in Hamburg on 27 April 1979.

II. Jurisdiction

254. In accordance with Article 2 of the Convention, it shall apply whenever judicial or arbitral proceedings related to matters dealt with in this Convention are brought in a State Party.

Besides, if there is no salvage agreement, or if the salvage agreement contains no stipulation as to the salvage reward, this issue shall be decided by the competent bodies.

Under the MNA (*Second Additional Provision*), the competent bodies to determine the awards and remunerations for salvage and towing are two: the *civil jurisdiction* and the administrative *maritime arbitration system* under the responsibility of the Navy. The civil jurisdiction shall hear the relevant claims, except if the parties agree to submit to an administrative maritime arbitration system due to it being salvage of goods abandoned at sea and of unknown ownership.

The competent bodies of the Navy that shall hear actions regarding salvage bounties and remuneration for salvage towing are the *Maritime Arbitration Council* and the *Maritime Arbitration Auditors*. Their composition, legal regime, territorial scope and other particulars required for their operation shall be established in the implementing regulations. The parties with an interest in such proceedings may opt to resort to said bodies of the Navy or to the ordinary civil jurisdiction.

If an agreement is not reached between the parties concerned, the ordinary civil jurisdiction shall prevail, which shall be substantiated according to the ordinary declaratory or verbal proceedings envisaged by the Civil Procedure Act, as appropriate according to the sum claimed (Articles 248 ff.).The classes of declaratory proceedings are: *Declaratory actions* and *Oral trials*. Any claims whose amount may exceed EUR 6,000 and any whose economic interests cannot be calculated in even a relative fashion shall likewise be decided upon in a declaratory action. Any claims whose amount does not exceed EUR 6,000 shall be decided upon in an oral trial.

Until constitution of the Maritime Arbitration Council and the Maritime Arbitration Auditors, the Central Maritime Tribunal and the Permanent Maritime Courts shall continue to perform their present duties (*First Transitional Provision MNA*).

III. Application to State Ships

255. The 1989 Convention does not apply to warships or other non-commercial vessels owned or operated by a State and entitled, at the time of salvage operations, to sovereign immunity under generally recognized principles of international law unless that State decides otherwise.

Under Article 5, the Convention shall not affect any provisions of national law or any international convention related to salvage operations by or under the control of public authorities. Nevertheless, salvors carrying out such salvage operations shall be entitled to avail themselves of the rights and remedies provided for in the Convention in respect of salvage operations. The extent to which a public authority under a duty to perform salvage operations may avail itself of the rights and remedies provided for in the Convention shall be determined by the law of the State where such authority is situated.

On this subject, the MNA states in Article 359 (*Application to State ships*), that the rules on salvage shall apply to services provided to State ships and vessels as defined in Article 3 of the MNA (*State ships and vessels are those assigned to National Defence and others that are owned or used by the public authorities, as long as these exclusively provide services of a non-business nature*). However, in these cases, the bounty shall be applied for through the appropriate administrative procedure, without the rules on withholding or arrest of the ships or goods salvaged being applicable.

These rules shall also apply to salvage performed by State ships and vessels, in which case the relevant bounty shall be made available to the administration or body they are assigned to, that shall provide for its equitable application.

IV. Compulsory Salvage

256. Under the MNA and the Convention, the service of salvage must be rendered *on a voluntary basis*. Compulsory salvage must be considered another institution. There are two kinds of compulsory salvage: salvage ordered by a public authority and salvage imposed by law.

A. Salvage Ordered or Supervised by a Public Authority

257. According to Article 360 of the MNA, the public authorities that order or supervise a salvage operation, or their officers, shall not be entitled to any bounty whatsoever.

However, the salvagers who perform operations ordered or supervised by these shall be entitled to bounty pursuant to the terms provided in the MNA.

In Spain, there is a public institution created to promote safety of life at sea: SASEMAR.

B. Salvage Imposed by Law

258. Saving life in danger at sea is an obligation provided for both in law and in international treaties and therefore this kind of service *is not rendered on a voluntary basis.*

The master shall be bound to take measures to save human lives in danger at sea, as long as he may do so without severe danger to the ship, its crew or passengers, and in all cases, shall leave a record of the proceedings in the Captain's Log (Article 183 (3) MNA).

Accordingly, reward for salvage of life at sea is denied in principle. Therefore, no remuneration is due from persons whose lives are saved. However, if several salvors took part in the same salvage operation, and some of them have salved only the persons while the others have salved the vessel or other property, the salvor of human life who has taken part in the services rendered on the occasion of the accident giving rise to salvage has the right to a reasonable share with the salvor of property in the salvage payment.

259. The Spanish Maritime Authorities shall in all cases be empowered to intervene in salvage operations performed within the Spanish maritime areas, in order to safeguard the safety of navigation, human life at sea and the environment, against maritime pollution. To that end, the Administration may direct or issue instructions related to the salvage operations that the master, ship operator or its representative, the consignor and salvor shall necessarily obey. When, as a result of direct action by the Maritime Authorities, bounties or compensation were to be earned, these shall be deposited directly at the Exchequer, and a credit may be generated for performance of activities that have caused such deposit. When the Administration performs the activities referred to above through private or public entities, it may agree formulas to arrange the said bounties or compensations in the appropriate service provision agreements (Article 367 MNA).

260. Finally, under the *Convention for the Unification of Certain Rules of Law with respect to Collisions between Vessels* of 1920, after a collision, the master of each of the vessels in collision is bound, so far as he can do so without serious danger to his vessel, her crew and her passengers, to render assistance to the other vessel, her crew and her passengers (Article 8).

V. Prohibition on Performing Salvage

261. The persons who proceeded in the salvage operation despite the express and reasonable prohibition of the master of the vessel in danger, are not entitled to the reimbursement of fees or costs for their performance.

Services provided in spite of specific, reasonable prohibition by the ship operator or the master of the ship assisted, or the owner of any of the goods in danger that are not, or have not been on board the ship, do not give rise to the right to reward (Article 364 MNA).

VI. Salvage Contract

262. In many of the salvage operations, the service is rendered in accordance with a salvage agreement concluded between the salvor and the salved party. In practice, in fact, there will usually be a salvage contract, particularly in circumstances where professional salvors are involved. But it must be underlined that salvage law is not a branch of the law of contract, since the reward for salvage is not based upon a contractual right.

The salvage contracts are usually concluded on the basis of standards forms in order to expedite the conclusion thereof. Several standard forms of salvage agreement are in use. The form by far more widely used in Spain is the *Lloyd's Open Form of Salvage Agreement 'No Cure-No Pay'* (LOF). The form has been revised several times since its introduction in the nineteenth century. The most recent version is *LOF 2011*, that separates the basic agreement (LOF) from the detail provisions, which are now set out in *Lloyd's Standard Salvage and Arbitration Clauses* (LSSA Clauses).Under LOF 2011, the salvor is bound to use their best endeavours to save the vessel, life, and property while performing the salvage services to prevent or minimize damage to the environment. There is, in fact, a close relationship between the 1989 Convention and LOF. The Convention adopted certain features which had appeared in LOF 80. Moreover, some Convention provisions were incorporated in LOF 90 before the 1989 Convention had the force of law, particularly, Article 1 (definitions), Article 8 (duties of salvor, owner and master), Article 13 (criteria for fixing the reward), and, mainly, Article 14 (special compensation).

Statutory provisions on property salvage shall apply unless otherwise provided for by the salvage contract. According to Spanish Law, the parties interested may freely contract the salvage conditions, with no further limit than their inexcusable obligation to act with the necessary diligence to avoid or reduce damage to the environment as much as possible (Article 361 (1) MNA).

263. Besides, the rules and provisions governing the salvage contract contained in the Convention (Articles 6 and 7) shall apply as provisions of basic law to salvage contracts. Therefore, upon request by one of the parties, a salvage agreement or any terms thereof may be annulled or modified if:

1. The contract has been entered into under undue influence or the influence of danger and its terms are inequitable; or
2. The payment under the contract is in an excessive degree too large or too small for the services actually rendered.

Therefore, the contract for salvage concluded in time of risk and under its influence can be cancelled or modified by the court upon request by anyone who has an interest if the content is unfair, especially if the agreed fee is manifestly excessive or disproportionate to the service offered. If no agreement is reached, the fee is then to be set by the court.

264. A contract for salvage operation at sea is concluded when an agreement has been reached between the salvor and the salved party regarding the salvage operation to be undertaken. In this regard, the master of the ship and the ship operator has power to enter into a salvage contract on behalf of the owner of the goods that are on board (Article 361 (2) MNA). Moreover, the master shall have the authority to conclude contracts for salvage operations on behalf of the owner of the vessel. The master or the owner of the vessel shall have the authority to conclude such contracts on behalf of the owner of the property on board the vessel (Article 6 (2) Convention).Thus, a salvage contract concluded by the master of the salved ship shall be binding upon the owners of the salved ship, and a salvage contract concluded by the master or owners of the salved ship shall be binding upon the owners of the cargo or other salved property on board the ship.

VII. Foreign Ships and Cargoes with Sovereign Immunity

265. Unless the flag State consents thereto, application of the rules on salvage set forth in the MNA shall exclude foreign State ships that, on providing aid, enjoy sovereign immunity pursuant to the generally recognized principles of International Law. It shall also exclude, except for consent by the owner State, the non-commercial goods owned by a foreign State that enjoy the immunity stated (Article 366 MNA). Under Spanish Law, with the exceptions foreseen under International Law and in the MNA, foreign State ships shall enjoy immunity, only being subject to the jurisdiction of their flag State.

VIII. Salvaged Goods with Unknown Owners

266. According to Article 368 of the MNA, those that, during navigation or from the coast, were to salvage unattended goods with unknown owners shall be bound to notify the Navy at the first port they put into.

The Navy will instigate proceedings to ascertain who are the legitimate owners, in the manner established by the implementing regulations, which shall necessarily include notification to the Consul of the flag country, if they are registered ships or vessels. Meanwhile, the salvor may withhold the goods salvaged, adopting the necessary measures for their adequate conservation.

Should the owner be located, the competent body of the Navy shall proceed to notify the salvor of its identity, that shall then be entitled to the rights envisaged by Article 8 (2) (c) of the *International Convention on Salvage* and in Article 365 of the MNA (to withhold the ship and other goods salvaged under its control), without prejudice to the relevant actions to claim conservation expenses and to obtain the appropriate reward for the salvage.

In the event of the owner not being ascertained within the term of six months from commencement of the administrative proceedings, the Navy shall take the appropriate measures to assess the goods salvaged. If their value does not exceed EUR 3,000, the salvor shall become the owner thereof once it has paid the procedural costs. Should their value exceed said amount, the goods shall be sold at public auction and, once the procedural costs are paid, in addition to that amount, the salvor shall receive one-third of the price obtained that exceeds EUR 3,000, plus the expenses it has incurred. The remainder, if any, shall be deposited at the Public Exchequer.

§3. Salvage Reward

267. The salvage reward is the payment that the salvor is entitled to for his salvage service rendered to ship or other recognized property. What is paid as a salvage reward depends on the circumstances.

Traditionally, the determination of salvage reward follows the principle of *no cure, no pay*. In other words, the basic principle of salvage is that the person who *successfully* rescues and preserves the property of another from danger at sea deserves a reward.

Under Article 12 of the Convention, salvage operations which provided a useful result give right to a reward. Except as otherwise is provided, no payment is due under the Convention when the salvage operations have had no useful result, in the meaning that all or part of the value of property is salved.

Salvage operations that yielded a useful result shall entitle the salvors to a reward, the amount of which *may not exceed the value of the ship and other goods saved* (Article 362 (1) MNA).

268. The reward shall be fixed with a view to encouraging salvage operations. Criteria for fixing the salvage reward are defined in Article 13 of the Convention, without regard to the order in which they are presented below:

1. the salved value of the vessel and other property;
2. the skill and efforts of the salvors in preventing or minimizing damage to the environment;
3. the measure of success obtained by the salvor;

4. the nature and degree of the danger;
5. the skill and efforts of the salvors in salving the vessel, other property and life;
6. the time used and expenses and losses incurred by the salvors;
7. the risk of liability and other risks run by the salvors or their equipment;
8. the promptness of the services rendered;
9. the availability and use of vessels or other equipment intended for salvage operations;
10. the state of readiness and efficiency of the salvor's equipment and the value thereof.

Payment of the reward shall be made *for all the interests linked to the ship and the other goods salvaged in proportion to their respective values*, without prejudice to the bounty being paid by the operator of the ship salvaged, notwithstanding its right to repetition against the rest of the interests of the goods on board salvaged for their respective contributions, or as appropriate in the case of general average. In the case of salvage of assets that are not on board, or that have not been transported by a ship, the debtor of the bounty shall be the owner of such property (Article 362 (2) MNA).

A reward shall be owed even if the salvor and the ship salvaged belong to the same owner.

Where two or more salvors take part in the same salvage operation, the total salvage reward shall still be fixed by virtue of the criteria contained in Article 13 of the Convention.

269. Regarding the securities for Salvage Payment, the salvor shall be entitled to withhold the ship and other goods salvaged under its control, in the port or place to which they have been taken after conclusion of the salvage operations, while a sufficient guarantee is not constituted in its favour for the amount of the reward claimed. The ship operator of the ship salvaged, at the request and expense of the salvor, shall be bound to condition delivery of the goods transported on that ship to constitution by the consignee of a sufficient guarantee to respond for the bounty they may be due. In the case of breach of this obligation, the ship operator shall be liable for the damages to the salvor arising therefrom (Article 365 MNA).

The claim for a salvage reward is protected by a maritime lien (Article 122 (1) MNA).

270. Regarding *Special compensation*, Article 14 of the Convention states that *if the salvor has carried out salvage operations in respect of a vessel which by itself or its cargo threatened damage to the environment and has failed to earn a reward under Article 13, at least equivalent to the special compensation assessable in accordance with this article, he shall be entitled to special compensation from the owner of that vessel equivalent to his expenses as herein defined.*

However, if under those circumstances the salvor by his salvage operations has prevented or minimized damage to the environment, the special compensation payable by the owner to the salvor may be increased up to a maximum of 30% of the expenses incurred by the salvor.

Though, the tribunal, if it deems it fair and just to do so and bearing in mind the relevant criteria set out in Article 13, paragraph 1, may increase such special compensation further, but in no event shall the total increase be more than 100% of the expenses incurred by the salvor.

§4. Reward to the Crew

271. According to Article 15 (1) of the Convention on Salvage 1989, the distribution of the remuneration among the beneficiaries is determined by the law of the state of the flag the ship flies.

For Spanish ships, Article 363 of the MNA states that the salvage reward, excluding the party due to compensate for damages, expenses or losses to the salvor, shall be distributed between the operator of the ship salvaging and its crew in a proportion of one-third and two-thirds respectively, except if otherwise agreed. Distribution of the part due to the crew among its members shall be performed in proportion to the base wage of each category.

This rule shall not apply to tugs or those ships fitted and equipped for salvage (professional salvors), on which the crew rights shall be regulated by the terms established in their respective boarding contracts or collective bargaining agreements.

In the case of foreign ships, the above rules of distribution shall apply except if the flag law provides otherwise.

§5. Liability and Limitation of Liability of Salvors

272. Under Spanish Law, the liability of the salvor is established in the Convention on Salvage (Article 8 (1) and Article 18).

The salvor shall owe a duty to the owner of the vessel or other property in danger:

1. to carry out the salvage operations with *due care*;
2. in performing the service, to exercise due care to prevent or minimize damage to the environment;
3. whenever reasonably required by the circumstances, to seek assistance from other salvors; and
4. to accept the intervention of other salvors when reasonably requested to do so by the owner or master of the vessel or other property in danger; provided however that the amount of his reward shall not be prejudiced should it be found that such a request was unreasonable.

A salvor may be deprived of the whole or part of the payment due under the Convention to the extent that the salvage operations have become necessary or more difficult because of fault or neglect on his part or if the salvor has been guilty of fraud or other dishonest conduct.

Moreover, the Spanish Civil Code provisions (Articles 1902 et seq.) are applicable: the person who, as a result of an action or omission, causes damage to another by his fault or negligence shall be obliged to repair the damaged caused. This obligation shall be enforceable not only as a result of one's own actions or omissions but also of those of such persons for whom one is liable. The owners or managers of an establishment or undertaking shall be liable for damages caused by their employees, in the service in which they are employed or in the performance of their duties. But the person who pays damages caused by his employees may recover from the latter the amount paid.

273. The salvor, and his servant or agent, are listed as persons who can avail of statutory limitation of liability in the Convention *on Limitation of Liability for Maritime Claims* 1976 (LLMC), Articles 1 (1), 1 (3) and 6 (3). The corresponding provisions of this Convention, by the terms set forth in the Protocol of 1996, are incorporated in Title VII *on limitation of liability* (Articles 392–405 MNA). On the other hand, a shipowner may not limit his liability as against a salvor (Article 3 (1) LLMC).

Therefore, shall be subject to limitation the claims for death or bodily injuries, or for losses or damage to property, including damage to port works, navigable channels, aids to navigation and other property of the maritime or port domain, that may take place on board or be directly linked to operation of the ship or to the salvage operations, as well as damages arising from any such causes (Article 396 (1) MNA).

§6. Removal of Wrecks

274. Generally, wreck removal and the recovery of sunken objects directly or closely concerns the *public interests of safety at sea* and the marine environment.

That is why wreck removal regulation is in the first place a matter of *administrative law* that deals mainly with *compulsory wreck removal and other public law obligations regarding ships that are shipwrecked or sunken*. But wreck removal can also be done *voluntarily* and based upon a *contract* concluded between the owner of the wreck and a wreck removal company and the owners or managers of the wreck.

Spanish shipwreck regulation has mainly the purposes of determining the status of the goods affected, the property rights thereto, and the regime of extractions that are subject to the relevant administrative authorization.

Spain is not a party to the *Nairobi International Convention on the Removal of Wrecks*, adopted on 18 May 2007 and entered into force on 14 April 2015.

275. The growing importance of wreck removal was recognized by the publication of two standard wreck removal agreements, WRECKCON and WRECKHIRE, in 1993. In 1999, new agreements were produced by the ISU (*International Salvage Union*) and adopted by BIMCO: WRECKSTAGE 99 (which replaces WRECKCOM and provides for lump sum remuneration with stage payments), WRECKHIRE 99 (which replaces WRECKHIRE and provides for payment on a daily rate) and WRECKFIXED 99 (a new contract, under which payment is a fixed sum, no cure, no pay). Nowadays, the new versions of these documents are: WRECKSTAGE 2010, WRECKHIRE 2010 and WRECKFIXED 2010. The background to this last revision is that in early 2009 the International Group of P&I Clubs Salvage Sub-committee approached BIMCO with a request to help initiate a revision of the more widely used Wreck Removal Agreements. The Clubs felt that although those documents had served the industry well over the past ten years, certain amendments were necessary to introduce better cost control, to restore to the contract a more equal balance between the parties, and to incorporate current commercial practice.

I. Compulsory Wreck Removal and Other Public Law Obligations Regarding Ships That Are Shipwrecked or Sunken

276. According to Article 370 of the MNA, masters and ship operators of vessels that are shipwrecked or sunken within the Spanish maritime areas are *obligated to notify* the Maritime Authorities of such events pursuant to the terms and to the ends determined by the implementing regulations.

The same obligation shall befall the owners of other shipwrecked goods that are not transported on board ships or vessels.

The Maritime Authorities shall proceed of their own motion to inform the owners of ships and other damaged property of their location in order that they may adopt the urgent measures convenient to their interests (Article 371 MNA).

277. The MNA also establishes the *duty to mark and prevent pollution*: ship operators of ships, and the owners of shipwrecked or sunken goods, are bound to immediately perform the marking operations, as well as those to prevent pollution that may be necessary to safeguard Spanish interests. To that end they shall comply with the instructions and orders issued by the Maritime Authorities (Article 372).

The regulation of administrative nature on compulsory removal of wrecks and sunken objects is laid down in SPMNA (Article 304). The removal of all sorts of sunken and stranded objects representing a hazard to the environment or to the safety at sea is compulsory. The competent body for the procedure of determination of hazard is the *Capitán Marítimo* (Maritime Authority). The public authorities must intervene in the event that the owner is unknown or if he fails to respond in timely and appropriate manner.

278. The owner's liability for the costs of locating, marking and removal of a hazardous wreck or a sunken object is strict and unlimited (Article 304 (6) SPMNA).

II. Voluntary Recovery of Wrecks

279. The provisions of Spanish Law on voluntary raising and recovery of wrecks and sunken objects are contained in the MNA and SPMNA and they comprise both administrative provisions, regulating the procedure of issuance of the recovery licence, and private law provisions which deal with the law of finds, acquisition of ownership over abandoned wreck or sunken object and with the issue of liability of the contractor performing recovery operations.

In practice, it is difficult to draw a line between salvage and wreck removal. In order to solve this situation, the MNA contains a provision (Article 369) regarding the applicable cases and relation to the salvage regime.

According to that rule, the regulations of the MNA *on shipwrecked or sunken goods* (Articles 369–383), shall apply to all operations *aimed at recovery of shipwrecked ships* or other goods located in the bottom of the navigation zones stated in each case, without prejudice that they may be subject to salvage, in which case the relations between the owner and salvor shall be governed by the rules of Salvage.

280. The exploration, tracking and location operations for ships and shipwrecked or sunken goods in internal waters and the Spanish territorial sea *shall require authorization* from the Navy, which shall grant such to whoever evidences ownership or, in other cases, discretionally and non-exclusively.

Moreover, the extraction operations of ships and shipwrecked or sunken goods in internal waters or in the Spanish territorial sea shall require prior authorization from the Navy, which shall set the terms and conditions to perform them. The holders of the authorization shall be bound to report on commencement and conclusion of the operations, as well as to allow inspection and supervision by the Navy.

281. The authorization of an extraction right may be applied for by owners of ships or shipwrecked or sunken goods, who duly evidence their ownership. If there are several owners, their application has to be made by agreement between them, or with specific renunciation by those who are not interested in extraction thereof. In the case of extraction of ships and goods on board, the initiative of the extraction proceedings shall lie with the owner of the ship.

Regarding the extraction contracts, the MNA states that the extraction application may be submitted by third parties other than the owner that arranged a salvage contract with it, or any other legally valid class (Article 379 MNA).

When ownership of the ships or goods lies with the State, and if it does not deem direct extraction or use to be appropriate, the Navy may grant this by tender pursuant to the laws on the assets of the Public Administrations (Ley 23/1982, de 16 de junio, *reguladora del Patrimonio Nacional/National Heritage*).

Extraction of weapons, ammunition, explosives or other military hardware that may affect National Defence, as well as objects belonging to the underwater cultural heritage and other goods whose trade is prohibited or restricted, shall be subject to the applicable special regulations and the regime that is established in such cases in the public authorization or contract for the relevant extraction thereof.

III. Property Rights

282. Ownership of ships or other shipwrecked or sunken goods shall not be affected by the sole fact of their shipwreck or sinking, thus they shall not be deemed as abandoned unless this is the specific will of their owner. The owners of such goods may also dispose of them and, especially, abandon them to the insurer where appropriate (Article 373 MNA).

283. The MNA also states a prescription in favour of the State: the State shall acquire the ownership of any ship or asset that is shipwrecked or sunken in the internal waters or Spanish territorial sea once three years have elapsed since the shipwreck or sinking, except for State ships and vessels. It shall also acquire the ownership of ships or goods that, once the term stated expires, are located in the exclusive economic zone or in the high seas and are owned by Spaniards.

The prescription term shall be interrupted at the moment of requesting extraction, as long as this is commenced within the term granted for the purpose. It shall elapse once more if the work is suspended or the term granted for such work expires.

IV. Shipwrecked or Sunken State Ships and Vessels

284. Without prejudice to the terms set forth in Articles 358 (4) and 359 of the MNA, regardless of the time at which the loss took place and the place where they may be located, shipwrecked or sunken Spanish State ships and vessels, their remains and their equipment or cargo, appertain to the State public domain, may not be disposed of, shall not prescribe and may not be seized, enjoying immunity of jurisdiction.

Exploration, tracking, location and extraction operations of shipwrecked or sunken Spanish State ships and vessels shall require authorization from the Navy, which holds full powers for their protection, without prejudice to the terms set forth in the laws on historical and cultural heritage, as appropriate.

285. The remains of foreign warships sunken or shipwrecked in Spanish maritime areas enjoy immunity of jurisdiction pursuant to the terms set forth in Article 50 of the MNA (*With the exceptions foreseen under International Law and in this Act, foreign State ships shall enjoy immunity, only being subject to the jurisdiction of their flag State*). Notwithstanding this, exploration, a tracking, location and extraction operation of these assets has to be agreed between the competent bodies of the flag State and the Ministry of Defence. In such case, those operations shall be subject to the terms established in the Convention on Protection of the Underwater Cultural Heritage of 2 November 2001.

V. Underwater Cultural Heritage

286. Except for specific provision otherwise in the regulations of the MNA, its rules shall not be applicable to the underwater cultural heritage, which shall be governed by its specific implementing regulations.

Those specific provisions are mainly in Article 383 of the MNA, which contains a regulation regarding objects belonging to the underwater cultural heritage *located beyond the territorial sea.*

Regulation and authorization of activities related to the underwater cultural heritage in the Spanish contiguous zone, as well as authorization of activities related to underwater cultural heritage in the exclusive economic zone and on the continental platform shall be governed by the terms set forth in the *Convention on Protection of the Underwater Cultural Heritage* of 2 November 2001 and other treaties to which Spain is a party, as well as the specific legislation.

In all cases, administrative authorization shall be required to extract archaeological or historical objects located on the seabed of the Spanish contiguous zone. Recovery of such goods without the required authorization shall be penalized as an offence committed in Spanish territory (Articles 321 et seq. Criminal Code: *On felonies against historical heritage assets*).

Chapter 9. General Average

§1. Historical Introduction

287. The origins of the earliest laws on general average that are among the oldest ones in the area of maritime law, cannot be identified precisely, but it is generally acknowledged that these very old maritime customs have been widely applied in Mediterranean maritime communities for centuries. The main principle of this custom can be basically stated as follows: if the common undertaking consisting of the ship and the cargo is exposed to a peril at the sea, the losses and expenses which are intentionally incurred to save the common adventure from that risk should be shared by the saved interest in proportion to their values.

The most complete ancient written trace on general average is the *Lex Rhodia de jactu* (Rhodian Law on Jettison) in the Justinianian Digesta, from the sixth century AC.

The Greek and Roman provisions on general average were adopted in the statutes of many maritime cities in the Mediterranean basin and along the Atlantic coast of Europe, as in the *Consulat de la Mer* compiled in the fourteenth century in Barcelona and the *Rolles d'Oléron* compiled in the twelfth century in Western France.

In later times, the provisions on general average entered into French *Ordonnance de la Marine Marchande* of 1681 and *Code de commerce* of 1807. By the ways of national codification, the ancient laws of general average were incorporated into a number of national legal systems, as in Spain by the Commercial Codes of 1829 and 1885.

In the latter half of the nineteenth century a strong need for international unification in this area was needed, and efforts were made to impose on a common interpretation. As a result, the YAR were born. These Rules are not an international convention, but are incorporated by reference into contracts of carriage and have in fact imposed a quite remarkable measure of uniformity on the basis of average adjustments around the world.

288. The YAR are administered by the *Comité Maritime International* (CMI). There have been various collections of YAR over the years, the most recent dated 2004. The YAR consist of a group of lettered rules, followed by a set of numbered rules. The lettered rules from A to G state the general principles, while the numbered rules (I–XXIII) are specific and deal with commercial practicability.

§2. Statutory Provisions

289. The YAR (which constitute a practical, simple, effective regulation) are in most cases used by free decision of the parties and their clauses are included in shipping documents. Almost all bills of lading and charter parties contain a clause making the YAR applicable as a part of the agreement.

For that reason, the MNA non-compulsory rules on the general average (Chapter II, Articles. 347–356) are only to apply unless stipulated otherwise.

To the extent that these Rules are not self-sufficient, other matters are regulated, such as the right to withholding of the effects that shall contribute, or the limitation of actions. Liquidation of such common claims shall be performed by a private liquidator appointed by the ship operator; although a procedure has been provided for cases in which an agreement is not achieved by the parties concerned over this point.

§3. Definition and Characteristics of General Average

290. The act of general average is defined in Article 347 of the MNA (*Concept and requisites of the event*) as one that arises when, in an intentional, reasonable manner, damage or extraordinary expense is caused for common salvage of goods committed to a sea voyage when these are all threatened by a danger.

The YAR of 2004 do not contain a definition of general average, but stipulate that '*there is a general average act when, and only when, any extraordinary sacrifice or expenditure is intentionally and reasonably made or incurred for the common safety for the purpose of preserving from peril the property involved in a common maritime adventure*'.

According to the definition of the MNA and to the provisions of the YAR, general average displays the following features:

1. The act must be intentional and reasonable for common salvage of goods.
2. There must also be areal and common danger.
3. There must also be an extraordinary damage, sacrifice or expenditure.

If the danger common to the ship, her cargo and the freight is the result of fault committed by one party giving rise to his liability by virtue of contract of carriage of goods by sea or charter party or the applicable international convention or national law, MNA contains a special rule in Article 351: when the situation of danger that justifies the general average event is one for which any of the parties with an interest in the voyage is to blame, all the damages and expenses caused shall be borne by the guilty party, and contribution by innocent parties shall not be appropriate.

The rules on general average serve to encourage masters and others involved in the trip to take the best possible actions to save the common undertaking from perils without regard to the interest sacrificed knowing that the losses will be compensated by all interests.

§4. Application of the YAR 1974 as Amended in 1990

291. By virtue of the optional nature of the provisions of the MNA dealing with general average, Spanish Law does not impose obstacles to the direct application of the YAR, if the parties so decide.

According to Article 356 of the MNA, those that hold an interest in the voyage may pact freely regarding the rules according to which the liquidation is to be performed. In the event of lack of specification otherwise, the most recent version of the York and Antwerp Rules shall be deemed to apply and, failing the choice of any rules, the provisions established by law shall be applicable. They may also agree the private settlement of a general average by a liquidator appointed by the ship operator.

In that regard, the parties may choose whatever legal system they wish, including the mutual abolition of any general average adjustment in their relations.

§5. General Average Adjustment

292. The settlement of the average occurs at the final port of discharge or at the port where the journey was interrupted, and is conducted by the average adjuster, in accordance with the average adjustment rules agreed upon between the parties.

If the YAR are incorporated into the contract, they will govern the adjustment of general average. They provide a complete code and, by the general rule of interpretation, they shall apply to the exclusion of any law and practice inconsistent with them, if the parties to a contract have adopted them.

Those that hold an interest in the voyage may also agree the private settlement of a general average by a liquidator appointed by the ship operator, with absence of formalities. Without prejudice to the terms set forth in the MNA with regard to the obligations of the master regarding the Captain's Log, the duty to notify a general average is not subject to fulfilment of any formal requisite on board (Article 350).

The MNA contains no special provisions on the adjustment of general average, but it is stated that *private settlement of damages*, and except if the title originating such has established something to the contrary, lacks binding force upon the parties concerned, who may dispute it through the relevant judicial proceedings (Article 353)

Should private settlement not take place, the claim shall be settled according to the proceedings of liquidation by public certification file, established in Articles 506–511 of the MNA.

§6. Receiving Fund

293. By virtue of Article 348 of the MNA on admissible sacrifices in general average, the active assets to which general average is applied shall only allow damage or expenses that are a direct or foreseeable consequence of the circumstances of the failure.

§7. Contributing Fund

294. According to Article 349 on contribution to general average, the damage or expenses caused by the general average shall be borne by the holders of the interests at risk at the moment of the failure, in proportion and within the limit of value salvaged of each one of these.

295. The contributing fund shall include the property saved in general average, the value of the property sacrificed and the reduced value of damaged property.

The ship operator may withhold the goods transported on board or on land until the parties with an interest in them do not deposit a sufficient guarantee to honour their obligation to contribute. They shall also sign a commitment to compensate the damage, in which the relevant goods and their value are detailed (Article 352 MNA).

296. The right to demand contribution to a general average expires one year after conclusion of the voyage on which it took place, it being deemed to end for each lot of goods at the moment of their definitive discharge. That term is interrupted by commencement of a private procedure or public certification for liquidation thereof (Article 355 MNA).

§8. Proceedings

297. Should private settlement not take place, the claim shall be settled according to the proceedings of liquidation by public certification file, established in Articles 506–511 (Chapter III. *On liquidation of the general average*).

Article 506 sets the object of the file and legitimation: in the event of the parties with an interest in a maritime voyage not reaching an agreement on private settlement of the general average, any of them may refer to a Notary Public to request the proceedings regulated in the MNA.

The writ of application of the general average settlement shall state a list of particulars of the facts that have occurred, of the expenses and damages caused and documents that evidence the request, as well as a list naming the parties holding an interest therein.

Once the application is admitted, the Notary Public shall notify all the parties with an interest in the maritime voyage, in the ship or in the cargo, informing them of their right to intervene in the proceedings.

The Notary Public shall appoint a liquidator in order to perform the liquidation, within a reasonable term to prepare the liquidation, which shall be established according to the difficulties of the case and may not exceed four months, except for a justified cause, at the request of the liquidator himself.

298. All the parties concerned shall be bound to provide the liquidator appointed the required collaboration in order to obtain information and documentation.

When liquidation of the general average is submitted by the liquidator, or his negative finding regarding the appropriateness of liquidation, the Notary Public shall notify this to the parties concerned, who may state their approval or challenge it within the thirty days following.

Once the approvals or the motions to challenge are received, the Notary Public shall notify the liquidator, who shall be bound, within the term of thirty days, to issue a reasoned finding on their suitability and, where appropriate, suggest the amendments he proposes to the original liquidation.

Considering the writs by the parties concerned and the finding by the liquidator, the Notary Public shall hand down a reasoned resolution approving, amending or rejecting the liquidation.

299. The resolution may be appealed with suspension effects before the competent Commercial Court. In that case, when the appeal is admitted, the Court Clerk shall appoint a new liquidator to perform the liquidation in the manner and within the terms stated in the MNA. Once the motions to challenge are received from the parties concerned, or the thirty-day term has elapsed from them being informed of the liquidation, the Court Clerk shall call a hearing to be held with the formalities of verbal trial.

The final resolution shall be a sufficient title to dispatch enforcement against the parties concerned who do not pay the contribution stated in the decision within the term of fifteen days, as well as against those who guaranteed their obligation, within the limits of the guarantee provided.

Chapter 10. Collisions

§1. Definitions

300. The MNA (Article 339) contains a legal definition of collision between ships: collision shall be construed as when ships, vessels or naval artefacts run into each other, causing damage to any of the parties, or to persons or property.

This definition covers all cases of direct collisions. It means that under Spanish Law, collision is, in a strict sense, an accident arising from the *touching* (actual impact between hulls, or ships' apparel, or appurtenances like the anchors or the anchor chains)of ships at sea.

However, the damage that a ship, vessel or naval artefact causes to another without contact due to an incorrect manoeuvre in navigation shall also be regulated by the rules set forth in the MNA. Thus, the law of collisions is applied to cover damage caused even if no physical touching between the ships have actually taken place, which is usually referred to as indirect or immaterial collisions. Therefore, physical contact between ships is not necessary to be under the scope of the law of collisions.

301. Finally, the provisions of the MNA shall not apply to collisions involving State ships. Foreign State ships shall enjoy immunity, only being subject to the jurisdiction of their flag State (Article 50 MNA).

§2. Statutory Provisions

I. Incorporation of Treaty Law

302. According to Spanish Law, collision shall be regulated by the terms set forth in the *Convention for the Unification of Certain Rules of Law with respect to Collisions between Vessels*, done at Brussels, on 23 September 1910, the other conventions on such matters to which Spain is a party, and by the provisions of Articles 339–346 of the MNA.

The Kingdom of Spain is also a party to the *International Convention for the Unification of Certain Rules of Law Relating to Civil Jurisdiction in Matters of Collision*, drafted by the *Comité Maritime International* and signed in Brussels 1952, and the *International Convention for the Unification of Certain Rules of Law Relating to Criminal Jurisdiction in Matters of Collision and Other Incidents of Navigation*, signed in Brussels, 1952.

Spain has also ratified the *Convention on the International Regulations for Preventing Collisions at Sea* (COLREG 1972), which entered into force on 4 December 1991. This Convention provides the rules in order to avoid collisions.

Moreover, the administration of the Kingdom of Spain, as flag State signatory of the UNCLOS (Article 94 (7)), is obliged to conduct investigations for the purpose of determining the cause of collisions, with the objective of reporting causes and seeking changes in international and national regulations that will aid in preventing such collisions in the future.

303. The provisions of national law dealing with collision liability are contained in Title VI (*Accidents in navigation*), Chapter I (*on collision*) of the MNA. In order to address some doubts regarding interpretation declared in Spanish's recent Case Law, the scope of application of this special regulation is to cover the criminal or administrative proceedings requiring an asset-based liability as subsidiary to the criminal or disciplinary, as substantive regulation of such matters is not to vary due to the simple fact of the liability being demanded by one procedural channel or another. Therefore, the provisions of the MNA on collisions shall apply in all cases to the responsibility for damages arising from collision, notwithstanding the fact of that liability being demanded in civil or criminal Court proceedings, or in administrative proceedings (Article 345 MNA).

However, those provisions shall not apply to relations between parties bound by a charter party or passage or labour contract, which shall be governed by their specific rules.

The wrongful collision of ships is a specific form of tort. Therefore, the rules governing tort liability contained in the *Civil Code* are also applicable as provisions of basic law to collision of ships to the extent they are not in contradiction to the MNA. As a general rule, the person who, as a result of an action or omission, causes damage to another by his fault or negligence shall be obliged to repair the damaged caused (Article 1902 *Civil Code*). This obligation is enforceable not only as a result of one's own actions or omissions but also of those of such persons for whom one is liable.

II. Damages and Procedure

304. In cases of collision, civil liability is based upon fault or negligence. Such negligence is based on the failure of skill and care which should ordinarily be expected of a competent seaman. Collisions may give rise to civil liability for personal and property injury or damage, within the law of tort, which may include administrative sanctions.

Under Spanish Law, the regime of collisions refers to the *Convention for the Unification of Certain Rules of Law with respect to Collisions between Vessels* of 1910 (Articles 3 and 5). It thus establishes the liability for *proven fault*, *exclusion of force majeure* and *classification of effective blame* (that shall never cover the contractual relations between the parties to a labour, passage or charter contract) when such blame has a shared nature.

According to Article 340 of the MNA, on *Grounds for liability*, liability for collision damage will rest on the ship or ships which have been proved to have caused the damage: the ship operator in charge of the ship, vessel or naval artefact to blame for the collision shall compensate the damages and losses suffered by the other and by the individuals and things on board thereof, always those caused outside these.

A substantial basis, though not the only one, for establishing fault on the part of a vessel for causing a maritime collision is the *International Regulations for the Prevention of Collisions at Sea*. These regulations have the force of law in the Kingdom of Spain.

305. In Spanish Law there is no in rem action and thus a ship being an object cannot be taken as a defendant in a case of ship's collision. The ship's collision liability shall be borne by the ship operator in charge of the ship. In the case of sports or recreational vessels, this obligation shall befall their holder or owner. The liability of the owner or ship operator spring from the fact that the owners or managers of an establishment or undertaking shall be liable for damages caused by their employees, in the service in which they are employed or in the performance of their duties (Article 1903 *Civil Code*).

306. The burden of proof rests on the claimant: the causal relation and the blame for the collision shall be proven by the party claiming the compensation. No presumptions of fault are raised by violation of a statute or regulation. Unless the plaintiff can establish such a prima facie evidence, he cannot hope to succeed.

In the case of collision caused by *fault shared* by both ships, the responsibility of their respective ship operators shall be classified in proportion to the degree of blame attributed to each ship or, where appropriate, vessel or naval artefact (Article 341 MNA). According to Article 1103 of the *Civil Code*, liability arising from negligence is enforceable in the performance of all kinds of obligations; but may be moderated by the Courts on a case-by-case basis.

When the degree of fault may not be established due to the circumstances of the event, or when the failures committed are equivalent, the liability shall be attributed to both ship operators in equal parts.

307. For better protection of third parties, the MNA declares the joint and several liability of both ship operators: both ship operators share joint and several liability in cases of collision due to shared blame with regard to damage suffered by third parties, be this personal harm or material damage (Article 342).

The ship operator that has paid the compensation by virtue of that joint and several liability shall be entitled to be reimbursed against the other ship operator in proportion to the degree its ship is to blame.

The ship operator sued in cases of shared blame may validly raise exceptions before third parties that, by extension, could be used by the other ship operator, especially those arising from contractual title that might exist between them, or those applicable due to limitation of liability (Article 343 MNA).

308. If a collision was the consequence of force majeure, or of an unknown cause, the damages shall be borne by those who suffered them (Article 2 Convention 1910).

309. Actions for compensation for collision damage shall be time-barred after the expiry of two years from the date of the accident(Article 7 Convention 1910).

310. As regards procedural matters, the MNA only contains an article forbidding any requirement of formal requisites: the right to demand compensation for collision shall not be subject to fulfilment of any formal requisite, without prejudice to the burden of proving the facts constituting the claim (Article 344). Notwithstanding this, the parties involved in a collision shall reciprocally facilitate inspection of the damages suffered. After a collision, the master of every ship that collided must also make known to the other ship the data of his ship (name, port of registration, port of departure and destination).

311. Finally, Article 346 of the MNA establishes that pollution damage arising due to a collision shall be regulated by the terms set forth in Articles 384–391 of that Act (Chapter V, *On civil liability for pollution*).

III. Limitation of Liability

312. The collision liability is subject to the general rules of limitation of liability for maritime claims (Article 2 of the *Convention on Limitation of Liability for Maritime Claims*, done at London on 19 November 1976), contained in Articles 392–405 of the MNA.

Chapter 11. Marine Pollution

§1. Introduction

313. Spain's membership of the European Union involves high standards in matters of liability for maritime pollution. Therefore, the national regulation on this topic is fully subject to the environmental principles included in Article 191 of the *Treaty on the Functioning of the European Union*, which involves greater quality in the building and maintenance of ships to hinder pollution processes, and attributing liability to the party that causes such pollution according to the principles of *prevention at source* and *the polluter pays*.

Marine Pollution has become a topic of paramount importance in the maritime world since the major accidents of the *Torrey Canyon*, the *Amoco Cadiz* and the *Erika*. Since the beginnings of the international response, two separate concepts have operated: first, the civil liability, the other being the purpose of the law to prevent pollution.

§2. Statutory Provisions: Sources of Law

314. Legislation on maritime pollution is both preventive as well as repressive and can be found on a civil, criminal, administrative and disciplinary level. It can generally be classified in two categories:

I. Regulations on Marine Environmental Protection

315. The principle of environmental protection has a constitutional status in Spain. According to Article 45 of the Spanish Constitution, everyone has the right to enjoy an environment suitable for the development of the person, as well as the duty to preserve it. Therefore, the public authorities shall watch over a rational use of all natural resources with a view to protecting and improving the quality of life and preserving and restoring the environment, by relying on an indispensable collective solidarity.

Consequentially, environmental protection is one of the state's fundamental policies in Spain. Legislation is aimed at strict prevention of all types of marine pollution and all the competent public bodies must emphasize the implementation of laws and regulations in this field, especially in the area of marine environmental protection.

The main provisions dealing with the various aspects of marine pollution prevention are contained in the MNA. Further provisions are contained in the SPMNA, which regulates the respective duties of shipowners and of crew members and shipmasters, on board vessels.

The safety requisites and those related to prevention of pollution by Spanish ships and vessels shall be determined and controlled according to the nature and purpose of the services provided and the navigation they perform (Article 97 MNA).Technical control of the safety requisites and those required to prevent pollution shall be performed by the competent bodies of the Maritime Authorities through the regulatory inspection and control plans and programs established. Inspections of ships or vessels, whatever their nature and purpose, shall be performed at the expense of the ship operator, except if they prove unwarranted.

316. Spain is a part of *the International Convention for the Prevention of Pollution from Ships* (MARPOL 73/78), the fundamental international text covering prevention of pollution of the marine environment by ships from operational causes and accidental discharges, and is bound by all its subsequent tacit acceptance procedure amendments. Where MARPOL 73/78 is applicable, its provisions concerning the discharge of pollutants by ships shall be complied with.

The Kingdom of Spain is also a party to a number of other international treaties dealing with the prevention of marine pollution, such as OILPOL 1954, the *Intervention Convention* 1969/73 (*International Convention relating to Intervention on the High Seas in cases of Marine Pollution*), the *Ballast Water Management Convention* 2004, the OPRC Convention (*International Convention on Oil Pollution Preparedness, Response and Cooperation*, signed in London in 1990) or the *Rio de Janeiro Convention* 1992.

317. Ships shall have on board the required certificates and documents of prevention of marine environmental pollution. According to MARPOL, the issuance of a certificate of compliance to the Regulations of MARPOL and its Annexes is provided along with the obligation of all parties to accept the certificates issued by another party of the Convention as equally valid and are attributed the authority to deny entrance of a ship in their ports or offshore terminals, if the ship does not carry a valid certificate, or does not carry it at all, in accordance with the provisions of the Regulations. The parties of the Convention have also the authority to inspect the ships entering their inland waters and in case a violation is detected, they are entitled to take measures altering the ship's sail (Articles 18, 78 MNA).

The Spanish Maritime Authorities shall inspect foreign ships and vessels departing from Spanish ports in the cases envisaged by the international treaties and conventions, in the European Union provisions and, in all cases, when there are reasonable doubts concerning their seaworthiness or those concerning protection of the marine environment or compliance with the Maritime Labour Convention (Article 104 MNA).

Should the inspections or controls stated in the national or international regulations show that the ship or vessel is not seaworthy or does not comply with the safety and contamination provisions, provision of its services or navigation may be suspended, until the ship operator has corrected the defects (Article 100 MNA).

318. The Maritime Authorities shall grant the relevant safety and pollution prevention certificates to Spanish ships and vessels that comply with the conditions foreseen in the applicable laws (Article 101 MNA).The Maritime Authorities may authorize reputable organizations to perform material actions and, where appropriate, to issue or renew the relevant certificates, in the cases and conditions foreseen in the implementing regulations. In cases when the inspectors declare the ship or vessel may not sail or perform its service under due conditions of safety of the individuals aboard and for the environment, the Maritime Authorities may prevent its departure, performance of its activity, or adopt the appropriate measures, until correction of the defects found, reporting this to the Consul of the flag State.

Ship safety and pollution prevention certificates shall be displayed on board, in a properly visible and easily accessible location (Article 102 MNA).

Regarding the effect of the certificates, by virtue of Article 103 of the MNA, the certificates issued presuppose the correct state of the ship with regard to its object, except for proof to the contrary. Lack or expiry of the certificates means that the ship shall be prevented from navigation or performing the services for which it is intended, with the exceptions that the implementing regulations may establish in special circumstances. The liability for lack or expiry of the ship's certificates shall lie with the ship operator and, pursuant to subsidiary terms, with the persons appointed pursuant to the provisions set forth in the International Safety Management Code (ISM).

319. Preventive measures and procedures, as well as response measures, are further regulated by a great number of other laws and regulations (e.g., Act No 26/2007, on environmental responsibility, or Royal Decree 1892/2004).

320. Finally, at EU level, the Commission proposed a number of measures. The packages of these measures are known as Erika I, II, and III. The *Erika I package* contained measures on port state control, classification societies and double-hull oil tankers. The *Erika II package* consists of measures on monitoring, controlling and setting up an information system, a fund to compensate victims of oil pollution and the creation of a Maritime Safety Agency. The *Erika III package* was adopted by the European Parliament on 11 March 2009.

Moreover, the Directive 2004/35/CE of the European Parliament and of the Council of 21 April 2004, *on environmental liability with regard to the prevention and remedying of environmental damage*, put in place an EU-wide framework for remediation of environmental damage, the scope of which is limited to damage to surface water. It is completed by Directive 2013/30/EU of the European Parliament and of the Council of 12 June 2013, *on safety of offshore oil and gas operations and amending Directive 2004/35/EC*, so that the ambit of damage covers all EU waters including the EEZ and the continental shelf where the coastal Member States exercise jurisdiction.

II. Regulations on Liability for Marine Pollution

321. By virtue of Article 45 (3) of the Spanish Constitution, for those who infringe the provisions on environmental protection, criminal or, where applicable, administrative sanctions shall be imposed, under the terms established by the law, and they shall be obliged to repair the damage caused.

The Kingdom of Spain has ratified the 1992 CLC and the 2001 Bunker Convention. The national basic provisions dealing with liability and compensation for pollution are contained in the MNA (Articles 384–391).

§3. Liability for Marine Pollution

I. Administrative and Criminal Liability

322. Title IV of the SPMNA specifies the administrative liability imposed on violators of the regulations on marine environmental protection.

For example, by virtue of Articles 305–310 of the SPMNA, the authorities may impose liabilities on the offenders in the following cases:

1) discharge into the sea of pollutants or other substances which are prohibited to discharge;
2) dumping into the sea of wastes without dumping permit;
3) failure to take immediate measures in the case of marine pollution incident.

In particular, the SPMNA regulates the duties of the shipmaster on board. In the event of a dangerous occurrence, the shipmaster has to apply any reasonable measure for the protection of the environment, to enter in the ship's logbook the description of the event endangering the environment and to submit a report to the competent authorities.

323. In some cases, the violation of the regulations on marine environmental protection may result in criminal liability. According to Article 325 of the *Criminal Code*, whoever, breaking the law or other provisions of a general nature that protects the environment, directly or indirectly causes or makes pollution that may seriously damage the balance of the natural systems shall be punished with a sentence of imprisonment for two to five years.

Investigation for criminal liabilities shall be done in accordance with the Criminal Procedural Code (*Ley de Enjuiciamiento Criminal*) by judicial organs.

II. Civil Liability

A. *Introduction*

324. The general rules on tort liability are clearly inadequate to offer a compensation response to pollution damages. Therefore, the international community solution was to offer an alternative compensation regime (CLC and FUND 1992). These rules are operative in Spanish Law.

However, the Kingdom of Spain has also its own complementary regimen on marine pollution. The Spanish regulation on civil liability for oil pollution is established in Chapter V, Title VI, MNA: *On civil liability for pollution* (Articles 384–391).

While 1992 CLC regulates civil liability for pollution damage caused solely by oil from ships and is not concerned with pollution damage to marine environment caused by other pollutants, Spanish civil liability regime extends to other substances. This regime imposes a *quasi*-strict liability of the ship operator or the owner of the artefact that causes the pollution, in addition to demanding the relevant mandatory insurance, pursuant to the applicable international conventions to which the MNA refers, especially the *International Convention on Civil Liability for Oil Pollution Damage 1992* (Civil Liability Convention, 1992) and the *International Convention on Civil Liability for Bunker Oil Pollution* (BUNKER, 2001). Thus, extensive application of the international principles is achieved in cases of pollution damage other than that specifically considered in the uniform laws in force.

However, by virtue of Article 391 of the MNA (on *Pre-emptive application of international conventions*) if any of the terms set forth in the international conventions to which Spain is a party on matters of civil liability for pollution damage by petrol or by noxious, hazardous or toxic substances, or by ship bunker, the provisions of such international treaties shall apply with priority in their respective scope. CLC has its specified scope of application with regard to the ship, oil and geographical limit (Article II: *This Convention shall apply exclusively: (a) to pollution damage caused: (i) in the territory, including the territorial sea, of a Contracting State, and (ii) in the exclusive economic zone of a Contracting State, established in accordance with international law, or, if a Contracting State has not established such a zone, in an area beyond and adjacent to the territorial sea of that State determined by that State in accordance with international law and extending not more than 200 nautical miles from the baselines from which the breadth of its territorial sea is measured; (b) to preventive measures, wherever taken, to prevent or minimize such damage*).

325. The terms set forth in the MNA shall not apply to damage caused by radioactive or nuclear substances, which shall be regulated by the specific provisions thereof.

326. The Spanish regulations on civil liability arising from pollution apply to any damage to the Spanish coasts and maritime areas that comes from ships, vessels, naval artefacts and fixed platforms, wherever they may be located (Article 384 MNA). Thus, that regime shall apply exclusively to the pollution damage caused in the territory of the Kingdom of Spain, including the territorial sea, and in its exclusive economic zone established in accordance with international law.

B. Subjects Liable

327. Regarding the subjects liable, following the criteria commonly contained in modern maritime conventions, Spanish legislation also establishes the channelling of liability to a single person, but in a different way to CLC. Article 385 of the MNA states that *the ship operator* of the ship or holder of the use or operation of the naval artefact or platform at the moment of the event causing pollution shall be bound to compensate for the pollution damage, notwithstanding its right to be reimbursed by the persons who are to blame for that event.

When the event causing pollution involves various ships, their ship operators shall be jointly and severally bound to compensate the pollution damage, unless this may be reasonably and exclusively attributed to one of the ships.

C. *Grounds for Liability*

328. According to the MNA (Article 386 on *Grounds for liability*), the ship operator is strictly liable for the damages caused, irrespective of any fault or wrongful act, and can only be exonerated for the events exhaustively mentioned in the Law. The ship operator shall be held liable for pollution damage due to the mere fact of it taking place. Notwithstanding this, it shall be exonerated if it proves that the damage has been caused by unavoidable force majeure, by negligence by any authority that is responsible for maintenance of lights or other aids to navigation, or by another intentional action or omission by a third party, notwithstanding the liability of the latter. The burden of proof is on the ship operator.

Without prejudice to the applicable international conventions, liability shall be demanded on the basis of the principles of caution and preventive action, the principle of correction, preferably right at the source of damage to the environment and the principle that *the polluter pays*. So the persons who have suffered loss do not have to prove negligence on the part of the ship operator.

Thus, the owner's liability is strict, with a restricted list of reasons for exoneration, as contained in Article 387 of the MNA (on *Fault of the damaged party*): should the ship operator prove that the pollution damage arose, fully or partially, due to a wilful or negligent action or omission of the person affected, it shall be fully or partially exonerated of its liability to that person.

D. *Scope of the Compensation*

329. The scope of the compensation is regulated in Article 388 of the MNA: losses or damages caused by pollution of the ship shall be duly compensated.

Besides, the cost of measures reasonably adopted by any person after the claim has taken place in order to prevent or minimize pollution damage shall also be duly compensated.

Damage compensation comprises not just the value of the loss suffered, but also that of the gain which the creditor has failed to obtain (Article 1106 *Civil Code*).If the obligation should consist of the payment of an amount of money, and the debtor should incur in default, damages shall consist of paying the agreed interest and, in the absence of an agreement, the legal interest.

E. *Limitation of Liability*

330. To counterbalance the strict form of liability established in the MNA and in the CLC, the operator of the ship is entitled to limit his liability in respect of any incident. The quantitative limitation of the tanker owners' liability is provided in the MNA and in the CLC, with the establishment of a financial fund that is addressed to fully indemnify and compensate the victims of oil pollution (Article 4 of the *Fund Convention*).

The owner of a ship shall be entitled to limit his liability under the CLC in respect of any one incident to an aggregate amount calculated as follows:

(a) 4,510,000 units of account for a ship not exceeding 5,000 units of tonnage;
(b) for a ship with a tonnage in excess thereof, for each additional unit of tonnage, 631 units of account in addition to the amount mentioned in subparagraph (a); provided, however, that this aggregate amount shall not, in any event, exceed 89,770,000 units of account.

Of course, if the harmful incident occurred as a result of the actual fault of privity of the owner, then the liability limitation does no longer apply (Article V (2) of CLC: *the owner shall not be entitled to limit his liability under this Convention if it is proved that the pollution damage resulted from his personal act or omission, committed with the intent to cause such damage, or recklessly and with knowledge that such damage would probably result*).

331. However, a public law liability may arise under EC legislation that exceeds the amount of compensation payable under CLC and FUND (*Commune de Mesquer v. Total France SA and Total International Limited*, Case C-188/07, Grand Chamber, 24 June 2008). In this case, the ECJ held that for the purposes of applying Article 15 of Directive 75/442, as amended by Decision 96/350, to the accidental spillage of hydrocarbons at sea causing pollution of the coastline of a Member State, the national court may regard the seller of those hydrocarbons and charterer of the ship carrying them as a producer of that waste. Moreover, if it happens that the cost of disposing of the waste produced by an accidental spillage of hydrocarbons at sea is not borne by the International Oil Pollution Compensation Fund, or cannot be borne because the ceiling for compensation for that accident has been reached, and that the national law of a Member State, including the law derived from international agreements, prevents that cost from being borne by the shipowner, even though they are to be regarded as 'holders' within the meaning of Article 1 (c) of Directive 75/442, as amended by Decision 96/350, such a national law will then, in order to ensure that Article 15 of that directive is correctly transposed, have to make provision for that cost to be borne by the producer of the product from which the waste thus spread came.

F. Mandatory Insurance

332. Finally, by virtue of Article 389 of the MNA, a mandatory insurance system of civil liability for pollution damage to the coast and navigable waters is adopted. The conditions and minimum coverage of this insurance are determined by the *Royal Decree* (*Real Decreto*) 1892/2004. According to this regulation, each ship carrying more than 2,000 metric tons of oil must carry a *Certificate of Insurance or Other Financial Security in Respect of Civil Liability for Oil Pollution Damage* attesting that insurance or other financial security is in force in accordance with the provisions of 1992 CLC. Without such a certificate, each contracting state shall not allow the ship to operate, whether the ship is engaged in international trade or domestic trade. This form of compulsory insurance is in force in maritime business since 1969, when for the first time in the history of ocean carriage, this rule was prescribed for sea carriers of crude oil.

In order to ensure the effectiveness of compulsory insurance, those harmed by pollution damage shall be entitled to *direct action* against the insurer for civil liability up to the limit of the sum insured. The insurer may raise the same exceptions as the ship operator would be entitled to pursuant to the MNA and also that of the pollution being due to an intentional act by the ship operator itself. Use of the applicable limitation on liability may also be made.

The Maritime Authorities shall prohibit navigation by ships or vessels and activity with naval artefacts or fixed platforms that do not hold the mandatory insurance coverage of civil liability for pollution damage (Article 390 MNA). It shall also refuse entry to or departure from Spanish ports, anchorage zones or terminals located in internal maritime waters or the territorial sea, by foreign ships, vessels or artefacts that lack the aforementioned insurance coverage.

§4. Marine Pollution Control and Cooperation

333. Spain is a party to the *International Convention relating to Intervention on the High Seas in cases of Marine Pollution* 1969. According to its rules, States, other than the flag State of the vessel, may take action beyond their territorial seas to prevent, mitigate, or eliminate imminent danger to their coastline against escape of oil from a vessel. The Convention was extended to substances other than oil by a 1973 Protocol.

334. The basic provisions of national law dealing with the various aspects of marine pollution control and cooperation are contained in Articles 32–36 of the MNA.

By virtue of Article 32 of the MNA (on *Plans for preparation and to combat pollution*), the Maritime Authorities shall establish a national plan for preparation and to combat maritime pollution to deal promptly and effectively with contamination events by petrol or other noxious or potentially harmful substances.

Moreover, the masters of Spanish ships must notify the Spanish Maritime Authorities and the competent authority of the nearest coastal State without delay of all pollution events by petrol, or by noxious or potentially hazardous substances, that come to their knowledge during navigation, pursuant to the procedures set out in the implementing regulations. The same obligation shall affect the masters of foreign ships navigating the Spanish maritime areas (Article 33 MNA).

335. Regarding international collaboration, the MNA establishes that without prejudice to the terms set forth in the applicable specific treaties, when the Spanish Maritime Authorities are required by another coastal State in whose waters acts of pollution have taken place, they shall collaborate with the authorities of that State when this is possible and reasonable. The assistance may consist of participation in operations to combat pollution or in intervention in proceedings to investigate the claim and in inspection of the documents, or of the ship supposedly responsible for the pollution, when it is in port or in the Spanish internal waters. Such assistance shall also be provided at the request of the flag State. When there is a real danger of pollution of the Spanish maritime areas, which may spread to the waters of another State, the latter shall immediately be informed.

The collaboration envisaged by the MNA may be subjected to the principle of reciprocity in all cases.

336. Spanish Law also contains special measures to be adopted in the contiguous zone. Whenever a competent Public Administration has knowledge that a foreign ship located in the contiguous zone has breached, is breaching or intends to breach the laws and regulations on this zone, it shall be entitled to intercept it, to request information or perform the appropriate inspection. Where necessary, other necessary and proportional measures may be adopted to prevent or penalize the offence, including arrest and escorting it to port.

337. Finally, a compensation system is established for cases of undue detention. The Maritime Authorities shall do everything possible to prevent ships suffering unnecessary detention or delay due to measures taken as foreseen in the MNA. Should an unnecessary arrest or delay occur, it shall bind the Administration responsible to measures to compensate the damages and losses that may be proven (Article 36 MNA).

Chapter 12. The Arrest of Ships

§1. Sources of Law

338. Under Spanish Law, the seizure of goods may occur:

1. As an enforcement execution proceedings (*embargo ejecutivo*), when the creditors claim is embodied in a final and irrevocable judgment.
2. As an interim measure in order to restrict the debtors' rights to manage, possess, use, and dispose the property (*embargo preventivo*), as a compulsory measure for property preservation that may be sought at any point before or during the litigation. The pre-judgment attachment, aimed at ensuring the enforcement of judgments ordering the delivery of amounts of money or yields, rents and fungible goods that can be estimated in cash by applying fixed prices. A pre-judgment attachment shall also be appropriate if it proves to be the most suitable measure and cannot be replaced by another measure that is equally or more efficient and less damaging for the defendant. Both kinds of seizures are regulated in the *Code of Civil Procedure* (*Ley de Enjuiciamiento Civil* de 2000).

In addition, the provisional seizure of ships, or arrest of ship, as a means of securing *maritime claims* or *other credits* is regulated by the MNA. In Spanish Law, a ship could be arrested as a security for any claim against its owner, whether maritime or not. But under no circumstance may arrest be applied to assure enforcement of a judgment that has already been handed down, or of an arbitration award already issued.

339. Chapter II, Title IX, of the MNA (*On arrest of ships*, Articles 470–479) contains the regime of arrest of ships, which refers to the *International Convention on Arrests of Ships*, done at Geneva on 12 March 1999, the rules of which it completes. Therefore, the Convention is the primary source of law on arrest of ships in Spain.

By virtue of Article 470 of the MNA (on *Nature and regulation of the measure*), the injunctive measure of arrest of ships, both Spanish as well as foreign, shall be governed by the *International Convention on the Arrest of Ships* 1999, by the terms set forth in the MNA and, under supplementary terms, by those established in Act No 1/2000, of 7 January, on *Civil Procedure*. Such a measure shall necessarily involve immobilization of the ship in the port where it is located.

According to the criteria of the MNA of not reiterating in the Act what is already foreseen in the international conventions, this regulation of Chapter II is limited to completing the procedural specialties, for example, setting the criteria that have to be used by a Court to determine the amount of the guarantee that shall be demanded to decree the arrest, which must be at least 15% of the amount of the maritime credit.

The provisions foreseen in the MNA are also applicable to vessels.

§2. ARREST FOR MARITIME CREDITS

340. *Arrest* means any detention or restriction on removal of a ship by order of a Court to secure a maritime claim, but does not include the seizure of a ship in execution or satisfaction of a judgment or other enforceable instrument (Article 1 (2) *Convention on Arrest 1999*).

The applicant must be a claimant of one of the maritime claims listed in Article 1 of the *Convention on Arrest 1999.*

According to Article 472 of the MNA, to decree arrest of a ship for maritime credit as defined in Article 1 of the *Convention on Arrest 1999, it shall suffice to allege the right or credits claimed*, the cause that gives rise to these and that the ship may be arrested.

341. In all cases, the Court shall demand a guarantee for a sufficient sum to respond to the damages, losses and costs that may arise.

That guarantee may be of any of the classes recognized by law, including a bank guarantee.

Once that guarantee is established, which shall be at least 15% of the amount of the maritime credit alleged, the Court may review its amount, of its own motion or at the request of a party, according to the carriage and the size of the ship, the cost arising from the ship staying in the port, its market price by day, whether or not it is on a regular line, whether it is loaded or not, as well as its contractual commitments.

342. Effective arrest of the ship is assured through the Maritime Authority, without the need to accredit the maritime credit, nor the hazard of procedural delay and urgency, referring in all non-specific matters to the *Civil Procedure Act* (Article 728).

I. Ship Subject to Arrest

343. All ships with regard to which a maritime credit is alleged may be arrested pursuant to the terms and within the scope of the *Convention on Arrest 1999* (Article 475 MNA). The basic rule on this topic is that the ship must be owned by the person liable for the claim at the time the maritime claim arose.

It means that arrest is permissible of any ship in respect of which a maritime claim is asserted if:

(a) the person who owned the ship at the time when the maritime claim arose is liable for the claim and is owner of the ship when the arrest is effected; or
(b) the demise charterer of the ship at the time when the maritime claim arose is liable for the claim and is demise charterer or owner of the ship when the arrest is effected; or
(c) the claim is based upon a mortgage or a *hypothèque* or a charge of the same nature on the ship; or
(d) the claim relates to the ownership or possession of the ship; or

(e) the claim is against the owner, demise charterer, manager or operator of the ship and is secured by a maritime lien which is granted or arises under the law of the State where the arrest is applied for.

344. Arrest is also permissible of any other ship or ships which, when the arrest is effected, is or are owned by the person who is liable for the maritime claim and who was, when the claim arose:

(a) owner of the ship in respect of which the maritime claim arose; or
(b) demise charterer, time charterer or voyage charterer of that ship.

This provision does not apply to claims in respect of ownership or possession of a ship.

The arrest of a ship which is not owned by the person liable for the claim shall be permissible only if, under the law of the State where the arrest is applied for, a judgment in respect of that claim can be enforced against that ship by judicial or forced sale of that ship.

II. Maritime Credits

345. In International Conventions, the basic criterion on which maritime claims are distinguished from other claims is their connection with a ship. For the purposes of the *Convention on Arrest 1999*, a maritime claim is a claim arising out of one or more of the following:

(a) loss or damage caused by the operation of the ship;
(b) loss of life or personal injury occurring, whether on land or on water, in direct connection with the operation of the ship;
(c) salvage operations or any salvage agreement, including, if applicable, special compensation relating to salvage operations in respect of a ship which by itself or its cargo threatened damage to the environment;
(d) damage or threat of damage caused by the ship to the environment, coastline or related interests; measures taken to prevent, minimize, or remove such damage; compensation for such damage; costs of reasonable measures of reinstatement of the environment actually undertaken or to be undertaken; loss incurred or likely to be incurred by third parties in connection with such damage; and damage, costs, or loss of a similar nature to those identified in this subparagraph (d);
(e) costs or expenses relating to the raising, removal, recovery, destruction or the rendering harmless of a ship which is sunk, wrecked, stranded or abandoned, including anything that is or has been on board such ship, and costs or expenses relating to the preservation of an abandoned ship and maintenance of its crew;
(f) any agreement relating to the use or hire of the ship, whether contained in a charter party or otherwise;
(g) any agreement relating to the carriage of goods or passengers on board the ship, whether contained in a charter party or otherwise;

(h) loss of or damage to or in connection with goods (including luggage) carried on board the ship;
(i) general average;
(j) towage;
(k) pilotage;
(l) goods, materials, provisions, bunkers, equipment (including containers) supplied or services rendered to the ship for its operation, management, preservation or maintenance;
(m) construction, reconstruction, repair, converting or equipping of the ship;
(n) port, canal, dock, harbour and other waterway dues and charges;
(o) wages and other sums due to the master, officers and other members of the ship's complement in respect of their employment on the ship, including costs of repatriation and social insurance contributions payable on their behalf;
(p) disbursements incurred on behalf of the ship or its owners;
(q) insurance premiums (including mutual insurance calls) in respect of the ship, payable by or on behalf of the shipowner or demise charterer;
(r) any commissions, brokerages or agency fees payable in respect of the ship by or on behalf of the shipowner or demise charterer;
(s) any dispute as to ownership or possession of the ship;
(t) any dispute between co-owners of the ship as to the employment or earnings of the ship;
(u) a mortgage or a *hypothèque* or a charge of the same nature on the ship;
(v) any dispute arising out of a contract for the sale of the ship.

§3. Arrest for Other Credits

346. Arrest of Spanish ships that are physically within the Spanish jurisdiction, ordered on application by persons who have their usual residence or main establishment in Spain, or who have acquired the credit concerned by cession or subrogation of such, may be decreed both for the maritime credits *as well as for any other rights or credits against the debtor pertaining to the ship or ships whose seizure is requested* (Article 473 MNA).

Spanish ships may also be arrested by the competent administrative body pursuant to the terms set forth in the specific provisions applicable (SPMNA and the implementing regulations).

In the arrests for any other rights or credits, *the immobilization may be replaced, at the discretion of the competent jurisdictional or administrative body, by an annotation of the measure on the Register of Moveable Assets* and, where appropriate, of prohibition on disposal.

347. Arrest of ships flying the flag of a State that is not a party to the *Convention on Arrest 1999*, shall be governed by the provisions of that Convention, notwithstanding it being possible for them to be arrested both for maritime credits as well as for any other credits.

348. Arrest of a ship shall also be appropriate for the purposes of obtaining a guarantee although, by virtue of the existence of a contract or another document with an arbitration clause, or a jurisdiction clause, the maritime credit for which the arrest is requested shall be subject to a hearing by a foreign jurisdiction or arbitration tribunal (Article 474 MNA, on *Arrest and a submission to foreign jurisdiction*).

349. It shall be assumed that arrest of ships arises due to the danger of procedural delay and urgency mentioned in Articles 728 (1) (Injunctions may only be decided if the applicant justifies that, in the case at hand, failure to do so could, during the course of the proceedings, lead to situations preventing or hindering the effectiveness of the protection that may be granted in case an affirmative judgment is eventually passed. No injunctions shall be decided if it is their aim to alter de facto situations that the applicant has been accepting during a prolonged period, unless the latter duly justifies the reasons for which the said measures have not been requested until then), 730 (2) and 733 (2) of the Civil Procedure Act (Article 476 MNA).The applicant must indicate the items of the maritime claim concerned, the reasons of the application and the ship to be arrested.

§4. JUDICIAL PROCEDURE FOR CONSERVATORY ARREST

350. The conservatory arrest of ships in Spain falls within the jurisdiction of the *Commercial Courts.*

The Court that has objective competence to hear the main claim, or that of the port or place where the ship is located, or that where the ship is expected to arrive, as chosen by the plaintiff that requests adoption of the injunctive measure, shall be competent to decree the arrest of a ship. Notwithstanding this, if the ship does not reach the port expected, the Court of that port shall lose its competence (Article 471 MNA).

When arrest of a ship is ordered, if a Spanish Court is competent to hear the substantive matter, the measure resolved shall be maintained as long as the suit is filed within the term set by the Court in keeping with the circumstances of the case.

The competent jurisdiction to decree the arrest shall be, at the choice of the claimant, that of the port where the ship is moored, that where its arrival is awaited, or that of the Court with competence to hear the main claim.

351. By virtue of Article 470 of the MNA, arrest of ships shall necessarily involve immobilization of the ship in the port where it is located.

Regarding the implementation of the arrest, the MNA states that once the arrest has been ordered, the Court shall notify the Maritime Authority of the port where the ship is located, or that where it is expected to arrive, by the swiftest means, and he shall adopt the necessary measures to arrest and prohibit departure by the ship. To that end, the Maritime Authorities may withdraw the ship's documentation, as well as obtain collaboration by the Port Authority, by the Security Forces and Corps and public entities dedicated to coastal surveillance, which shall be bound to provide the required cooperation pursuant to their respective powers (Article 477 MNA).

The terms set forth in the MNA do not affect the rights or powers that, pursuant to the applicable administrative legislation and international conventions, are the responsibility of the public and port administrations, to retain a ship or otherwise prevent it from setting sail within their jurisdiction.

Once the arrest is resolved and carried out, and the arrest guaranteed, the master or shipping agent acting for the ship shall be notified, delivering a copy of the suit filed and the order that resolves it(Article 478 MNA).

352. In cases in which according to the terms set forth in Article 7 of the *Convention on Arrest 1999*, the Spanish Courts are not competent to hear the substantive related to a ship arrested in Spain, the Court that performed the arrest shall, of its own motion or at the request of the party, set a term of no less than thirty days, nor exceeding ninety, for the holder of the maritime credit to evidence commencement of proceedings before the competent Court or arbitration tribunal. If the proceedings are not initiated within the term set, on request by the party, the Court shall order release of the ship arrested or cancellation of the guarantee provided (Article 479 MNA).

353. The arrest may be lifted when sufficient security has been provided in a satisfactory form in an amount sufficient to cover the principal claim, as well as interest and legal costs. The security may be provided by way of depositing cash or other assets with the court, or by way of submitting other sureties (bank guarantee, liability insurer's letter of undertaking), as long as it is freely disposable and transferable in favour of the claimant. In the absence of agreement between the parties as to the sufficiency and form of the security, the Court shall determine its nature and the amount thereof, not exceeding the value of the arrested ship. Any request for the ship to be released upon security being provided shall not be construed as an acknowledgement of liability nor as a waiver of any defence or any right to limit liability (Article 4 Convention 1999).

Chapter 13. Carriage of Passengers

§1. Introduction: Applicable Laws

354. The Spanish regulation relating to the carriage of passengers and their luggage by Sea, after the entry into force of the MNA is a complex framework, where national, international and UE laws are operating.

Carriage of passengers in Spain is regulated by the *International Convention relating to the Carriage of Passengers and their Luggage by Sea*, done at Athens on 13 December 1974 (PYE/PAL), the Protocols that amend it, to which Spain is a party, the provisions of the European Union and the MNA.

The uniform rules on the subject are now the main source of law. The Kingdom of Spain is a party to 1974 PAL and its 2002 Protocol, which is in force throughout the EU. Moreover, the EU Law has extended the scope of application of PYE/PAL in internal transportation at European level, by virtue of Annex I of the Regulation 329/2009, whereby the status of liability as defined in the International Convention of Athens 1974 apply also in the internal transportation of passengers in the EU Member States. The 2002 Protocol entered into force on 23 April 2014. The implementation legislation in the EU was already in force at that time.

However, the application of the Athens Convention meets several limitations: its aim is not to establish a comprehensive legal regime of the contract of carriage. It is confined exclusively to contemplate the carrier's liability and compensation for injury or damage caused as a result of an accident. Therefore, it does not address other issues such as the carrier's liability for breach of the obligation to transport, defective performance of the contract, delay damages, etc. To cope with these subjects, national and EU law have to be applied.

355. In Spanish Law, the carriage of passengers by sea is based upon contract. The basic regulation of this contract is in the MNA (Chapter III. *On the passage contract.* Articles. 287–300). But there are other sources of regulation on this subject: in addition, the remaining regulations of private law will be applied (Articles 1254 et seq. *Civil code*).

356. Besides, a number of EU regulations are applicable to the carriage of passengers by sea at EU level:

(a) Regulation No 392/2009, of 23 April 2009, on the liability of carriers of passengers by sea in the event of accidents.
(b) Regulation No 1177/2010, of 24 November 2010, concerning the rights of passengers when travelling by sea and inland waterway and amending Regulation (EC) No 2006/2004.
(c) Council Directive 98/41/EC, of 18 June 1998, on the registration of persons sailing on board passenger ships operating to or from ports of the Member States of the Community

357. As a general rule, the provisions of law regarding carriage of passengers by sea apply compulsorily in order to protect the interests of passengers.

Specifically, the provisions of the MNA shall imperatively apply to all maritime passage contracts. Contractual clauses that are directly or indirectly aimed at attenuating or avoiding the liability of the carrier to the detriment of the holder of the right to demand compensation shall be null and void (Article 298 (2) MNA).

The same rule applies in international maritime law. According to Article 18 of the PYE/PAL: *any contractual provision concluded before the occurrence of the incident which has caused the death of or personal injury to a passenger or the loss of or damage to the passenger's luggage, purporting to relieve any person liable under this Convention of liability towards the passenger or to prescribe a lower limit of liability than that fixed in this Convention except as provided in Article 8, paragraph 4, and any such provision purporting to shift the burden of proof which rests on the carrier or performing carrier, or having the effect of restricting the options specified in Article 17, paragraphs 1 or 2, shall be null and void, but the nullity of that provision shall not render void the contract of carriage which shall remain subject to the provisions of this Convention.*

§2. Contract of Carriage of Passengers by Sea

I. Concept

358. The contract of carriage of passengers by sea (or *Passage Contract*) is defined in Article 287 of the MNA: by means of a passage contract, the carrier undertakes, in exchange for payment of a price, to transport an individual and, where appropriate, his luggage, by sea.

According to that definition, the *carrier* and the *passenger* are the two parties to a contract of carriage of passengers by sea. The carrier is the person by or on behalf of whom a contract of carriage has been concluded, regardless of whether the carriage is actually performed by him or by a performing carrier. The 'carrier' is thus the party that promises to perform the carriage, not necessarily the party that does perform the carriage. Virtually every carrier today subcontracts with separate companies to perform specialized aspects of the carriage. For the definition of the performing party, Article 278 of the MNA must be applied: the party that effectively performs the carriage with its own resources.

Moreover, the carriage of passenger's luggage is covered by a passage contract (Article 294 MNA). The carrier shall transport the luggage along with the travellers and included in the price of the tickets, within the limits of weight and volume set by the carrier or usual practice. That exceeding the limits stated shall be subject to special stipulation, with the obligation to previously inform the passenger of these limitations of luggage and cost thereof.

359. The luggage shall be considered to include the items or cars transported by the carrier by virtue of the passage contract, excluding those that are under a goods transport contract, or live animals (Article 295 MNA).

Luggage include *cabin luggage* and *hold luggage*.

Cabin luggage is considered exclusively that which the passenger has in the cabin, or in the vehicle transported, or on it, or that he conserves in his possession, custody or control.

Hold luggage shall be considered cars and items delivered to the carrier. When the luggage is admitted, the carrier shall record the following data on the ticket or a complementary stub:

a) Number and weight of the items or vehicles;
b) Name and seat of the main establishment of the carrier;
c) Name of the passenger;
d) Port of departure and destination;
e) Eventual declared value.
f) Transport price.

360. The MNA also states what must not be considered as a passage contract: the provisions of this contract shall not apply to amicable transport or clandestine passage. Notwithstanding this, it shall apply to free transport provided by a maritime passenger carrier.

II. The Passage Ticket

361. The carrier must inexcusably extend a *passage ticket* (Article 288 MNA). It serves as evidence of conclusion of a contract of carriage of passenger by sea.

The passage ticket shall compulsorily contain at least the following mentions:

a) Place and date of issue;
b) Name and address of the carrier;
c) Name of the ship;
d) Class and number of the cabin or accommodation;
e) Price of the transport or free nature thereof;
f) Place of departure and destination;
g) Date and time of boarding, as well as that of arrival or estimated duration of the voyage;
h) Summary indication of the route to be followed, as well as the stops foreseen;
i) The remaining conditions under which the transport shall be performed.

The foregoing notwithstanding, for vessels that provide port and regular services inside the zones defined by the maritime authorities, the passage ticket may be replaced by a *ticket* that shall state the name of the carrier, the service provided and its amount.

The passage ticket may be issued *to the bearer* (the passenger is the bearer and it is transferable by a simple handing over of the document) or to a *specific individual* (indicating the name of the passenger, being transferable by assignment). In the latter case, it may only be conveyed with the carrier's consent (Article 289 MNA).

III. Obligations of the Carrier

362. The main obligation of the carrier under a passage contract is to begin the voyage at the time as indicated in the passenger ticket and carry the passenger and the luggage to the agreed port of disembarkation within the agreed or reasonable time on the agreed or customary route.

Moreover, the carrier shall provide the passengers the ship at the place and time agreed, as well as the spaces dedicated to those of their class and, where appropriate, the accommodation places acquired by the passengers (Article 290 MNA).

The carrier shall ensure the ship is put into and kept in a state of seaworthiness and duly fitted out, equipped and provisioned to perform the transport agreed and to guarantee the safety and comfort of the passengers on board, according to the conditions that are usual on the type of voyage contracted.

Regarding the obligation to perform the voyage, the carrier shall commence the voyage and complete it to the destination without unjustified delay and on the route agreed or, should an agreement not exist, by that most appropriate according to the circumstances.

Likewise, it shall provide complementary services and medical assistance in the manner established in the regulations or usual practice.

If the voyage is interrupted by failure of the ship before reaching the destination port, the carrier shall bear the maintenance and accommodation expenses of the passengers while the ship is repaired. If the ship is definitively incapacitated or the delay may severely harm the passengers, the carrier shall provide transport to the agreed destination at its expense, notwithstanding the relevant liabilities (Article 292 MNA).

The carrier shall transport the luggage along with the travellers and included in the price of the tickets, within the limits of weight and volume set by the carrier or usual practice. That exceeding the limits stated shall be subject to special stipulation, with the obligation to previously inform the passenger of these limitations of luggage and cost thereof.

363. The MNA expressly states that the passenger shall be entitled to demand that the carrier fulfils the obligations upon it according to the rules of the European Union (Article 293 MNA). Passengers' rights are delimited by Regulation (EU) No 1177/2010: rights of disabled persons and persons with reduced mobility and obligations of carriers and terminal operators in the event of interrupted travel. Regulation (EU) No 1177/2010 also includes some general rules on information and complaints.

This Regulation shall not apply in respect of passengers travelling:

(a) on ships certified to carry up to twelve passengers;
(b) on ships which have a crew responsible for the operation of the ship composed of not more than three persons or where the distance of the overall passenger service is less than 500 meters, one way;
(c) on excursion and sightseeing tours other than cruises; or

(d) on ships not propelled by mechanical means as well as original, and individual replicas of, historical passenger ships designed before 1965, built predominantly with the original materials, certified to carry up to thirty-six passengers.

IV. Obligations of the Passenger

364. The passenger shall pay the price of the passage, arrive on time for boarding and abide by the rules established to maintain proper order and safety on board (Article 293 (1) MNA.

First of all, the passenger shall pay the fare. If the passenger does not comply with this obligation, the carrier has a lien and withholding right (Article 296 MNA). The luggage shall be assigned preferentially to payment of the fare, delays and other expenses arising from their carriage until their delivery and during fifteen days thereafter, except if conveyed to a third party in good faith within the latter term. The carrier shall be entitled to withhold the luggage carried in its possession until it receives the fare, delays and other expenses arising from such carriage. It may also resort to deposit proceedings and sale of goods and luggage, requesting a Notary Public to sell the goods.

The passenger must not take contraband or hazardous goods on board. Hazardous goods may not be loaded without prior declaration of their nature to the carrier, and without its consent to transport such, and in any event, they shall be marked and labelled by the consignor pursuant to the rules in force for each class of such goods (Articles 295 (4) and 232 MNA).

Should the passenger load hazardous goods without prior declaration of their nature to the carrier or without its consent to transport such, he shall be held liable to the carrier and before the other consignors for all damages and losses caused. Moreover, such goods may be unloaded, destroyed or transformed to make them harmless at any time, as required by the circumstances, without right to compensation.

Even in the case of correctly declared loading of hazardous goods, these may be unloaded, destroyed or transformed to make them harmless at any time if they become a real hazard to individuals or property, without right to compensation, unless the carrier is responsible for the situation of danger.

Finally, the passenger must collaborate with the carrier in the execution of the contract. In case the passenger fails to embark on time, the carrier has no contractual obligations towards him and the passenger is obliged to pay the entire fee.

V. Termination of the Contract

365. The contract shall be terminated in the following cases (Article 297 MNA):

a) When the passenger does not board on the date established, in which case the price of the passage shall be forfeited to the carrier, except if the cause of failure to board is the death or illness of the passenger or relatives accompanying him and that is notified without delay, or it has been possible to replace the passenger with another.

b) When, for a fortuitous reason, the voyage becomes impossible or delayed, in which case the carrier shall refund the price of the passage and being exempt of liability.
c) For all major amendment of fees, foreseen stopovers, diversion of the ship from the agreed route, accommodation places acquired by the passenger and the comfort conditions agreed, in which case, if the passenger opts for termination, he shall be entitled to reimbursement of the total price of the passage, or the proportional part thereof for the distance still to be covered, and compensation of damage and losses, if the modification is not for justified reasons.
d) If, prior to commencing the journey or during execution thereof, war were to break out that might expose the ship or passenger to unforeseen risks, in that case both parties may request termination without compensation.
e) If, once the journey has commenced, the passenger cannot continue for a fortuitous reason, in which case the carrier shall be entitled to the proportional part of the price according to the route covered.

§3. Liability and Limitation of Liability

I. Basis for Liability

366. The regime of liability is established in Article 298 of the MNA: *the liability of the carrier shall be governed, in all cases, by the International Convention relating to the Carriage of Passengers and their Luggage by Sea, done at Athens on 13 December 1974 (PYE/PAL), the Protocols that amend it to which Spain is a party, the provisions of the European Union and this Act.*

The 2002 Protocol introduced a system of primarily strict liability of carriers for death and personal injury, limited to an amount of 250,000 SDR. For other claims and claims exceeding 250,000 SDR, the basis of liability is negligence with reverse burden of proof.

This can be described as a mechanism to assist passengers in obtaining compensation, based on well-accepted principles applied in existing liability and compensation regimes dealing with environmental pollution. These include replacing the fault-based liability system with a strict liability system for shipping related incidents, backed by the requirement that the carrier take out compulsory insurance to cover these potential claims.

367. Regarding the *liability for death of or personal injury to a passenger* caused by a shipping incident, Article 3 of PYE/PAL applies: for the loss suffered as a result of the death of or personal injury to a passenger caused by a shipping incident, the carrier shall be strictly liable. But this strict liability does not apply if the carrier proves that the incident resulted from an act of war hostilities, civil war, insurrection or a natural phenomenon of an exceptional, inevitable and irresistible character, or that it was wholly caused by an act or omission done with the intent to cause the incident by a third party (e.g., an act of terrorism).

Moreover, strict liability may be reduced or even cease if a passenger has contributed to the situation by his own carelessness or while under the influence of alcohol.

If and to the extent that the loss exceeds the above limit, the carrier shall be further liable unless the carrier proves that the incident which caused the loss occurred without the fault or neglect of the carrier.

For the loss suffered as a result of the death of or personal injury to a passenger not caused by a shipping incident, the carrier shall be liable if the incident which caused the loss was due to the fault or neglect of the carrier. The burden of proving fault or neglect shall lie with the claimant. A passenger claim for death and personal injury will often be secured by a maritime lien.

The *Shipping incident* in which strict liability applies, correspond to incidents where the burden of proof was reversed under the 1974 PAL Convention: shipwreck, capsizing, collision or stranding of the ship, explosion or fire in the ship, or defect in the ship (including breakdown of steering and emergency appliances).

368. Regarding *material damages*, liability is negligence-based: Article 3 PYE/PAL establishes that for the loss suffered as a result of the loss of or damage to cabin luggage, the carrier shall be liable if the incident which caused the loss was due to the fault or neglect of the carrier. The fault or neglect of the carrier shall be presumed for loss caused by a shipping incident.

For the loss suffered as a result of the loss of or damage to luggage other than cabin luggage, the carrier shall be liable unless the carrier proves that the incident which caused the loss occurred without the fault or neglect of the carrier.

Thus, the burden of proof is reversed if the carrier has the goods in his possession, but for cabin luggage the burden of proof is straight.

369. The liability of the carrier under PYE/PAL only relates to loss arising from incidents that occurred in the course of the carriage. The burden of proving that the incident which caused the loss occurred in the course of the carriage, and the extent of the loss, shall lie with the claimant. If notice of damage is not given at the end of the voyage, it is for the passenger to prove that his luggage was damaged during the carriage by sea.

II. Limitation

370. In the matter of *limitation of liability*, the MNA refers to PYE/PAL (Article 299 MNA): *Liability of the carrier is limited to the sums established in the Athens Convention relating to the Carriage of Passengers and their Luggage by Sea and Protocols that amend it and are in force in Spain.*

The limits of liability have been raised significantly under the 2002 Protocol, to reflect present day conditions and the mechanism for raising limits in the future has been made easier.

By virtue of Article 7 of the PYE/PAL, the liability of the carrier for the death of or personal injury to a passenger shall in no case exceed 400,000 units of account per passenger on each distinct occasion. Where, in accordance with the law of the court seized of the case, damages are awarded in the form of periodical income payments, the equivalent capital value of those payments shall not exceed the said limit.

As far as loss of or damage to luggage is concerned, the carrier's limit of liability varies, depending on whether the loss or damage occurred in respect of cabin luggage, of a vehicle and/or luggage carried in or on it, or in respect of other luggage.

With regard to the limit of liability of the carrier for loss of or damage to luggage and vehicles, Article 8 of the PYE/PAL states that such liability for the loss of or damage to cabin luggage shall in no case exceed 2,250 units of account per passenger, per carriage.

The liability of the carrier for the loss of or damage to vehicles including all luggage carried in or on the vehicle shall in no case exceed 12,700 units of account per vehicle, per carriage.

The liability of the carrier in respect of other luggage in no case exceeds 3,375 units of account per passenger, per carriage.

371. The carrier and the passenger may agree that the liability of the carrier shall be subject to a deductible not exceeding 330 units of account in the case of damage to a vehicle and not exceeding 149 units of account per passenger in the case of loss of or damage to other luggage, such sum to be deducted from the loss or damage.

If the luggage is transported with declared value, accepted by the carrier, the limit to their liability shall match that value (Article 299 (2) MNA).

§4. Compulsory Insurance

372. The new Article 4*bis* of the PAL Convention (2002 Protocol) introduces compulsory insurance to cover passengers on ships. It requires carriers to maintain insurance or other financial security, such as the guarantee of a bank or similar financial institution, to cover the limits for strict liability under the Convention in respect of the death of and personal injury to passengers. The limit of the compulsory insurance or other financial security should not be less than 250,000 SDR per passenger on each distinct occasion.

Any liability that is not covered by compulsory insurance may still be insured.

373. Ships are to be issued with a certificate attesting that insurance or other financial security is in force and a model certificate is attached to the Protocol in an Annex. The model shall contain the following particulars:

(a) name of ship, distinctive number or letters and port of registry;
(b) name and principal place of business of the carrier who actually performs the whole or a part of the carriage;
(c) IMO ship identification number;
(d) type and duration of security;
(e) name and principal place of business of insurer or other person providing financial security and, where appropriate, place of business where the insurance or other financial security is established; and

(f) period of validity of the certificate, which shall not be longer than the period of validity of the insurance or other financial security.

The certificate shall be in the official language or languages of the issuing State. If the language used is not English, French or Spanish, the text shall include a translation into one of these languages, and, where the State so decides, the official language of the State may be omitted.

The certificate shall be carried on board the ship, and a copy shall be deposited with the authorities who keep the record of the ship's registry or, if the ship is not registered in a State Party, with the authority of the State issuing or certifying the certificate.

374. According to this regulation, the MNA (Article 300, on *Mandatory insurance*) states that the effective carrier that executes transport of a ship transporting more than twelve passengers shall be bound to subscribe mandatory liability insurance for death or bodily harm to the passengers transported, with a limit for each passenger and each accident that is no lower than those established in the conventions and in the provisions of the European Union. The implementing regulations shall govern the details of such mandatory insurance and the certificate it is mandatory for the ships to carry on board (Regulation 270/2013 *on the certificate of insurance or financial guarantee of civil liability in the carriage of passengers by sea in the event of an accident* and Regulation 1575/1989, *on Compulsory Insurance of Travellers*).

375. Moreover, the party damaged shall be entitled to *direct action* against the insurer up to the limit of the sum insured. The insurer may raise the same objections as those to which the carrier is entitled pursuant to Article 3 of the PAL Convention and, where appropriate, the fact of the accident being fraudulently caused by the insured. In all cases, it may also oppose the limit of liability established in Article 7 of the Convention, even in the event of the insured having lost it pursuant to Article 13 of the Convention.

The defendant may invoke the defence that the damage resulted from the wilful misconduct of the assured, but the defendant cannot invoke any other defence which the defendant might have been entitled to invoke in proceedings brought by the assured against the defendant. The defendant shall in any event have the right to require the carrier and the performing carrier to be joined in the proceedings.

Any sums provided by insurance or by other financial security maintained in accordance with PAL Convention shall be available exclusively for the satisfaction of claims under the Convention, and any payments made of such sums shall discharge any liability arising under the Convention to the extent of the amounts paid.

376. By virtue of Regulation 270/2013 on the certificate of insurance or financial guarantee of civil liability in the carriage of passengers by sea in the event of an accident, a ship under Spanish flag cannot operate at any time unless that certificate has been issued.

Part III. Other Transport

Chapter 1. Transport by Road

by Achim Puetz

§1. Introduction

377. The Kingdom of Spain deposited the instrument of accession to the Convention on the Contract for the International Carriage of Goods by Road (CMR) on 12 September 1973,[10] and the Convention entered into force on its territory on 13 May 1974. It also acceded to the Protocol thereto, made in Geneva on 5 July 1978, which replaced the (Germinal) gold franc by the International Monetary Fund's SDR in Article 23 CMR,[11] as well as to the Additional Protocol concerning the Electronic Consignment Note of 27 May 2008.[12]

On a national level, the main private law regulation dealing with the carriage of goods by road is Act No 15/2009, of 11 November, on the Contract for the Carriage of Goods by Land (COGLA). It imports many of the solutions contained in the CMR Convention into Spanish law, in a way similar to that engaged by other European countries, although it establishes some important innovations that serve to fill the gaps left by the international legal instrument. They shall briefly be described hereunder. Furthermore, it should be noted that, on 1 August 2012, the Ministry of Public Works and Transport issued the Order FOM/1882/2012, establishing general conditions of contracts for the carriage of goods by road.[13] Pursuant to Article 2 of the Order, the general conditions contained therein shall apply to all contracts for the carriage of goods by road, unless the parties to the contract specifically exclude their application. Where amendments to these general conditions are made in a standard form contract, modifications are only admissible to the extent that they are beneficial for the party adhering to the pre-established contractual terms.

378. Absent any international convention on the contracts for the carriage of passengers – the 1973 Convention on the Contract for the International Carriage of

10. *B.O.E.* No 109, of 7 May 1974. An extensive corrigendum of the Spanish translation of the Convention has been published in *B.O.E.* No 142, of 15 Jun. 1995.
11. *B.O.E.* No 303, of 18 Dec. 1982.
12. *B.O.E.* No 141, of 14 Jun. 2011.
13. *B.O.E.* No 214, of 5 Sept. 2012.

Passengers and Luggage by Road (CVR) has neither been ratified nor acceded to by Spain – such agreements are governed by national law. However, since Spain is a Member State of the European Union, the provisions contained in Regulation (EU) No 181/2011, of 16 February 2011, concerning the rights of passengers in bus and coach transport, directly apply to most contracts of carriage of passengers by road. This fact is implicitly recognized by the Spanish national legislation, when it establishes that the maximum amount of the compensation due in case of incidences with the luggage is that laid down in the EU Regulation, 'unless limits or conditions which are more favourable for the passenger are agreed' (Article 23 of Act No 16/1987, on the Administrative Organisation of Land Transport (AOLTA)).

§2. The Contract for the Carriage of Goods by Road under National Law

I. Introduction

379. The 2009 Carriage of Goods by Land Act applies to all contracts for the carriage of goods by both road and rail for reward, by virtue of which the carrier undertakes to carry goods from one place to another and to deliver them to the consignee mentioned in the contract (Articles 1 and 2 COGLA). As a general rule, its provisions are of a dispositive nature, unless the Act itself states otherwise, which is the case of the carrier's liability (Article 46 COGLA) and the rules on limitation of actions (Article 78 COGLA).

380. Article 5 COGLA refers to intermediation when contracting the carriage of goods. It is well known that such intermediation is usually carried out by freight forwarders who contract the carriage in the name of their client, so that they are liable only for the diligent election of the carrier, unless they carry out the transport with their own means; offer the transport service for a fixed price; or group together the consignments of more than one sender. However, freight forwarding in the aforementioned sense is not possible in Spain. This is so because carriers, cooperatives that offer transport services, transport marketing companies, transport operators and agencies, freight forwarders, warehousers, logistic operators and, in general, all those who usually celebrate contracts of carriage or intermediate in their celebration are obliged to celebrate them in their own name. If they fail to do so, Act No 16/1987, on the Administrative Organisation of Land Transport, provides for the imposition of a fine and, additionally, Article 5 (1) COGLA establishes that such contracts of carriage are 'supposed' to be celebrated in the contractor's own name. The precise meaning of the verb is unclear, but it seems that such contracts are considered to be celebrated in the contractors own name (prima facie evidence), unless exceptionally it is proven that the intermediation was done free of charge,[14] with the consequence that the intermediary is liable for the correct performance of the contract of carriage, i.e., he is normally considered to be a contracting carrier.

14. *See* the judgment of the Spanish Supreme Court No 158/2015, of 1 April.

381. Furthermore, the Act also envisages those situations, very frequent in practice, in which the contracting carrier entrusts the performance of the carriage, in whole or in part, to another carrier, the performing or substitute carrier. Absent any special rule on the liability of such performing carrier *vis-à-vis* the sender or the consignee (which disappeared during the parliamentary processing of the draft Act), Article 6 COGLA merely states something which is obvious: on the one hand, the contracting carrier shall be liable for the performance of the transport as a whole, even if he does not carry it out in full or in part; on the other hand, the contracting carrier occupies the position of the sender in the (sub) contract of carriage with the performing carrier. As a consequence, and without prejudice to what will be said later on the standing to be sued of the substitute carrier, the latter is liable only *vis-à-vis* the contracting carrier who, in turn, is responsible for the performance of the transport as a whole *vis-à-vis* the sender and the consignee.

II. Rights and Obligations of the Parties

A. *The Carrier*

382. The (contracting) carrier is the person who assumes in his own name the obligation to carry out the transport operation, with independence of whether he performs it with his own means or subcontracts the execution with one or more performing carriers (Article 4 (2) COGLA). Although he will usually carry out the service with his own means, this is no essential feature of the contract, because the obligation is generally fungible, so that subcontracting is doubtlessly possible. However, the (contracting) carrier shall be responsible for the acts and omissions of his agents and servants (e.g., the driver) and any other person whose services he makes use of for the performance of the carriage (Article 47 (3) COGLA).

383. During the *initial phase of carriage* (i.e., the reception of the goods), the carrier shall furnish a vehicle that is adequate under the circumstances of the case, according to the information provided by the sender, at the place and time agreed. If he fails to do so, the sender is entitled to avoid the contract, immediately search another carrier and, where the case may be, claim compensation for the damages caused to him by the delay (Article 18 COGLA). On the other hand, the carrier has the right to require the goods, correctly packed and identified, to be handed over to him at the place and time agreed. In case of breach of this obligation by the sender, the carrier shall be entitled to compensation equivalent to the carriage charges (or a part thereof, if the goods are delivered only partially to the carrier), or to another transport under similar conditions that is immediately available (Article 19 COGLA). Furthermore, pursuant to Article 22 COGLA, the carrier is also entitled to compensation in concept of paralysation of the vehicle if he has to wait more than two hours for the goods to be handed over to him. Since both provisions contradict each other, their coordination is not easy, but it seems that the carrier has the right to choose between the compensation envisaged by Articles 19 and 22 COGLA.

While the CMR is quiet about the obligation to load and stow the goods, the Carriage of Goods by Land Act provides for a complete regulation in Article 20. Pursuant to this provision, it is the obligation of the sender to load and stow the goods on board the vehicle, unless the carrier expressly assumes such obligations *before* the vehicle arrives at the place of loading.[15] Where the sender is obliged to load and stow, he shall also bear the consequences of any damage arising therefrom, unless improper stowage is due to the sender following instructions of the carrier. There is, however, a special rule for parcel and similar services in Article 20 (3) COGLA, according to which loading operations shall be at the carrier's expense, unless otherwise agreed, while stowing corresponds, in any case, to the carrier.

Although, strictly speaking, there is no legal obligation to do so, the carrier does well to check the goods and their packing at the moment of taking them over from the sender. If the packing, the identification or the documentation of the goods is insufficient, the carrier is entitled to refuse to receive them (Article 27 (1) COGLA), and if their apparent condition or the number of the packages or their marks and numbers do not match the indications in the consignment note he shall make (specific) reservations on the consignment note (Article 25 (2) COGLA). Since such unilateral reservations do not bind the sender, the carrier is entitled to make the admission of the goods contingent upon acceptance of the reservations made in the consignment note (Article 27 (2) COGLA). Finally, pursuant to Article 14 (2) COGLA, the absence of reasoned reservations in the consignment note – or on a separate document, signed by both the sender and the carrier – shall be prima facie evidence that the carrier has received the goods and their packing in the condition described in the consignment note, and that they bear the marks and numbers indicated therein.

384. During the *carriage phase in a strict sense*, the carrier is responsible for the custody of the goods and the breach of his obligation to do so triggers the liability regime of the carrier for loss and damage. Furthermore, he is obliged to carry the consignment following the agreed itinerary or, absent any agreement on this particular issue, the itinerary that best fits the circumstances of the case and the nature of the goods (Article 28 (2) COGLA). He also has to carry the goods within the agreed time limit or, where an agreement on such time limit does not exist, within the term reasonably employed by a diligent carrier to perform the carriage, taking into account the circumstances of the case (Article 33 (1) COGLA).

Finally, the carrier is obliged to ask for instructions in case the carriage becomes impossible and to comply with the instructions received (Article 31 COGLA), as well as with those he is given in exercise of the right to dispose of the goods (Articles 29 and 30 COGLA). As a general rule, such right of disposal belongs to the sender who may, in particular, order the carrier to stop the goods in transit, to return them to their origin or to deliver them at a place or to a consignee other than those indicated on the consignment note. Similarly to what happens under the CMR,

15. With this last provision, the Act aims at preventing certain abuses that used to be frequent in practice, where senders obliged the driver to load and stow the goods even though no such obligation existed, thus shifting the liability for damages caused when loading or stowing the goods from the sender to the carrier.

the right of disposal of the sender shall cease to exist when the second copy of the consignment note is delivered to the consignee or when the latter claims delivery of the goods or exercises the rights that correspond to him in case of loss or delay in delivery. From that moment onwards the right of disposal belongs to the consignee, and it shall also correspond to the latter from the time of the taking over of the goods by the carrier when expressly agreed by the carrier and the sender. In order to exercise the right to dispose of the goods, both the sender or the consignee have to produce the first copy of the consignment note on which the new instructions to the carrier have been entered. The carrier is then obliged to carry out the instructions, whenever their execution is possible at the time they are notified to him and does not negatively affect the normal operation of the carrier's business or the consignees of other consignments. If such conditions are fulfilled, the carrier who fails to execute the instructions given to him or who executes them without requiring the first copy of the consignment note shall be liable for any damage caused thereby.

385. During the *phase of termination of the carriage* (i.e., upon arrival at the place of destination), the carrier shall deliver the goods to the consignee in the same conditions in which he received them and within the established time limit (Article 34 (1) COGLA). The obligation to unstow and to unload the goods lies with the consignee, unless otherwise agreed before the vehicle is presented for unloading. As an exception, with respect to parcel and similar services the obligation to unload (and, in any case, to unstow) the goods belongs to the carrier, subject to contractual clauses to the contrary.

Where delivery is impossible due to the fact that the consignee is not to be found at the mentioned address or refuses to receive the goods, to unload them or to sign the receipt thereof, the carrier shall ask the sender for instructions. If such instructions are not received from the sender in good time, the carrier may unload the goods and hold them on behalf of the person entitled to dispose thereof, although he may also entrust them to a third party, in which case he shall be under no liability but for the diligent choice of such third party (Article 44 COGLA). Finally, he may also deposit them with a judicial body or with the Arbitral Board for Transportation, who may proceed to sell the goods if justified by their perishable nature or their condition; if the expenses for their custody are excessive in relation to their value; or if the carrier does not receive, in a reasonable time, instructions from the person entitled to the right of disposal the execution of which is proportionate to the circumstances of the case.

B. The Sender

386. The sender or shipper is the person who celebrates the contract of carriage in his own name and with whom the carrier assumes the obligation to perform the transport, i.e., while all vicissitudes of private contracts are admissible (e.g., representation, without prejudice to what has been said about freight forwarding in Spain), the sender is always the person in the name of which the contract with the carrier is stipulated. Although it usually is also the sender who hands the goods over to the carrier, there may exist a third person that physically hands them over to the carrier on behalf of the sender. Since the only relevant data that qualifies a person as sender is the celebration of the contract of carriage, both the legal situation that links the sender with the goods to be carried (e.g., a property right) and the relationship of the sender with the consignee (e.g., a sales contract) are widely irrelevant.

387. As has been shown above, the sender is under an obligation to hand over the goods to the carrier at the agreed place and time, the breach of which entitles the carrier to avoid the contract and/or to claim a compensation (Articles 19 and 22 COGLA). The sender shall also provide for adequate packing, unless otherwise agreed, and submit the required administrative documents (Articles 21 and 23 COGLA). As regards the operations of loading and stowing, it has already been said that, unless otherwise agreed before the vehicle is presented for loading, the obligation to load and stow belongs to the sender, with the exception of parcel and similar services, where it lies with the carrier.

Apart from the duties related to the handing over of the goods, the main obligation of the sender is to pay the carriage charges. Given its importance for day-to-day practice, this obligation, which has not received hardly any attention by the CMR, is extensively regulated in the Carriage of Goods by Land Act. Pursuant to Article 37 COGLA, unless otherwise agreed, it is the sender who shall pay the carriage charges. If they are to be paid by the consignee, he assumes this obligation with the acceptance of the consignment, although the sender remains liable for the payment of the charges in case the consignee refuses to pay them. Article 39 COGLA then establishes that, unless otherwise agreed, the charges are to be paid upon completion of the transport operation. In absence of payment, the carrier is entitled to refuse the delivery of the goods, unless a sufficient security is provided, and may even request their sale from a judicial body or the competent Arbitral Board of Transportation to cover the transport charges and the expenses incurred. Furthermore, unless otherwise agreed in writing, the carrier is entitled to increase in a proportionate way the charges initially agreed in case the gas price augments between the day of conclusion of the contract and the time the carriage is performed (Article 39 COGLA). If the carriage charges are paid more than thirty days after the performance of the service (or, in any case, after the time agreed, which may not exceed sixty days) the person obliged to pay the charges is under an obligation to pay default interest for the period of delay (Article 40 COGLA in relation with Act No 3/2004, of 29 December, establishing measures to fight against default in commercial operations).

Finally, there is one more provision worth mentioning in relation to the payment of the carriage charges: the sixth additional provision of Act No 9/2013, of 4 July, that modifies Act No 16/1987, of 30 July, on the Administrative Organisation of Land Transport and Act No 21/2003, of 7 July, on Air Safety. Pursuant to this provision, in case of intermediation in the contracting of land transport, where the carriage charges are not paid to the performing carrier by the person who subcontracted the execution of the contract with him, the carrier who actually carried out the transport will have direct action for the unpaid part against the main sender and all those who, if appropriate, have preceded him in the subcontracting chain.[16] Due to its unclear wording, the provision raises one fundamental doubt of interpretation: does the main (or first) sender has to pay the carriage charges due to the performing carrier even where he has already paid the contractual carrier? Unfortunately, the answer given by courts is not univocal. Although there is a (rather informal) agreement among the magistrates of Commercial Courts in Spain that the sender only has to pay once, the Supreme Court has recently adopted the opposite approach.[17]

It is also unclear whether the direct action envisaged by Act No 9/2013 can be exercised where the carriage is subject to CMR. Since the Convention is silent on this issue, it seems that the resulting gap has to be filled by recourse to national law. Thus, where the conflict-of-law rules of the forum declare the (subsidiary) application of Spanish domestic law to the main contract of carriage, the performing carrier should arguably be allowed to avail himself of such direct action, at least against the main sender.

388. As to the rights of the sender, he is entitled to demand the carriage to be executed on the agreed itinerary and within the agreed time limit. And he also is the 'natural' holder of the aforementioned right to dispose of the goods and may do so unless he has renounced to his right in favour of the consignee; the second copy of the consignment note has been handed over to the consignee; or the consignee has required delivery from the carrier or exercised his rights in case of loss or delay (Articles 29 and 30 (3) COGLA).

C. *The Consignee*

389. The consignee is the person to whom the carrier shall deliver the goods at the place of destination. He is usually not a party to the contract of carriage, although nothing prevents the sender and the consignee from being the same person, for example, because the sender wants the goods to be carried to another establishment of his own, or because it is the consignee who organises the carriage (e.g., as a consequence of an ex-works sale). If he has not celebrated the contract of carriage by himself, he shall be considered alien thereto, in which case the contract is considered to be a contract in favour of a third party, the consignee. As such, he is under no obligation deriving from the contract of carriage, although he is entitled to extract certain rights therefrom. In particular, pursuant to Article 35 COGLA, the consignee has the right to require the delivery of the goods and the consignment note upon their arrival at the place of destination and to enforce in his own name

16. The rule is based on the 1998 Gayssot Act in France, that modified Art.L132-8 of the Code de Commerce and gave it the following wording: 'La lettre de voiture forme un contrat entre l'expéditeur, le voiturier et le destinataire ou entre l'expéditeur, le destinataire, le commissionnaire et le voiturier. Le voiturier a ainsi une action directe en paiement de ses prestations à l'encontre de l'expéditeur ou du destinataire, lesquels sont garants du paiment du prix du transport. Toute clause contraire est réputée non écrite.'

17. Judgment of the Spanish Supreme Court No 644/2017, of 24 November, pursuant to which the original sender may have to pay twice. The only possibility he has to prevent double payment is to forbid subcontracting by the contractual carrier.

the rights against the carrier. However, by accepting the consignment he also accepts the obligations that derive for him from the contract of carriage, so that he can only claim delivery, where the case may be, against payment of the (carriage and other) charges due.

III. The Consignment Note

390. Although the contract of carriage is usually documented in writing (the consignment note) and the Carriage of Goods by Land Act is silent on its perfection, it is nonetheless a consensual contract that becomes binding for the parties upon (even verbal) acceptance of an offer. It is not surprising, therefore, that there are no formal requirements for the validity of the contract and the absence, irregularity or loss of the consignment note does not affect the existence or the validity of the contract (Article 13 (1) COGLA). The consignment note rather serves the function of a privileged document of proof as regards the existence of the contract and its content, as well as of a receipt of the goods by the carrier (Article 14 (1) COGLA).

Pursuant to Article 10 (1) COGLA, either party to the contract may require the other to issue a consignment note and shall be entitled to avoid the contract if the other party refuses to do so. The consignment note shall include the following particulars: (*a*) As regards the note itself, it shall contain the date and place at which it is issued, as well as the signature of both the carrier and the sender; (*b*) With respect to the personal elements of the contract, the name and address of the sender, of the carrier and of the consignee (and, where applicable, a notify address); (*c*) As regards the goods to be carried, their gross weight or the number of packages, the description of the nature of the goods, the marks and numbers to identify them, the method of packing etc.; and (*d*) With relation to the conditions of the performance by the carrier, the payment of the carriage charges (carriage paid or due), place and time of taking over of the goods, place and (where applicable) time limit for delivery, instructions for administrative formalities, etc. Furthermore, the consignment note may also contain optional data, e.g., a declaration of value or special interest in delivery, a prohibition of trans-shipment, a 'cash on delivery' clause, instructions regarding the insurance of the goods, a list of documents handed over to the carrier, etc.

As shown above, the absence, irregularity or loss of the consignment note does not affect the existence or validity of the contract, neither does it prevent the note to be considered a document of proof with respect to the data that have been included (Article 13 (2) COGLA). However, for the only purpose of administrative control, every domestic carriage of goods in Spain has to be documented in writing (Order of the Ministry of Public Works and Transport No 2861/2012, of 13 December), and the consignment note usually serves this purpose (although it would also be enough with a packing list). The breach of the obligation to document the shipment may thus entail administrative sanctions (the imposition of a fine), but does not have major consequences from a private law point of view, apart, of course, from the lack of the single most important document of proof.

The consignment note is issued in three original copies, signed (even by mechanic means) by the carrier and the sender, the first of which is handed over to the sender; the second travels with the consignment; and the third stays with the carrier (Article 11 COGLA). Where the parties agree, the note can also be issued by electronic means, in which case it must consist of an electronic record of data that can be transformed into legibly written signs (Article 15 COGLA). Under Spanish law, the consignment note cannot be configured as a negotiable document. It does, however, serve a 'blocking' function with respect to the right of disposal, in the sense that the sender who gives away the first copy of the consignment note may no longer exercise his right to dispose of the goods (Article 30 (1) (a) COGLA).

IV. Liability of the Carrier in Case of Loss, Damage or Delay in Delivery

391. As has already been pointed out, the rules on the liability of the carrier under Spanish law closely follow the model envisaged by the CMR Convention. The relevant provisions are to be found in Chapter V of the 2009 Carriage of Goods by Land Act (Articles 46–63). Pursuant to Article 46 in relation to Article 3 COGLA, the regulation contained therein is mandatory and any clause that aims at reducing the liability of the carrier is null and void. This, however, does not mean that no deviation whatsoever from the liability regime is permitted, but such deviations are admissible only when allowed by the Act itself (e.g., a declaration of value or of a special interest in delivery, Article 61 COGLA).

A. *Basis of the Carrier's Liability*

392. Articles 47–51 COGLA outline the basis of the carrier's liability. According to Article 47 (1) the liability of the carrier is presumed: he shall be liable for total or partial loss of or damage to the goods (including containers and other means of cargo consolidation when furnished by the sender), occurring between the taking over of the cargo and its delivery at the place of destination, as well as for any delay in delivery. He shall, however, be relieved from liability when the breach is not attributable to him, i.e., when the cause of damage fits into one of the grounds for relief envisaged by Article 48 ('ordinary' grounds for relief) or Article 49 ('presumptions of relief' or 'special risks').

393. The so-called ordinary grounds for relief match those in Article 17 (2) CMR and the carrier shall be relieved from liability if the loss, damage or delay is due to a wrongful act or neglect of the sender or the consignee; to instructions of the former or the latter given otherwise than as the result of a wrongful act or neglect on the part of the carrier; to inherent vice of the goods; or to circumstances which the carrier could not avoid and the consequences of which he was unable to prevent. As well as under Article 17 (3) CMR, the defective condition of the vehicle employed shall never supply a ground for relief for the carrier (Article 48 (2) COGLA), and in case that the loss, damage or delay is only partly due to a cause not attributable to the carrier, he shall only be liable to the extent that the factors for which he is liable have contributed to the damage (Article 48 (3) COGLA).

Such circumstances receive the name of 'ordinary' grounds for relief due to the fact that the rules of evidence are the ordinary ones, as envisaged by Article 217 of Act No 1/2000, of 7 January, on Civil Procedure: the claimant (sender or consignee) has to prove: (*a*) the existence and validity of the contract of carriage; (*b*) the loss or damage to the goods, or the delay in delivery; and (*c*) that the loss or damage occurred during the period of liability, i.e., between the taking over of the goods and their delivery at the place of destination. The carrier then has to prove: (*a*) the existence of one of the grounds for relief laid down in Article 48 COGLA; and (*b*) the causal relation (*nexus*) between the event not attributable to him and the loss, damage or delay.

394. In comparison, the rules of evidence as regards the 'presumptions of relief' or 'special risks' are far more beneficial for the carrier. While the claimant has to prove once again the existence of the contract, the loss or damage and that such loss or damage occurred during the period of liability, the carrier shall only have to prove:(*a*) the existence of one of the special risks found in Article 49 COGLA; and (*b*) that, according to the circumstances of the case, the loss or damage (but not the delay, liability of which can only be eluded in case an 'ordinary' ground for relief is available) *could* be attributed to one of such special risks. Causality shall then be presumed, without prejudice to the right of the claimant to prove that the loss or damage is not, or only partly, attributable to one of these risks (Article 49 (2) COGLA).

The 'special risks' envisaged by Article 49 COGLA almost literally match those in Article 17 (4) CMR: (*a*) the use of open unsheeted vehicles, whenever their use has been agreed (or is consistent with prevailing customs, a –useful– precision which is absent under Article 17 (4) CMR); (*b*) the lack or defective condition of packing in the case of goods which, by their nature, are liable to wastage or damage when not (properly) packed; (*c*) handling, loading, stowage or unloading of the goods by the sender or the consignee, or by a person acting on behalf of one or the other; (*d*) the nature of certain goods which exposes them to total or partial loss or damage, especially through breakage, rust, internal and spontaneous deterioration, wastage, leakage, desiccation, or the action of moth or vermin (where the carriage is performed in vehicles specially equipped to control temperature, humidity of the air or other environmental circumstances, the carrier can only invoke this special risk when he proves that he took all steps incumbent on him under the given circumstances with respect to the choice, maintenance and use of such equipment and that he complied with any special instructions issued to him, Article 51 COGLA); (*e*) deficient identification or marking of the goods; and (*f*) the carriage of livestock, although the carrier shall only be entitled to benefit of this last provision when he proves that he took all steps normally incumbent on him in the circumstances and that he complied with any special instructions given to him with respect to the animals (Article 50 COGLA).

B. Compensation in Case of Loss, Damage or Delay in Delivery

395. As regards partial or full loss or damage, only *direct damages* are subject to compensation, i.e., such compensation is calculated on the basis of the value of those goods that have been damaged or have not been delivered. The relevant value is that of the goods at the place and time at which they were accepted for carriage (Articles 52 and 53 COGLA). It shall be determined taking into account the current market price or, where unavailable, the normal value of goods of the same kind and quality (Article 55 COGLA). With respect to the situation under CMR, Article 55 COGLA contains a relevant innovation: where the goods have been sold prior to shipment, it shall be presumed, unless the contrary is proved, that the current market price is that shown on the sales invoice, deduction made of the freight and other transport charges that, if appropriate, appear on the invoice.

While in case of loss the amount of the compensation due coincides with the value of the goods the carrier failed to deliver (Article 52 COGLA), where the cargo has been damaged, the carrier shall be liable for the depreciation, i.e., the amount by which the goods have diminished in value, with respect always to the value of the goods at the place and time at which they were accepted for carriage (Article 53 (1) COGLA). No reparation in kind is due by the carrier; neither shall the cost of reparation of the damaged goods be taken into account.

In both cases, the compensation due by the carrier is limited to the amounts envisaged by the Carriage of Goods by Land Act. Where the consignment is (wholly or partially) lost, compensation shall not exceed the third part of the daily rate of the so-called Public Income Indicator for Multiple Effects (*Indicador Público de Renta de Efectos Múltiples – IPREM*) per kilogram of gross weight short or damaged. The said Indicator is updated on a yearly basis in the State Budget Act that, for the year 2017, establishes a daily rate of EUR 17.93, so that the amount of the compensation is limited to EUR 5.98 per kilogram of gross weight short or damaged (Article 57 (1) COGLA). Where the goods are damaged, Article 53 (2) and (3) establishes, furthermore, that the compensation shall not exceed the amount payable in the case of total loss if the whole consignment has been damaged; or that payable in the case of loss of the part affected when only part of the cargo has been damaged (i.e., one-third of the daily rate of the IPREM per kilogram of gross weight).

In case of delay in delivery, only *indirect* or *consequential damages* are subject to compensation (e.g., loss of profit, production stoppage, etc.), the *quantum* of which has to be proven by the claimant (Article 56 COGLA). In this case, the amount of the compensation is limited to the carriage charges (Article 57 (2) COGLA). Where the claimant is entitled to compensation by virtue of both damage or partial loss and delay (e.g., because the consignment arrives late and has, furthermore, suffered damages during the carriage), the compensation shall not exceed the amount due in case of total loss (Article 57 (3) COGLA).

396. Under certain circumstances, the law allows the claimant to consider the goods to be lost albeit no proof thereof can be established. This issue is addressed by Article 20 CMR, according to which '(t)he fact that goods have not been delivered within thirty days following the expiry of the agreed time-limit or, if there is no agreed time-limit, within sixty days from the time when the carrier took over the goods, shall be conclusive evidence of the loss of the goods, and the person entitled to make a claim may thereupon treat them as lost'. In sight of the – usually – shorter distances of domestic carriage, the national counterpart of Article 20 CMR reduces the relevant deadlines to twenty days after the expiry of the agreed time limit or, where there is none, thirty days from the time the carrier took over the consignment (Article 54 (3) COGLA). But the Carriage of Goods by Land Act goes a step further and also allows the claimant to treat the goods as lost (i.e., to 'abandon' the consignment to the carrier) in case there is a partial loss and he proves that he is unable to use the goods that have been delivered without the part that has been lost; or when the damages suffered by the goods render them useless for sale or consumption, taking into account the nature and current use of the assets in question (Article 54 (2) and (3) COGLA).

397. Furthermore, the person entitled to a compensation for loss or damage (not, therefore, in case of delay in delivery) can also claim the refund of the carriage charges and other charges incurred in respect of the carriage of the goods. There are hardly any court decisions on this issue in Spain, but it seems that only those charges that would have accrued in the same way if the transport had been carried out normally and which, as a rule, increase the value of the goods at destination (e.g., packing, loading and stowage costs, when generated after the carrier has taken over the goods; charges associated with the removal of impediments to carriage not related to the incident; charges for storage and preservation of the goods, provided that they are not the consequence of the incident, costs of a cargo insurance,[18] etc.). To the contrary, charges incurred as a result of the loss or damage are consequential damages that the carrier does not have to compensate (e.g., the cost of repairing or replacing the goods, or to destroy those which are useless; legal and expert expenses related to the incident, etc.) (Article 58 (1) COGLA). Although the relevant costs are consequential damages that should not be recoverable under Article 58 (1) COGLA, the law itself entitles the claimant to the reimbursement of the so-called salvage costs (Article 58 (2) COGLA), i.e., those that are necessary or convenient in order to re-dispatch the goods, at least when they are reasonable and proportionate.

398. Finally, whenever the claimant receives a compensation for loss of the goods, he may request in writing that he shall be notified in case that they are recovered in the course of the year following the payment. Upon the receipt of the notification of such recovery, he is entitled (but not obliged) to claim the delivery of the goods, against payment of the charges shown in the consignment note and against refund of the compensation he received, less any charges included therein. However, he retains his right to claim a compensation for the delay in delivery. If after recovery of the goods – and notification thereof to the claimant – the latter does not claim the delivery of the consignment, the carrier is entitled to freely dispose of the goods (Article 59 COGLA).

18. On the insurance costs, *see* the judgment of the Spanish Supreme Court No 1023/2004, of 25 October, albeit in relation to Art. 23 (4) CMR.

399. Pursuant to Article 58 (3) COGLA, no other damages are to be compensated. However, the Carriage of Goods by Land Act itself envisages different means to claim compensation that exceeds the limits indicated above. On the one hand, Article 61 (1) COGLA provides for the possibility to make a declaration of value, in the consignment note and against payment of a surcharge, that allows to elevate the maximum amount payable in case of loss or damages (which is substituted by the declared value). On the other hand, the second paragraph of Article 61 COGLA allows the parties to agree on the declaration of a special interest in delivery, in the consignment note and against payment of a surcharge, by way of which the claimant is entitled to both a compensation that exceeds the carriage charges in case of delay and the compensation of indirect or consequential damages in case of loss or damage. Finally, Article 61 (3) COGLA declares, notwithstanding the possibility to declare the value of the goods or a special interest in delivery, that the parties may also agree to increase the upper limits of the amount of compensation in case of loss or damage (one-third of the daily rate of the IPREM); an agreement that apparently need not be shown on the consignment note but entitles the carrier to a surcharge.

A fourth possibility to overcome the limits to the liability is to prove the wilful misconduct of the carrier. Pursuant to Article 62 COGLA, the provisions of the Act that exclude or limit the liability of the carrier or that invert the burden of proof shall not apply when the damage has been caused by him or by his servants or agents, with intent or with a conscious and voluntary breach of the legal duty assumed by him that produces damages that, without being directly sought, are a necessary consequence of the action. Despite the unclear wording of the provision, according to a now consolidated interpretation of Article 62 COGLA only intentional behaviour (*dolus directus* and *dolus eventualis*), but not gross negligence, triggers the consequence envisaged by the precept, i.e., the loss of the benefit of limitation of liability.[19]

400. Finally, although claims in tort are, as a general rule, not subject to any limits under Spanish law, the liability regime (including the aforementioned limitations) shall apply whatever the procedure or the (contractual or non-contractual) basis of the claim, whether it is enforced against the carrier himself or against one of the persons for whom he is responsible (Article 63 COGLA). Thus, both the carrier and his servants and agents are entitled to avail themselves of the provisions of the Act that exclude their liability or limit the compensation due even where the claim is in tort; a rule which is similar to that in Article 28 CMR.

C. Claims and Reservations at Destination

401. In case of damage to or loss of (part of) the consignment, the consignee shall, upon receipt of the goods, express his *reservations* in writing to the carrier or his agents or servants, giving a general indication of the loss or damage. If such loss

19. Judgments of the Spanish Supreme Court No 382/2015, of 9 July; No 399/2015, of 10 July; and No 455/2016, of 4 July.

or damage is not apparent, reservations shall be made within seven days of delivery. Where no reservations are made, it shall be presumed, unless proof to the contrary (prima facie evidence), that the goods were delivered in the condition described in the consignment note (Article 60 (1) COGLA). However, the reservation – a unilateral declaration of the consignee, who puts on record the existence of a loss of or a damage to the goods – shall not be necessary when the carrier (or his agents or servants) and the consignee have *jointly checked* the goods and agreed on their condition and the reasons that led to a possible loss or damage. Where no agreement is reached, either on the condition of the goods or the reasons thereof, the expertise of a third party (a notary public, the president of the Arbitral Board for Transportation, an independent expert, etc.) may be requested (Article 60 (2) COGLA).

While the reception of the goods without making reservations shall only be prima facie evidence that the consignment was received in the condition described in the consignment note, the absence of reservations in case of delay, within twenty-one days from the day following the delivery to the consignee, entails the extinction of the claim (Article 60 (3) COGLA).

V. Liability of the Carrier in Case of Breach Different from Loss, Damage or Delay

402. Pursuant to Article 47 (2) COGLA, the carrier's liability for breach of other obligations arising from the contract of carriage is governed, absent any specific regulation in the Act, by the general rules on contractual liability. And certainly, apart from the main obligation to carry the goods unharmed and within the time limit, the Act contemplates a high number of accessory obligations, e.g., to issue a consignment note if the sender so requires (Article 10 (1)), to provide a suitable vehicle (Article 17) at the place and time agreed (Article 18), to correctly keep and use the documentation that accompanies the consignment (Article 23 (3)), to execute the instructions given under the right of disposal (Article 30 (2)), etc. Although on occasions a specific consequence is triggered by such breaches, the legal regime that applies to other cases of non-performance is that of the Civil Code in matters of contractual liability (Articles 1101 et seq.).

A detailed analysis of each of the aforementioned cases exceeds the scope of this general overview. However, three key issues should be kept in mind. First, the particular liability regime of the carrier only applies once the goods have been taken over by the carrier, so that damages and delays prior to this moment are not subject to the relevant provisions of the Act. Secondly, the carrier's liability regime cannot be circumvented with recourse to general categories of civil law (such as the avoidance for fundamental breach, Article 1124 of the Civil Code) in order to obtain full compensation of the damages caused. Finally, the compensation due in those cases in which the Civil Code applies is not limited in amount, but absent a rule similar to that of Article 46 COGLA (according to which the clauses attenuating the liability of the carrier are null and void), a limitation of liability by agreement between the carrier and the sender should be possible (except in cases of fraud).

VI. Standing

A. Standing to Sue

403. The standing to sue belongs to both the sender and the consignee: to the former, because he is the counterpart of the carrier in the contract of carriage; to the latter, because Article 35 COGLA assigns him such right. Pursuant to the aforementioned provision, the consignee shall be entitled to exercise the rights derived from the contract of carriage from the moment in which, the goods having arrived at the place of destination or having expired the time limit in which they should have done so, he requires the carrier to deliver the consignment.[20] From that moment on, he shall also be obliged to pay the carriage charges and other expenses made by the carrier or to provide sufficient security. In case of loss, damage or delay, he can also claim compensation, since it is a 'right derived from the contract of carriage'.

It is not clear, however, whether the standing to sue may belong simultaneously to the sender and to the consignee, or whether the acquisition of the right by the latter implies its loss by the former. The only court decision on this issue (a judgment of the Castellon Court of Appeal of 11 July 2003) links the standing *ad causam* to the right to dispose of the goods, so that simultaneous standing is not possible. However, the opposite solution is not prohibited by law and should not be ruled out, since the adoption of a system of exclusive standing (either of the sender or the consignee, but not both at a time) does not take into account who is the holder of the injured interest, so that the latter may find himself in a situation where he cannot claim compensation for the damage caused. Hence, in countries (like Germany) where the double standing of sender and consignee is even legally recognized, the solution is justified with the desire to avoid that the claim is dismissed because it is filed by a party that is not entitled to do so.

What distinguishes the contract of carriage from other contracts is the fact that, in case of loss or damage to the goods, it is sufficient to prove such loss or damage, without the need to demonstrate a specific damage to the claimant's assets (Articles 52, 53 (1) COGLA). The proof as to who has suffered the damage may thus not be required and, if simultaneous standing is admitted, there is a risk that the carrier is obliged to face a double compensation to both the sender and the consignee. However, even if they had simultaneous standing, the danger that the carrier would actually have to pay twice is low, because the sender and the consignee are joint and several creditors (Articles 1137, 1140, 1142 and 1143 (2) of the Civil Code), so that the carrier can argue either that he has already paid to one of them or that the claim is still pending. Whoever obtains compensation from the carrier will then be liable *vis-à-vis* the other on the basis of the *valuta* relationship (generally a sales contract).

Finally, it should also be borne in mind that by virtue of the subrogation ordered in Article 43 of Act No 5/1980, of 8 October, on the Insurance Contract, the standing to sue might also lie with the (civil liability or cargo) insurance company.

20. *See* the judgment of the Court of Appeal of Madrid (s. 28) No 167/2015, of 12 June.

B. Standing to Be Sued

404. Pursuant to Article 35 in relation with Article 4 (2) COGLA, the standing to be sued is held by the contracting carrier, i.e., the carrier that entered the contract of carriage with the sender. Furthermore, where several carriers promise by virtue of a single contract documented in a single consignment note to successively carry out different legs of the same contract, all of them shall be responsible for the performance of the transport as a whole (Article 64 (1) COGLA), but the sender or the consignee can only sue the first carrier, the last carrier or that which has executed the part of the transport in the course of which the event on which the action is based has occurred. However, this scenario, known as 'successive carriage', is hardly ever found in Spain,[21] since carriers are reticent not only when it comes to assuming such joint and several liability, but also to hand over the original consignment note containing commercial information on the transport (in particular, the carriage charges) to successive carriers.

More controversial is the standing to be sued of the performing carrier when the requirements of Article 64 COGLA are not met. To this aim, the draft Carriage of Goods by Land Act envisaged a direct action of the sender or the consignee against the performing carrier, similar to that which can be found in Article 27 COTIF-CIM and Article 40 of the Montreal Convention. However, the relevant provision disappeared during the procedure in Parliament and there is no rule whatsoever that declares the liability of the performing carrier *vis-à-vis* the sender or the consignee. This being true, it should not be discarded that the consignee is entitled, at least, to sue that (performing) carrier who delivered the goods to him: the subcontract between the contracting carrier and the performing carrier is a legally typical contract of carriage, so that the consignee should be entitled to invoke *vis-à-vis* the performing carrier the rule laid down in Article 35 COGLA, which allows him to exercise the rights that derive from the contract from the moment in which he claims delivery.

VII. Limitation of Actions

405. The Carriage of Goods by Road Act establishes a single limitation period of one year for all actions that arise from a contract of carriage by land, unless the carrier acted with *dolus* (*directus* or *eventualis*), in which case the limitation period shall be of two years (Article 79 (1) COGLA). It also pays attention to the *dies a quo*, which differs according to the situation at issue. If 'something' is delivered (partial loss, damage, delay), the limitation period shall begin to count from the

21. It should be noted, however, that the situation is different in other countries, where courts adopt more liberal positions and appreciate the existence of successive carriage even where the first (contracting) carrier has not even received the goods or signed the consignment note ('paper carriers', similar to non vessel-operating common carriers or NVOCCs in maritime transport) (*see*, e.g., the judgment of the Dutch Supreme Court of 11 Sept. 2015).

delivery of the goods to the consignee. To the contrary, if nothing is delivered (total loss), it shall commence the twentieth day after the expiration of the agreed time limit or, in the absence of such agreement, the thirtieth day from the date on which the goods were taken over by the carrier. In all other cases (e.g., payment of the carriage charges, compensation for vehicle standstill, cash on delivery, etc.) the period of limitation shall begin to run on the expiry of a period of three months after the making of the contract or, if later, from the date on which the action could be brought (Article 79 (2) COGLA).

Pursuant to Article 79 (3) COGLA, the period of limitation shall be *interrupted* for the reasons indicated in general for commercial contracts, i.e., a legal claim or any other kind of judicial interpellation to the debtor; by the recognition of obligations; or by the renewal of the document on which the creditor's right is based. As a consequence of the interruption, the period of limitation shall begin to count again in full from the day the obligation is recognized or from the date of the new document (fresh accrual). Instead, a written (out-of-court) claim shall *suspend* the period of limitation until such date as the carrier rejects the claim by notification in writing and returns the documents that accompanied the claim (if any).[22] In case of partial acceptance of the claim, the limitation period shall be resumed in respect of the part still in dispute.

406. Apart from these general provisions, the fourth paragraph of Article 79 COGLA introduces a specific rule for claims between carriers. In such cases, the period of limitation shall begin to run from the date on which a final decision or arbitral award has been rendered that establishes the compensation to be paid according to the provisions of the Act. In absence of such judgment or award, the period shall begin to count from the date on which the claimant carrier made the payment. This rule, which does not have a precedent in the CMR, is of great practical importance, since it addresses those issues where the contracting carrier subcontracts the carriage, wholly or in part, with a performing carrier who is responsible for the loss, damage or delay. In such cases, the contracting carrier who has paid compensation to the claimant (or has been ordered to do so by a court or arbitral tribunal) has an additional period of one year to require payment from the performing carrier.

Under CMR, the limitation period of such actions is calculated according to the general rules, i.e., it begins to count from the day when the goods have been delivered to the consignee, in case of partial loss, damage or delay, or, in case of total loss, on the thirtieth day after the expiry of the agreed time limit or on the sixtieth day from the date on which the goods were taken over by the carrier (Article 32 (1) CMR). It is thus perfectly possible that the subcontracting carrier's action against the performing carrier is time-barred even before he has paid compensation to the claimant.

22. *See* the judgment of the Spanish Supreme Court No 704/2016, of 25 November, declaring that a claim by e-mail has to be considered a written claim and suspends the limitation period.

VIII. Jurisdiction and Arbitration

407. As has already been pointed out, the jurisdiction for claims related to contracts of carriage of goods lies with the commercial courts, whose judgments are open to appeal before the Court of Appeal and, where the case may be, cassation or review before the Supreme Court. As a general rule, territorial jurisdiction lies with the courts at the domicile of the defendant (Articles 50 and 51 of the Act on Civil Procedure). However, in the case of an individual claim filed by a consumer, the competence lies with the courts at his domicile or that of the defendant, at the choice of the plaintiff (Article 52 (3) of the Act on Civil Procedure).

Choice of jurisdiction clauses is possible, unless they are contained in general conditions (Article 54 of the Act).

408. Finally, it should be taken into account that, pursuant to Article 38 (1) of the 1987 Land Transport Organisation Act, an arbitration agreement in favour of the so-called Arbitration Boards for Transportation (*Juntas Arbitrales del Transporte*) is presumed to exist provided that the amount of the dispute does not exceed EUR 15,000 and none of the parties to the contract expressly manifested to the other his will to the contrary before the transport has or should have started. The Arbitration Boards for Transportation are established by the Spanish Autonomous Regions and the tribunals are composed of a president (a civil servant who obligatory has to hold a law degree) and at least two vocals, one of which is designated by the shipping industry and the other one by the trucking industry (Article 8 of the Land Transport Organisation Regulation). Territorial jurisdiction lies then with the Board at the place of origin of the transport or at the place where the contract was celebrated, at the choice of the claimant (Article 7 (2) of the Regulation).

§3. International Carriage by Road under the CMR Convention

409. As stated in the introduction, the Kingdom of Spain acceded to the CMR on 12 September 1973 and, since its entry into force within its territory on 13 May 1974, the convention forms part of the national legal order (Article 96 (1) of the Spanish Constitution). It also acceded to the 1978 SDR-Protocol and the 2008 Additional Protocol concerning the Electronic Consignment Note.

The convention applies to any contract for the international carriage of goods by road for reward, unless expressly excluded by the CMR (i.e., postal transport, funeral consignments and furniture removal). The existence and validity of the contract depend on national law, which, in the case of Spain, requires legal capacity of both parties and a valid agreement on the object and the cause of the contract (Articles 1254 and 1261 of the Civil Code). The reference to contracts of 'carriage' in the title of the convention excludes, as a general rule, freight forwarding, charter and trucking contracts, but their content has to be analysed in order to determine whether they are or not contracts of carriage. Such carriage is international when the place of taking over of the goods and the place designated for delivery, as specified in the contract, are situated in different countries, one of which has to be a contracting party for the convention to apply; and has to be carried out in (or better 'with') vehicles, i.e., motor vehicles, articulated vehicles and trailers (Article 4 of the 1949 Road Traffic Convention). Finally, the convention only applies to contracts for the carriage of goods (i.e., all moveable goods, including money, containers, animals, etc.) by road (not by air, rail, sea or inland waterway).

If such requirements are met, the convention prevails over domestic legislation. However, the CMR is deliberately incomplete (according to its Preamble, it mainly focusses on the documents used for carriage of goods by road and the carrier's liability), and possible gaps are to be filled resorting to national law. Within the European Union, the applicable national law is determined with recourse to Regulation No 593/2008 of the European Parliament and the Council, of 17 June 2008, on the law applicable to contractual obligations (Rome I), according to which the law governing the contract may be chosen by agreement between the parties (Article 3); absent a choice of law, 'the law applicable shall be the law of the country of habitual residence of the carrier, provided that the place of receipt or the place of delivery or the habitual residence of the consignor is also situated in that country. If those requirements are not met, the law of the country where the place of delivery as agreed by the parties is situated shall apply'(Article 5 (1) Rome I).

I. The Consignment Note – Waybill

410. The CMR consignment note, which is a non-negotiable transport document, serves the same functions as the consignment note under national law. It is made out in three copies, too, the signature of which can be printed or replaced by stamps of the sender and the carrier if the law of the country in which the consignment note is made out so permits (Article 5 CMR). Pursuant to Article 11 (2) COGLA, such procedure is possible if the consignment note is made out in Spain, provided that the identity of the signatory is clear.

The note shall be prima facie evidence of the existence of the contract, its content and the receipt of the goods by the carrier. Absent any reservation made by the carrier on the document, it is presumed, unless the contrary is proved, that both the goods and their packing appeared to be in good condition when the carrier took them over.

II. Rights and Obligations of the Carrier, the Sender and the Consignee

411. The regime of rights and obligations in the convention is fragmentary and there are many gaps to be filled with recourse to national law. A first important issue is the question as to who is obliged to load and stow the goods at the place of origin, and to unload and unstow them at the place of destination. Where Spanish law applies, it has already been said that, as a general rule, it is the sender who is obliged to load and stow the goods on board the vehicle and that it is the obligation of the consignee to unstow and unload, unless the carrier expressly assumes such obligations before the vehicle arrives at the place of loading or unloading. As regards parcel and similar transport, such obligations lie with the carrier, although at least the obligation to load and unload can be assumed by the sender by way of an agreement with the carrier (Article 20 COGLA).

A second issue is the payment of the carriage charges and of other expenses related to the carriage. It is partially addressed by the CMR by stating that the consignee shall only be entitled to require the carrier to deliver the goods to him if he pays the charges shown to be due on the consignment note (Article 13 CMR). Any other question arising in relation to the obligation to pay such charges is thus to be answered according to national law.

A last issue that is not at all addressed by the convention refers to the consequences of a delay, not in the delivery of the goods, but in the presentation of the vehicle for loading, or those of a delay of the sender in handing over the goods to the carrier (or, where he is obliged to do so, in loading and stowing them in the vehicle). Once again, if Spanish law applies, the questions left open by the convention have to be solved with recourse to the detailed regime laid down in the Carriage of Goods by Land Act.

Finally, the convention does establish the rights of the consignee, who is entitled to require the carrier to deliver the goods to him, against payment, where the case may be, of the carriage charges and other expenses. But the consignee cannot only claim fulfilment of the contract; he can also claim compensation from the carrier in case of loss, damage or delay in delivery of the goods. The CMR, however, fails to clarify whether the sender loses his standing to sue in the moment in which the consignee acquires his own. As has already been pointed out, the only judicial decision in Spain that has addressed this issue (a judgment of the Castellón Court of Appeal of 11 July 2003) links the standing to sue with the right to dispose of the goods, so that simultaneous standing is not possible, a solution that seems to be prevalent also in Italy. Authors in most European countries, however, advocate for allowing a double standing of sender and consignee (e.g., Germany, the Netherlands, Belgium, France and, probably, the United Kingdom). It remains thus unclear how a Spanish court would decide the issue as of today.

The CMR also contains a detailed regulation of the right to dispose of the goods (Article 12 CMR) and the so-called impediments, i.e., circumstances hampering the carriage or preventing the delivery (Articles.14–16 CMR). The solutions are, however, identical to those found under national law, so that any further comment is unnecessary.

III. Liability of the Carrier

A. Basis of the Carrier's Liability

412. The liability of the carrier is regulated in Articles 17 et seq. CMR. Although it is debated whether the convention establishes a *quasi*-strict system of liability or a presumption of fault, it should be retained that the liability of the carrier shall be presumed in case there is a loss of or damage to the goods during the period of liability, or a delay in delivery. Both the period of liability and the time limit are calculated in the same way as under national law.

B. Exoneration of Liability

413. In the presence of loss, damage or delay the carrier's liability is thus presumed, so that he will be held liable unless he proves the existence of one of the grounds for relief listed in Article 17 (2) and (4) CMR. Such grounds are the same as under domestic law, and they can also be divided into 'ordinary' grounds for relief (those of Article 17 (2) CMR) and 'special risks'(those envisaged by Article 17 (4) CMR), the difference lying with the burden of proof. While in both cases the claimant (sender or consignee) has to prove: (*a*) the existence and validity of the contract of carriage; (*b*) the loss or damage to the goods, or the delay in delivery; and (*c*) that the loss or damage occurred during the period of liability, i.e., between the taking over of the goods and their delivery at the place of destination, the proof to be furnished by the carrier is less burdensome with respect to the so-called special risks: he shall only have to prove: (*a*) the existence of one of such special risks; and (*b*) that, according to the circumstances of the case, the loss or damage (but not the delay) *could* be attributed to one of such special risks, in which case causality (the *nexus*) shall be presumed (Article 18 (3) CMR). As well as under domestic law, the defective condition of the vehicle shall never supply a ground for relief of liability.[23]

C. Sharing of Liability Between the Claimant and the Carrier

414. Once again, the rule contained in Article 17 (5) CMR is identical to that under domestic law (Article 48 (3) COGLA), i.e., where 'the carrier is not under any liability in respect of some of the factors causing the loss, damage or delay, he shall only be liable to the extent that those factors for which he is liable (…) have contributed to the loss, damage or delay'.

D. Compensation Due in Case of Loss, Damage or Delay in Delivery

415. As well as under national law, in case of partial or full loss or damage only *direct damages* are subject to compensation, calculated on the basis of the value of the goods that have been lost or damaged at the place and time at which they were accepted for carriage (commodity exchange price, current market price or normal value of goods of the same kind and quality). In case of loss, the amount of the compensation matches the value of the goods that have not been delivered; where they arrive damaged at the place of destination, the carrier shall be liable for the depreciation, i.e., the amount by which the goods have diminished in value (Articles 23 (1) and (2), 25 (1) CMR).

Since Spain has acceded to the 1978 SDR-Protocol, the compensation due by the carrier, irrespective of whether the goods have been lost or damaged, is in both cases limited to 8.33 units of account (and not 25 Germinal francs as established by the

23. Judgment of the Spanish Supreme Court No 392/2011, of 14 June.

original version of the Convention) per kilogram of gross weight short or damaged. Such unit of account is the so-called special drawing right (SDR) of the International Monetary Fund and shall be converted into the forum's national currency by the court seized on the date of the judgment or the date agreed upon by the parties (Article 23 (3) and (7) CMR). In addition, where the goods are damaged, Article 25 (2) CMR establishes that the compensation shall not exceed the amount payable in the case of total loss if the whole consignment has been damaged; or that payable in the case of loss of the part affected when part only of the cargo has been damaged (i.e., 8.33 SDR/kg).

Indirect or consequential damages are only subject to compensation in case of delay in delivery, and their amount has to be established by the claimant. The compensation, however, shall be limited to the carriage charges (Article 23 (5) CMR).

416. As well as under national law, the claimant is under certain circumstances entitled to consider the goods to be lost although no prove thereof can be established (Article 20 CMR).[24] However, CMR only envisages the possibility to treat them as lost in case they 'have not been delivered within thirty days following the expiry of the agreed time-limit or, if there is no agreed time-limit, within sixty days from the time when the carrier took over the goods'. No reference is made, thus, to partial loss or damage (unlike what happens under Article 54 COGLA). Apart from that, the regulation is practically identical.

417. A last question that should be addressed in this paragraph is the possibility to overcome the limitations to the liability of the carrier established by the CMR. As well as the Spanish Carriage of Goods by Land Act, CMR also envisages declarations of value and of special interest in delivery (Articles 24 and 26 CMR), but the issue usually arises with respect to situations in which the actions of the carrier are particularly reprehensible. Such situations are regulated in Article 29 CMR, pursuant to which 'the carrier shall not be entitled to avail himself of the provisions of this Chapter which exclude or limit his liability or which shift the burden of proof if the damage was caused by his wilful misconduct or by such default on his part as, in accordance with the law of the court or tribunal seized of the case, is considered as equivalent to wilful misconduct'. The provision was already outdated in the moment the convention was adopted, because it copies a rule (Article 25 of the 1929 Warsaw Convention) that only one year before the CMR was signed had been replaced by the 1955 Hague Protocol, precisely because of the difficulties of its practical application. Furthermore, it makes a uniform application of the convention impossible. The new wording of Article 25 of the Warsaw Convention (WC) now reads that such limitations shall not apply 'if it is proved that the damage resulted from an act or omission of the carrier, his servants or agent, done with intent to cause damage or recklessly and with knowledge that damage would probably result', a formula that has later been incorporated into many international instruments (e.g., in Article 36 of the COTIF/CIM Uniform Rules).

24. And there is no need to provide proof thereof, since the mere passing of time is sufficient for the goods to be considered as lost: judgment of the Spanish Supreme Court No 265/2008, of 16 April.

A first problem raised by Article 29 CMR in practice is the fact that the two official versions (English and French) do not match completely, because the French concept of 'dol' (that also appears in the Spanish translation) is more restrictive than the common law concept of 'wilful misconduct'. Even more problematic is the fact that the provision refers to national law in order to determine whether there is or not a category of negligence that is considered 'as equivalent to' *dol* or wilful misconduct, which has given rise to *forum shopping* all around Europe. One of the most well-known examples is that of Germany and the Netherlands: while German courts usually follow an approach that can be described as 'strict' with road carriers and that in many cases results in judgments that declare the non-application of the limitations laid down in the Convention, the approach applied by Dutch courts is more lenient, since only intentional and consciously reckless misconduct (that very much resembles *dolus eventualis*) entails the obligation to pay full compensation. As a consequence, where allowed by the jurisdiction rules in Article 31 CMR, carriers may want to seek a 'negative declaratory judgment' from a 'friendly' forum that declares the absence of liability or, at least, the non-application of Article 29 CMR, a situation that has been referred to in occasions as 'Der Holländische Trick' or 'The Dutch Trick'.

Without prejudice to what will be said later about such 'negative declaratory judgments' in the light of the European Court of Justice's *Nipponkoa* decision of 2013, it should be pointed out that, from the entry into force of the 2009 Carriage of Goods by Land Act onward, the situation in Spain has shifted from a situation where the non-application of the limitations in the Convention was very frequent to a new framework in which, as has been shown when analysing the national legal system, the only default considered equivalent to *dol* by Spanish transport law is a conscious and voluntary breach of the legal duty assumed that produces damages that, without being directly sought, are a necessary consequence of the action, i.e., *dolus eventualis.*[25] This approach seems reasonable, since the normal situation should be the limitation of the carrier's liability (irrespective of whether the claim is in contract or in tort: Article 28 CMR) and only in cases where his conduct is especially condemnable such limitation should not apply.

IV. Time Limits for Complaint and Action

418. As regards claims and reservations at destination, Article 30 (2) CMR refers to those situations where the goods are checked jointly with the presence of both the consignee and the carrier or his driver. If damages are detected during such a bilateral exam, the consignee holds a valuable proof in case of conflict, but if no damages are found, evidence contradicting the result shall only be admissible in the case of loss or damage which is not apparent. As well as under national law, the consignee also has the possibility to make a unilateral declaration (i.e., a reservation)

25. *See* Art. 62 COGLA and the judgment of the Spanish Supreme Court No 455/2016, of 4 July. Prior to the entry into force of the Carriage of Goods by Land Act, the judgment No 78/1999, of 9 February, refused to apply the limitations to the liability of the carrier where the driver had acted with gross negligence only.

that puts on record the existence of a loss of or damage to the goods or a delay in delivery. Such reservations are to be made at the time of delivery in case of apparent loss or damage, or within seven days of delivery if the loss or damage is not apparent (Article 30 (1) CMR). Where the consignment is delivered with delay, reservations shall be made within twenty-one days from the time of delivery (Article 30 (3) CMR). However, the consequences of not making a reservation are different for loss or damage and delay. In the first case, it shall be presumed that the goods have been delivered in the condition described in the consignment note (a presumption that, precisely, is destroyed in case reservations are made), while the absence of a reservation as regards a delay in delivery entails the extinction of any claim against the carrier for this reason.

419. The period of limitation is of one year for all actions arising out of the contract of carriage, except from those based on wilful misconduct or equivalent fault, where they become barred after three years. The *dies a quo* is calculated in the same way as under national law and a written claim to the carrier shall suspend[26] the period of limitation until the carrier rejects the claim and returns the documents to the claimant. Since both the extension of the period of limitation and the fresh accrual of actions shall be governed by national law (Article 32 (2) CMR), the relevant provisions of the Spanish Civil and Commercial Code apply. Pursuant to Article 5 of the Civil Code, the periods that are calculated by years shall be counted from date to date, although the day on which the period of limitation begins to run shall not be included in the period (Article 32 (1) CMR). The fresh accrual of actions derived from commercial contracts, on its part, is envisaged by Article 944 of the Commercial Code, i.e., a legal claim or any other kind of judicial interpellation to the debtor;[27] by the recognition of obligations; or by the renewal of the document on which the creditor's right is based.

Absent any special rule on the limitation of the contracting carrier's action against the performing carrier in case the former has paid compensation for damage caused by the latter, the limitation regime should be the same for both the action of the sender or consignee against the contracting carrier and that of the latter against the performing carrier. Justification lies with the fact that this last action is an ordinary claim for damages and not an action for recovery, so that all actions based on the same carriage operation become barred at the same point of time. Recovery claims only exist in the infrequent case of carriages performed by successive carriers, where the *dies a quo* for claims between carriers is set on the date of the final judicial decision fixing the amount of compensation payable under the convention or, absent any such decision, the actual date of payment (Article 39 (4) CMR). There are, however, different judgments in Spain that apply Article 39 (4) CMR whenever

26. Although the Spanish translation of Art. 32 (2) provides that a written claim shall 'interrupt' the limitation period, it becomes clear from the original texts in English and French that such a written claim shall only suspend the period of limitation (*see also* the judgments of the Spanish Supreme Court No 327/2008, of 13 May; and No 704/2016, of 25 November).

27. *See* judgment of the Spanish Supreme Court of 10 Jun. 1985 (RJ 1985, 103).

a carriage is performed by more than one carrier, irrespective of whether it qualifies as a successive carriage or not.[28]

V. Jurisdiction of Courts

420. Pursuant to Article 31 (1) CMR, an action based on a carriage under the convention can be brought: (*a*) in any court or tribunal of a contracting country designated by agreement between the parties (e.g., by virtue of a jurisdiction clause in the consignment note[29]); (*b*) additionally –only prorogation, but not derogation of jurisdiction is possible– in the courts or tribunals of a country within whose territory the defendant is ordinarily resident, or has his principal place of business or the branch or agency through which the contract of carriage was made; or the place where the goods were taken over by the carrier or the place designated for delivery is situated. Where an action is already pending before a court that is competent according to the aforementioned rules (*lis pendens*) or a judgment has already been delivered by such a court (*res judicata*) with respect to a claim between the same parties and on the same grounds, no new action shall be started, unless the judgment of the first court seized is not enforceable in the country in which the fresh proceedings are brought (Article 31 (2) CMR). Finally, judgments entered by a court of a contracting country that have become enforceable in that country shall become enforceable in each of the other contracting states of the convention as soon as the formalities required in the country where enforcement is sought are fulfilled, although such formalities shall not permit to reopen the merits of the case (Article 31 (3) CMR).

Although the wording of the provision is clear, there are some debated issues. The first one is the relationship between Article 31 and Regulations No 44/2001 and No 1215/2012 (Brussels I and Brussels Ia). Certainly, the convention came into force on 2 July 1961, and has done so for virtually all Member States of the EU (except Cyprus and Malta) before the entry into force of Brussels I Regulation, so that Article 71 of Brussels Ia Regulation applies. Pursuant to this provision, the Regulation 'shall not affect any conventions to which the Member States are parties and which, in relation to particular matters, govern jurisdiction or the recognition and enforcement of judgments'. However, in its *TNT*-judgment of 4 May 2010 (C-533/08), the ECJ held that the rules on jurisdiction, *lis pendens* and enforcement laid down in such conventions on particular matters shall only apply if they are highly predictable, facilitate the sound administration of justice, enable the risk of concurrent proceedings to be minimized and ensure, under conditions at least as favourable as those in Brussels Ia Regulation, the free movement of judgments in civil and commercial matters and mutual trust in the administration of justice in the European Union (*favor executionis*). Although on that occasion the Court stated that it

---

28. *See*, e.g., the judgments of the Barcelona Court of Appeal (s. 15) No 407/2012, of 5 December; and No 410/2014, of 17 December. The judgment of the Supreme Court (Civil Chamber) No 611/2014, of 4 November, does not specifically refer to the limitation period, but applies Art. 37 CMR to the action 'of recovery' between carriers who do not seem to be successive carriers.
29. The jurisdiction clause has to be accepted by both parties: judgment of the Spanish Supreme Court of 21 Jan. 1986 (RJ 1986, 108).

had no jurisdiction to interpret the CMR, in its *Kintra*-judgment of 4 September 2014 (C-157/13) it nonetheless did so and held that, with respect to an international transport of goods by road, the fora envisaged by Article 31 (1) CMR apply, even though the precept establishes two 'places of performance' (the place of taking over of the goods and that designated for delivery) where Article 5 (1) Brussels I Regulation (Article 7 (1) Brussels Ia Regulation) only mentions one. And this is so because: (*a*) the Court itself had previously accepted that, under a contract of carriage, the claimant may have the choice between the courts of the place of departure and that of arrival;[30] and (*b*) the criteria of proximity, predictability and legal certainty are fulfilled, since the competent courts are easily identified and the applicant's choice is limited to two possible judicial fora.

421. With respect to *lis pendens*, a recurring problem is the aforementioned 'Dutch trick,' where the carrier files a claim for a 'negative declaratory action' in a carrier-friendly forum before the person entitled to compensation files an action for damages in a forum that is not. The doubt arises because, while the cause of action (i.e., the facts and the rule of law relied on as the basis of the action) is doubtlessly the same, the object of the action (i.e., the end the action has in view) seems to be different. However, the Court of Justice held in its *Nipponkoa*-judgment[31] that Article 71 Brussels Ia Regulation precludes an international convention from being interpreted in a way that does not guarantee the objectives and principles that underlie the Regulation, so that Article 31 (2) CMR may not be interpreted in the sense that an action for a negative declaration does not have the same ground of action as an action for indemnity between the same parties. Thus, once a negative declaratory action has been filed, no fresh action can be brought between the same parties and the court seized in the second place has to stay the proceedings until a judgment is delivered by the court seized in the first place.

Finally, as regards the recognition and enforcement of judgments, it seems clear – the Convention refers to the 'formalities required in the country concerned', and these are those of Brussels Ia Regulation whenever both countries involved are Member States of the European Union – that an *exequatur* decision, which has been abolished by Brussels Ia Regulation, should not be required and recognition and enforcement can only be refused on the basis of the grounds envisaged by Article 45 Brussels Ia Regulation. In particular, the lack of jurisdiction of the court that has delivered the judgment is not among the grounds for denial of recognition[32].

Another problematic issue related to jurisdiction under the convention is the possibility to invoke Article 31 in the framework of a multimodal transport. The problem lies with the fact that CMR does not apply to multimodal transports as a whole, at least when different from a ro-ro or piggyback transport (Article 2 CMR), but it usually does apply to the international road leg when the damage was caused during the carriage by road. It is not clear, however, whether it applies autonomously

30. *See* the judgment of the ECJ of 9 Jul. 2009, case C-204/08, *Rehder*, although referred to carriage of passengers by air.
31. Judgment of 19 Dec. 2013, case C-452/12, *Nipponkoa*.
32. Judgment of the ECJ of 4 May 2010, case C-533/08, *TNT*.

or directly to such road leg. For the English Court of Appeal,[33] it seems to do so, although the relevant judgments refer to the application of Article 29 CMR. In the opinion of other national courts,[34] the rules on jurisdiction of the CMR do not apply 'directly' as regards the multimodal transport as a whole, and although there is an international road leg, Article 31 CMR cannot be invoked. At least as regards jurisdiction, the latter opinion seems preferable, because it is undesirable to give jurisdiction to all courts mentioned in any one of the sector-specific conventions and acts that may apply to a multimodal transport. Furthermore, if Article 31 CMR applied, it would not be clear which would be the 'place where the goods were taken over by the carrier' or the 'place designated for delivery' (those of the multimodal contract as a whole or those of the road leg): legal certainty and predictability, as required by the ECJ in its *TNT*-judgment, could not be guaranteed any more.

A last problem worth mentioning is that of connected claims and successive carriage under Article 34 CMR. It has already been said that the performance of carriage operations by successive carriers is only rarely to be seen in Spain, and courts have hardly ever appreciated such a situation in their judgments. However, the situation is slightly different in other countries, where the courts are more likely to estimate the existence thereof. Be that as it may, with respect to a carriage performed by successive carriers a claim can be brought (only) against the first or the last carrier, as well as against the carrier who performed the leg where the damage occurred (Article 36 CMR). But can an action be brought against all of them in the same court[35]? Arguably, this is only possible where a claim against all carriers mentioned in Article 36 can be filed with one single court according to Article 31, since Article 36 CMR only envisages standing to be sued, but contains no rule on jurisdiction. Thus, absent a binding jurisdiction clause, it does not seem possible to sue all carriers by way of a single action, since CMR does not refer to 'connected claims' in the sense of Article 8 (1) Brussels Ia Regulation. However, it is not a gap: an interpretation of CMR in the light of Brussels Ia Regulation would, in this case, affect the predictability of fora.[36] Finally, where there is a jurisdiction clause in favour of one specific court or tribunal, it can only be invoked with respect to successive carriers if they have accepted it (e.g., by accepting the consignment note containing the clause).

VI. Arbitration

422. Pursuant to Article 33 CMR, the claim may also be brought before an arbitration tribunal, whenever there is a valid arbitration clause that, furthermore,

33. *See* the judgments of 27 Mar. 2002, *Quantum v. Plane Trucking*; and of 29 November, *Datec v. UPS*.
34. In particular, the judgments of the German Bundesgerichtshof of 17 Jul. 2008 (I ZR 181/05) and of 25 Oct. 2012 (I ZR 167/11); and that of the Dutch Hoge Raad of 1 Jun. 2012 (*Goðafoss*).
35. The problem arises, e.g., because depending on which court is seized, import and excise duties or VAT are to be reimbursed or not by the carrier under Art. 23 (4) CMR. While in the Netherlands they are not (judgment of the Hoge Raad of 14 Jul. 2006), in England they are (judgment of the House of Lords of 9 Nov. 1977, *Buchanan v. Babco*).
36. Judgment of the UK Supreme Court of 28 Oct. 2015, *BAT v. Exel, Kazemiers and Essers*.

provides that the tribunal shall apply the CMR, so that only arbitration in law but not in equity is permitted. Although it is debatable, it seems that – contrary to what happens with a jurisdiction clause – the choice of an arbitration tribunal derogates the jurisdiction of national courts.

It should doubtlessly be possible to designate the Arbitration Boards for Transport envisaged by Article 38 of the Land Transport Organisation Act in the arbitration clause. However, the presumption of submission to the jurisdiction of the Boards, which applies to all domestic transports where the amount of the claim does not exceed EUR 15,000, is probably inapplicable, since it does not fulfil the requirements of Article 33 CMR.

§4. Carriage of Passengers by Road

I. Introduction: Applicable Law

423. The legal regime applicable to the carriage of passengers by bus and coach comes marked by the absence of a generally accepted international treaty, since the Convention on the Contract for the International Carriage of Passengers and Luggage by Road (CVR), of 1 March 1973, has not been ratified by Spain, nor by the majority of EU Member States. This led the European Union to take the lead and legislate in order to give greater protection to passengers in (domestic and international) road transport, adopting Regulation (EU) No 181/2011, of 16 February, concerning the Rights of Passengers in Bus and Coach Transport. The Regulation came into force on 1 March 2013 and envisages the rights of passengers in case of accident, cancellation and delay. It also contains rules on non-discrimination of disabled persons and persons with reduced mobility, as well as the provision of assistance to such persons, the minimum information to be provided to passengers, or the system of processing of complaints (Article 1).

Pursuant to its Article 2 the Regulation, shall apply in its entirety to passengers using regular services (i.e., those that are performed at specified intervals along specific routes) for non-specified categories of passenger (which excludes, e.g., schoolchildren when using transport means exclusively programmed for them) where the boarding or the alighting point is located in the territory of a Member State and where the scheduled distance of the service is 250 kilometres or more. By contrast, only some of its provisions shall apply to shorter distance and occasional services, and Member States are entitled to exempt domestic regular services for a maximum period of eight years from the application of certain rules. In general, the protection offered by the Regulation is less comprehensive than that established for other modes of transport, as the Regulation takes into account the specific characteristics of the sector, formed mostly by small and medium-sized enterprises. In addition, the Regulation has to be completed, where appropriate, with national law. Where Spanish legislation applies, the 1987 Land Transport Organisation Act only contains some few provisions, amended by Act No 9/2013 in order to adapt them to Regulation No 181/2011. The domestic Regulation developing the Land Transport Organisation Act (approved by Royal Decree 1211/1990, of 28 September), on its part, has not been adapted to EU legislation yet.

II. Liability in Case of an Accident

424. In case of death or personal injury resulting from an accident 'arising out of the use of the bus or coach' (Article 7 (1) of Regulation No 181/2011), two fundamental rights are granted to the passenger, irrespective of the cause that had originated the accident: the right to indemnity or compensation and the right to assistance. With regard to compensation, it should be noted that the determination of the basis of liability and the calculation of the amount of compensation (which must comprise, in any case, reasonable funeral expenses) are referred to national law. National law may establish, furthermore, a maximum amount of compensation (Spain has not made use of this faculty, so the amount of compensation is unlimited), which may not be less than EUR 220,000 per passenger (Article 7 (2) (a)).

425. Spanish domestic law lacks a specific rule governing the contract of carriage of passengers by bus or coach. Therefore, general rules of private contract law apply, especially those on the contract for services, as well as the recast of the General Act for the Defence of Consumers and Users (approved by Royal Legislative Decree 1/2007, of 16 November). Finally, one does also have to take into account the recast of the Act on Civil Liability and Insurance in the Circulation of Motor Vehicles, approved by Royal Legislative Decree 8/2004, of 29 October, that establishes a system of strict liability of the driver, that is extended to the transport undertaking as a vehicle owner. In case of death or personal injury, the only grounds for relief are the victim's fault and force majeure, external to the act of driving and the functioning of the vehicle (Article 1).

In its Article 2, the Act on Civil Liability establishes the obligation of the owner of the vehicle (i.e., the transport undertaking) to take out insurance that covers the aforementioned liability. Apart from this, the carrier must also hire the so-called compulsory insurance of passengers (*seguro obligatorio de viajeros – SOV*), a casualty insurance which is obligatory when performing carriage of passengers by land (road and rail) (Article 5 of the Regulation to the Land Transport Organisation Act).

As regards assistance to the passengers, it shall be adequate and proportionate to the immediate practical needs of the passenger after the accident, including, where necessary, accommodation, food, clothing, transportation and the provision of first aid. The carrier may limit the total cost of the accommodation to EUR 80 per night per passenger, for a maximum of two nights (Article. 8 of Regulation 181/2011).

III. Liability in the Event of Incidents in Relation to Luggage

426. Regulation No 181/2011 also envisages the liability of the carrier for loss of or damage to luggage. However, in this case the legal obligation to compensate remains limited to those cases in which the loss or damage is the result of an accident arising out of the use of the bus or coach, a concept that has to be interpreted widely. For the calculation of the amount of compensation, the Regulation once again refers to the provisions of national law, which may establish a maximum amount thereof (not less than EUR 1,200 per item of luggage, Article 7 (2) (b) of Regulation 181/2011).

To this effect, Article 23 AOLTA sets different limits depending on whether the transport is included or not in the scope of application of Regulation No 181/2011. In the first case, the limit of liability is set, precisely, at the amount of EUR 1,200 per item of luggage. For other transports (to which the Regulation does not apply), liability for damage to or loss of the baggage is limited to EUR 450 per item, unless a higher limit is agreed or the damage is due to a fraudulent action of the carrier or his agents and servants (Article 1102 of the Civil Code). Apart from this, the regulation of the basis of liability of the carrier is fragmented, because 'checked baggage' (that travels in the bus hold, a roof rack or in a trailer) is distinguished from hand luggage, but the Act only establishes rules for hand luggage. Indeed, since the custody thereof corresponds to the passenger, the carrier's liability is for fault: the passenger has to bear the damages undergone by hand luggage while it is on board, unless he proves negligence on the part of the carrier, in which case the abovementioned limitations to the liability of the carrier shall apply. By way of derogation of this rule, the carrier's fault is presumed unless proof to the contrary in case of loss or damage to hand luggage occurred when, on the occasion of a stop, all occupants had abandoned the vehicle (unless, immediately afterwards, the driver had closed the doors of access to the bus or coach).

Conversely, when what is claimed is loss of or damage to checked luggage, Article 23 AOLTA is silent on the basis of liability of the carrier, so that general rules apply: either those applicable to the loss of the asset due, pursuant to Article 1183 of the Civil Code, or the regulation that disciplines the liability of the debtor in result obligations. The solution is the same in both cases: the liability of the carrier shall be presumed, who will have to compensate the damages caused (with the above-mentioned limit) unless he proves that the circumstances that caused the damage are not attributable to him.

IV. Passengers' Rights in Case of Delay, Cancellation and Overbooking

427. In the event of cancellation, long delay in departure (more than 120 minutes) and overbooking of a regular service, Article 19 of Regulation No 181/2011 gives the passenger the right to choose between: (*a*) the continuation of the journey or re-routing to the final destination without additional cost and at the earliest opportunity, under conditions comparable to those stipulated in the contract of carriage; or (*b*) reimbursement of the ticket price and, where relevant, a return service free of charge at the earliest opportunity, to the first point of departure mentioned in the contract of carriage. Where the carrier does not offer the passenger this possibility of choice, he will have to compensate him with 50% of the ticket price, in addition to the reimbursement. Furthermore, if as a result of a breakdown of the bus or coach a journey that has already begun is interrupted, the carrier must provide either the continuation of the service with another vehicle from the point the inoperable vehicle is located, or transport from that point to a suitable waiting point or terminal from where continuation of the journey becomes possible (Article 19 (3)).

Only where the journey has a scheduled duration of more than three hours, the carrier is obliged, in case of cancellation or a delay in departure of more than ninety minutes, to provide free assistance to the traveller: (*a*) snacks, meals or refreshments in reasonable relation to the waiting or delay time, but only if they are available at the bus or station or can reasonably be supplied; and (*b*) a hotel room or other accommodation – and transfer thereto where necessary – in cases where a stay of one or more nights is necessary (the cost of which can be limited to EUR 80 per night and traveller, for a maximum of two nights).

Finally, the passenger has a right to information: the carrier (or the terminal managing body) is obliged to inform as soon as possible – and, at the latest, thirty minutes after the scheduled departure time – of the delay or cancellation, as well as of the estimated departure time, as soon as that information becomes available. Likewise, where travellers miss a connection due to a cancellation or delay, the carrier (or the terminal managing body) shall make reasonable efforts to inform the passenger about alternative connections (Article. 20).

428. As is the case with other means of transport, Regulation No 181/2011 only envisages a minimum framework of protection. As a consequence, Article 22 entitles passengers to request additional compensation, in accordance with national law, for the damages that have actually been suffered. Although the provision only mentions cancellation or delay (where the passenger may claim, e.g., compensation for the damages caused by late arrival at the place of destination pursuant to Article 1101 of the Civil Code), nothing should prevent it from being applied to cases of overbooking or overselling of tickets.

V. Jurisdiction of Courts

429. Absent any international convention on the carriage of passengers by road, the rules on jurisdiction of Regulation No 1215/2012, of 12 December 2012, on jurisdiction and the recognition and enforcement of judgments in civil and commercial matters apply (Brussels Ia Regulation). Apart from the general forum of the domicile of the defendant (Article 4), the Regulation envisages a special jurisdiction for matters relating to contract. Indeed, pursuant to its Article 7 (1), where a claim is based on contract, it may also be brought in the courts for the place of performance of the obligation in question. Such 'place of performance' is then defined, in the case of the provision of services, as the place in a Member State where, under the contract, the services were provided or should have been provided. Since transportation services, by their own nature, are 'performed' in different places, it was up to the Court of Justice to decide the question, who ruled (albeit in relation to air transport) that both the place of origin and that of destination are places of performance of the contract, so that a claim can be brought in either forum, at the applicant's choice.[37] *Mutatis mutandi*, the same should be true for contracts of carriage of passengers by road.

37. Judgment of the ECJ (Fourth Chamber) of 9 Jul. 2009, case C-204/08, *Rehder*.

Chapter 2. Transportation by Rail

by Maria-Victoria Petit-Lavall and Achim Puetz

§1. Statutory Provisions: Legislation

430. The law of carriage of goods by rail in Spain is regulated by Act No 15/2009, of 11 November, on the Contract of Carriage of Goods by Land (COGLA), together with the carriage of goods by road. The legislator has indeed chosen to regulate in a uniform manner the contract of carriage by road and rail. Thus, in principle, the provisions are common to both modes of transport, although specific solutions are offered for the carriage of goods by rail, when necessary or desirable. With respect to these specific solutions, the Act adapts Spanish domestic law to the relevant international convention on this subject, i.e., the Uniform Rules concerning the Contract of International Carriage of Goods by Rail (CIM UR), Appendix B to the COTIF convention.

431. As regards the carriage of passengers by rail, since Spain is a Member State of the European Union, it is bound by Regulation (EC) No 1371/2007 of the European Parliament and of the Council, of 23 October 2007, on Rail Passengers' Rights and Obligations. In fact, Article 23 of Act No 16/1987, of 30 July, on the Administrative Organisation of Land Transport (AOLTA), provides that the liability of the carrier in relation to the carriage of passengers by rail shall be determined in accordance with the provisions contained in the Regulation. Moreover, Regulation No 1371/2007 extends the system of liability for damages in respect of passengers and their luggage contained in the Uniform Rules concerning the Contract of International Carriage of Passengers by Rail (CIV UR), Appendix A to the COTIF, to all transports performed by railway undertakings licensed within the European Union, irrespective of whether the carriage is of an international or a domestic nature (Article 3 (1)).

432. Along with the above provisions, Act No 38/2015, of 29 September, on the Rail Sector (RSA) and its regulatory development, contained in the Rail Sector Regulation (RSR), approved by Royal Decree 2387/2004, of 30 December, have to be taken into account. Both legislative acts mainly address questions of public law, e.g., the liberalization of the rail sector imposed by the European Union. The Rail Sector Regulation, however, also contains some few private law rules applicable to the relationship between the rail carrier and the passenger. But it should be noted that such provisions have not been amended after the entry into force of Regulation No 1317/2007 and those precepts that are contrary to either the Rail Sector Act or to European Regulation are to be considered as tacitly suppressed.

§2. Carriage of Goods by Rail under National Law

433. As has been exposed, the 2009 Carriage of Goods by Land Act regulates carriage both by road and by rail. Their legal regime is virtually identical. Since the carriage of goods by road has already been analysed, only the particularities that have been established for rail transport shall be displayed here. In this sense, the Act contains two sector-specific provisions. The first is contained in Article 33 COGLA and refers to the time limit the carrier disposes of to perform the carriage. The second special rule is included in Article 47 (4) COGLA, which qualifies the managers of the railway infrastructure as auxiliaries of the carrier when determining the liability of the latter.

434. As regards the first question, Article 33 (1) COGLA provides the general rule for both road and rail transport: the carrier shall deliver the goods to the consignee at the place and time agreed in the contract or, in the absence of an agreed period, within the term reasonably employed by a diligent carrier to perform the carriage, taking into account the circumstances of the case. The second paragraph of Article 33 then establishes the maximum transit periods for rail transport, which only become applicable when the parties have not provided otherwise. The precept closely follows Article 16 (2) CIM UR and the maximum transport period shall be calculated as the sum of two different periods: one for the consignment of the goods and one for their carriage, depending on the distance as specified in the contract. More specifically, the transit period shall not exceed the following limits: (*a*) for wagon-load consignments, there is a period for consignment of twelve hours and a period for carriage of twenty-four hours for each 400 kilometres or fraction thereof; (*b*) for less than wagon-load consignments (parcel consignments), the period for consignment is of twenty-four hours, plus a period for carriage of twenty-four hours for each 200 kilometres or fraction thereof. Similarly as to what happens under Article 16 (3) CIM UR, the third paragraph of Article 33 COGLA entitles the carrier to extend those periods in two cases. First, when consignments are carried by lines of a different gauge, or by sea or by road absent a railway connection. Secondly, when there are extraordinary circumstances involving an abnormal increase of traffic or abnormal difficulties of exploitation.

435. With respect to the second particularity regulated in the Carriage of Goods by Land Act, Article 47 (4) establishes that 'the managers of the railway infrastructure on which the transport is performed will be considered, to these effects, auxiliaries of the carrier'. As a consequence, the rail carrier shall be liable for their acts and omissions when he takes recourse to their services to fulfil his contractual obligations with the consignor (or the passenger). This does of course not mean that the infrastructure manager is not liable at all; he is, but *vis-à-vis* the rail undertaking, on the basis of the relevant contract of use of infrastructure which, on an international level, is subject to the Uniform Rules concerning the Contract of Use of Infrastructure in International Rail Traffic (CUI – Appendix E to the COTIF) (*see* Article 8 (1) (c) CUI UR).

§3. CARRIAGE OF PASSENGERS BY RAIL

I. Liability for Damages to Passengers and Their Luggage

436. Pursuant to Article 3 (1) of Regulation (EC) No 1371/2007, the liability of railway undertakings licensed within the European Union for damages in respect of passengers and their luggage remains subject to the CIV Uniform Rules. The European Regulation applies both to intra-Community rail transport and to Spanish domestic rail transport, carried out by a railway undertaking licensed in any of the EU Member States. This derives expressly from the provision in Article 11 of the Regulation, according to which the liability of railway undertakings in respect of passengers and their luggage shall be governed by Chapters I, III and IV of Title IV, Title VI and Title VII of Annex I; and Annex I is nothing else than an excerpt of the CIV Uniform Rules. By incorporating the Rules into an EU legislative instrument, they are not only made extensible to purely domestic traffic; they are also open to interpretation by the European Court of Justice. It should be noted, however, that the provisions on jurisdiction contained in Article 57 CIV UR are not incorporated into the Regulation, a fact that causes some interpretative doubts that will be addressed later in the text.

Moreover, the 'substantive' part of Regulation (EC) No 1371/2007 envisages three measures that increase the protection afforded to passengers under the CIV Uniform Rules:

(a) First, Article 12 requires the railway undertakings to be adequately insured or to make equivalent arrangements for cover of their liabilities under the Regulation following Article 9 of Council Directive 95/18/EC of 19 June 1995 on the licensing of railway undertakings;
(b) Secondly, Article 13 obliges rail undertakings to make advance payments to the passenger in the case an accident occurs. If a passenger is killed or injured, the railway undertaking shall without delay, and in any event not later than fifteen days after the establishment of the identity of the natural person entitled to compensation, make such advance payments (not less than EUR 21,000 per passenger in the event of death) as may be required to meet immediate economic needs on a basis proportional to the damage suffered. The advance payment shall not constitute recognition of liability and may be offset against any subsequent sums paid on the basis of Regulation No 1371/2007, i.e., according to the CIV Uniform Rules. Moreover, it is not returnable, except in the cases in which damage was caused by the negligence or fault of the passenger or when the person who received the advance payment was not the person entitled to compensation.
(c) Finally, pursuant to Article 14, the railway undertaking shall make every reasonable effort to assist a passenger claiming compensation for damage from third parties.

The regime of Regulation (EC) No 1371/2007 is imperative. As provided by Article 6, obligations towards passengers pursuant to the Regulation may not be limited or waived, notably by a derogation or restrictive clause in the contract of carriage. Nonetheless, railway undertakings may, in any case, offer contract conditions that are more favourable for the passenger than the conditions laid down in the Regulation.

437. It should be highlighted that Spanish domestic law does not envisage an own regime of liability of railway undertakings in case of accident. Article 59 (2) (e) of Act No 38/2015, of 29 September, of the Rail Sector (RSA), generically entitles 'users' of railway transport services to compensation by the railway undertaking in the event of failure to comply with the obligations imposed on such undertaking by the Act and by the developing regulatory provisions, or in case of failure to fulfil the assumed contractual obligations. Thus, the law applicable to national carriage is Regulation (CE) No 1371/2007 and, by virtue of the reference in Article 11 of the Regulation, the system provided for in the CIV Uniform Rules. For if there were any doubts, Article 23 *in fine* AOLTA, recalls the mandatory application of the European Regulation to both international and domestic services.

As a result, railway undertakings are liable for death or personal injury, caused by an accident arising out of the operation of the railway, without limitation of the maximum amount of compensation. The carrier shall only be relieved of this liability if he proves the existence of a ground for relief, namely, inevitable circumstances, fault of the passenger and inevitable behaviour of a third party (Article 26 (2) CIV UR). However, another railway undertaking which uses this same infrastructure, or the infrastructure manager himself, are not considered third parties, so the carrier cannot be exempted from liability if the damage has been caused by them. With regard to compensation, certain expenses are considered as compensable damages by the Uniform Rules themselves. For example, in case of death of the passenger, those of transport of the body and the funeral expenses or, in case of personal injury or any other physical or mental harm, those of treatment and transport (Articles 27 and 28 CIV UR). The amount of damages to be awarded is not subject to any monetary limit under the rules and the liability of the carrier is, as a general rule, unlimited. However, Article 30 (2) CIV UR refers the determination of the amount of compensation to national law (that may envisage such limit), although it provides for a subsidiary limit: where national law provides for an upper limit of less than 175,000 SDR per passenger, the limit shall be set in any case at the latter amount. Since Spanish domestic law does not envisage any such upper limit, the compensation due is capped only by the amount of damages the victim proves to have undergone.

438. Chapter III of Title IV of the CIV Uniform Rules contains the carrier's liability regime in respect of hand luggage, animals, registered luggage and vehicles that, by virtue of its incorporation in Annex I of Regulation (EC) No 1371/2007, applies to national transport, too. With respect to hand luggage and animals the passenger brings with him, Article 33 CIV UR establishes a sort of 'automatic' liability for loss of or damage to such items (delay, of course, is not covered) in case of death of, or personal injury to, the passenger. In all other cases, the latter has to establish that such loss or damage has been caused by the fault of the carrier (or that of his agents and servants). Article 34 then limits the amount of the compensation due to 1,400 SDR per passenger.

The liability regime for registered luggage is necessarily different, since custody thereof is assumed by the carrier, who is liable for loss or damage resulting from the total or partial loss of, or damage to, registered luggage, as well as from delay in delivery (Article 36). Moreover, registered luggage is considered lost when delivery is delayed more than fourteen days. The basis of liability and the criterion of imputation also vary. While as regards hand luggage, the liability is for fault – except in case of death or injury of the passenger who brought the luggage – the liability is *quasi*-strict with respect to registered luggage. To be relieved of his liability, the carrier must prove that the loss, damage or delay in delivery has been caused by any of the risks mentioned in Article 36 (2) CIV UR, a list that lacks any reference to the proof of his diligence or lack of negligence. If the liability of the carrier for loss, damage or delay is established, his liability is limited to the amounts envisaged by Articles 41–43 CIV UR.

439. Irrespective of whether the carrier is liable for death, injury, or for loss, damage or delay of registered or hand luggage, the upper limits to compensation established either by the CIV Uniform Rules themselves or by domestic law shall not apply if the event giving rise to the damage has been caused, not by a negligent act or omission of the railway company, but by an act or omission which the carrier has committed either with intent to cause such loss or damage, or recklessly and with knowledge that such loss or damage would probably result (Article 48 CIV UR).

440. Finally, carriers against whom an action may be brought and the conditions and terms of exercise of the corresponding claims are those established by the CIV Uniform Rules, as incorporated into Annex I of Regulation (EC) No 1371/2007 (Title VI).

II. Liability for Delays, Missed Connections and Cancellations

A. *The Situation under Regulation No 1371/2007 and the CIV Uniform Rules*

441. Regulation (EC) No 1371/2007 contains a number of rail passenger rights that may not be limited or waived, notably by a derogation or restrictive clause in the contract of carriage (Article 6 (1)). However, an *enhancement* of rights either on the part of the railway undertaking (Article 6 (2)) or on that of the respective Member State remains possible. The rights awarded by the Regulation have thus the character of a minimum protection that has to be offered in any case.

The legal regime laid down in Regulation (EC) No 1371/2007 is confusing and sometimes obscure. On the one hand, it provides for specific rules in case of certain types of breach of contract (delays, missed connections and cancellations) in its Chapter IV (Articles 16–18). On the other hand, Article 15 generically refers to Chapter II of Title IV of the CIV UR (Annex I to the Regulation), which surprisingly contains only one provision (Article 32 CIV UR), on the liability of the rail carrier in case of failure to keep the timetable, *i.e.*, delay (here referred to as 'late running'), missed connections and cancellations. Article 32 CIV UR is thus to be applied to domestic rail transport services as well.

442. The minimum protection afforded to passengers in case of delays, missed connections and cancellations is contained in Articles 16–18 of Regulation (EC) No 1371/2007. Pursuant to these provisions, the passenger has the right to timely and continuous information (Article 18); the right to reimbursement or re-routing where a delay in arrival of over sixty minutes is reasonable to be expected (Article 16); the right to assistance (Article 18) when the waiting time due to delay, cancellation or a missed connection exceeds sixty minutes (Article 16); and the right to compensation (Article 17) when the cancellation or the missed connection causes an actual delay in the arrival of at least sixty minutes (excluding periods of delay due to cancellations or missed connections outside the territory of the EU).

Together with those precepts, Article 15 of Regulation No 1371/2007 incorporates the CIV UR provision on liability of railway undertakings where they fail to comply with the timetable, *i.e.*, in case of cancellations, delays or missed connections. Unlike Articles 16–18 of the Regulation, Article 32 CIV UR does not contain a regime of protection for passengers. It rather sets up a system of liability of railway undertakings complementing the minimum passenger rights, although in a somewhat confusing way.

Thus, whereas Article 18 (2) (b) of the Regulation establishes the obligation of the railway undertaking to *provide* free accommodation in cases where a stay of one or more nights or an additional stay becomes necessary (where and when it is physically possible), Article 32 CIV UR only obliges to *reimburse* the 'reasonable' costs of accommodation when – due to the cancellation, the late running of a train or a missed connection – the journey cannot be continued (or could not reasonably be required to continue because of given circumstances) the same day. Moreover, Article 32 CIV UR omits any reference to the supply of reasonable meals and refreshments, or the transport between the railway station and the place of accommodation (Article 18 of the Regulation).

However, Article 32 CIV UR does not prohibit that damages for harm other than accommodation and notification costs be claimed from the carrier (e.g., maintenance, or even lost profits or moral damages), but it refers for such actions to national law (Article 32 (3) CIV UR). What is much more important is that Article 32 (2) CIV UR establishes a series of cases in which the railway undertaking shall be relieved from his liability. However, it is not clear whether these grounds for relief shall apply also when compliance with one of the rights laid down in Regulation No 1371/2007 is claimed. Arguably, this is not possible and the obligations to reimburse the ticket price or to offer an alternative transport; to provide assistance; and to compensate according to Articles 16–18 of the Regulation have to be fulfilled even if the delay, cancellation or missed connection are due to force majeure or to fault of a third party. Not only does the Regulation not contemplate such grounds, neither directly or indirectly; they are also minimum rights that cannot be limited or waived (Article 6). Furthermore, this is the solution given by the Court of

Justice (First Chamber) in its judgment of 26 September 2013,[38] which grants the right to compensation *ex* Article 17 of the Regulation always and in any case, even if the delay in arrival is due to force majeure.

Hence, two are the aims pursued by the various provisions of the Regulation, which are not inconsistent with each other. Articles 16–18 grant passengers minimum inalienable *rights*. Article 32 CIV UR then adds a system of *liability* of the rail carrier, so passengers can seek compensation, both under Article 32 CIV UR itself and according to the applicable national law.

B. The Situation under Domestic Law

443. Passenger rights are regulated in a very deficient manner in Spanish domestic law. On the one hand, the legislative act that deals with such rights in some detail, the Rail Sector Regulation (RSR), was enacted before Regulation No 1371/2007 was passed and it has not been modified since in order to adequate its provisions to the wording of the European legal text.[39] On the other hand, the only provision that acknowledges the existence of the EU Regulation, Article 23 *in fine* AOLTA, merely states something that is obvious: 'The liability of the carrier, in the case of rail passenger transport, shall be determined according to Regulation (EC) No 1371/2007'. The resulting legal regime could not be more distressing. Once the mandatory application in Spain of Regulation (EC) No 1371/2007 has been determined, the regulation of rail passenger rights in the Spanish Rail Sector Regulation[40] is sometimes inconsistent with the European legal instrument. In such cases, given the priority awarded to European law, in general, and Regulation No 1371/2007, in particular, the provisions contained in Articles 88 and 89 RSR that are incompatible with the European standards shall be considered tacitly suppressed. However, if the rules envisaged by domestic law are more favourable to the passenger (e.g., Article 89 (1) (c) RSR, pursuant to which, in case of delay at destination of more than one hour, the passenger is entitled to compensation equivalent to half of the ticket price, a compensation that increases up to the full ticket price where the delay exceeds ninety minutes), the latter shall apply: the rights envisaged by Regulation No 1371/2007 are *minimum* passenger rights.

In conclusion, the conjugation of the provisions contained in the CIV Uniform Rules and in the Rail Sector Regulation with the minimum rights of passengers on a Community level is far from easy, since it requires a comprehensive interpretation of all three bodies of law. The lack of coordination between them should lead to a

38. Case C-509/11, *ÖBB-Personenverkehr AG*.
39. It is true that Art. 88 RSR has been modified, precisely, in 2007, by virtue of Royal Decree 810/2007, of 22 June (*B.O.E.* No 162, 7 Jul. 2007), but the reform is not only prior to the enactment of Regulation No 1371/2007, it does not even affect the matter before us. It merely introduces a stylistic improvement in para. 1 and adds a new para. 3 that allows railway undertakings that have paid compensation to a passenger to take recourse against the infrastructure manager if he considers that the latter is responsible for the cancellation or the interruption (or delay, it should be added) of the service.
40. Which is mostly reproduced in the general terms and conditions of the major Spanish railway undertaking.

profound reform of the legal texts in force; a reform that is all the more necessary due to the fact that, both the CIV Uniform Rules and the European Regulation limit themselves to establish minimum and inalienable rights of the passengers and refer, for any other question, to domestic law.

§4. Jurisdiction of Courts

444. Here again, the relationship between the rules on jurisdiction in the relevant international convention (COTIF) and those in Brussels Ia Regulation is far from clear, although the situation differs from that in road transport.

445. The COTIF Convention contains different rules on jurisdiction that vary depending on the object of the contract: goods or passengers. Pursuant to Article 46 (1) CIM UR, an action based on a carriage of goods under the Rules can be brought in any court or tribunal of an OTIF Member State designated by agreement between the parties (e.g., a jurisdiction clause in the consignment note). Additionally (so only prorogation, but not derogation of jurisdiction is possible), the claim can be brought in the courts or tribunals of a country within whose territory: (*a*) the defendant has his domicile or habitual residence, or has his principal place of business or the branch or agency which concluded the contract; (*b*) the place where the goods were taken over by the carrier is situated; or (*c*) the place designated for delivery is situated.

As can be observed, the rule is very similar to that in Article 31 CMR, but the CIM Rules came into force on 1 July 2006, that is, *after* the entry into force of Brussels I Regulation in 2002. Thus, arguably, Article 71 of Brussels Ia Regulation is not relevant[41] and Article 67 applies, which gives preference to provisions governing jurisdiction in instruments of the European Union. This is so because the Union may conclude agreements with international organizations, which are then binding upon the institutions of the EU and on its Member States (Article 216 TFEU), and such an agreement of accession of the European Union to the COTIF has been concluded in 2011.[42] Certainly, Article 2 of the Accession Agreement contains a so-called disconnection clause in favour of Union rules in the mutual relations between the Member States, but Brussels Ia Regulation is not even mentioned in the 'Declaration of competences' and its Article 67 specifically provides for the application of provisions in specific matters in instruments of the Union.[43] As a consequence, the fora envisaged by Article 46 (1) CIM UR should also apply to international transports within the European Union, taking preference over those in Regulation No 1215/2012.[44]

41. *See* the references in the ECJ's aforementioned decision in the *TNT*-case, as well as recital 36 of Brussels Ia Regulation.
42. *O.J.* L 51, of 23 Feb. 2013.
43. *See*, however, the judgment of the French *Cour de Cassation* of 29 Nov. 2016: due, precisely, to the 'disconnection clause' in Art. 2 of the accession agreement between the EU and the OTIF, Brussels I(a) Regulation and not COTIF applies in the mutual relations between EU Member States.
44. In any case, since such fora are almost identical to those in the CMR Convention, they doubtlessly fulfil the test established in the ECJ's 2010 *TNT*-judgment, especially the predictability criterion.

446. The situation is slightly different in the field of passenger transport, because the number of possible fora is smaller. Indeed, pursuant to Article 57 CIV UR, an action based on the CIV Rules can only be brought in a court of an OTIF Member State designated by agreement and, additionally, before the courts or tribunals of the OTIF Member State where the defendant has his domicile or habitual residence, or his principal place of business (or the branch or agency which concluded the contract of carriage). Since the European Union has declared its accession to the COTIF Convention as a whole, this rule should also apply per se to international carriages within the Union (Article 67 Brussels Ia Regulation), although Article 57 CIV UR has not been incorporated into Regulation No 1371/2007. To the contrary, and precisely because Article 57 CIV UR has been excluded from the passengers' rights Regulation, for claims based on a domestic carriage (and, arguably, for all those based on the Regulation itself) the private international rules of Brussels Ia Regulation apply, at least when the matter has 'cross-border implications' (otherwise, jurisdiction has to be determined according to national legislation).

Chapter 3. Inland Navigation

by Achim Puetz

§1. Carriage of Goods by Inland Waterways

447. Carriage of goods by inland waterways is of scarce importance in Spain. This has not always been the case, for great channels have been built in the eighteenth and nineteenth centuries to allow inland navigation on the dry mainland of the Iberian Peninsula: the Castille and Imperial Canals, now relegated in their use to irrigation and water supply for neighbouring populations. Inland navigation for the purpose of transportation of goods is limited, thus, to a single river, the Guadalquivir, in the south of Spain, that connects the port of Seville, the only commercial inland port in Spain, with the Atlantic Ocean. However, the proximity to the Atlantic Ocean and the fact that, with the recent opening of a new sluice of extraordinary dimensions, the port can now accommodate a large majority of the vessels currently used for the carriage of goods by sea, make that the transportation of goods exclusively by inland waterways remains marginal in Spain.

Where goods are to be transported by inland waterway, Additional Provision No 4 COGLA declares the application of the Carriage of Goods by Land Act: otherwise, absent any special regulation, it would be governed by the clearly inadequate Articles 1601–1603 of the Spanish Civil Code. Before the entry into force of the 2014 Maritime Navigation Act, this situation was liable to create problems where both maritime routes and inland waterways were used, which necessarily was the case for transports originating in or destined for Seville (with or without transhipment of the goods). In view of the fact that two different 'means' of transport were used, one subject to the Carriage of Goods by Land Act and the other to the (then) relevant maritime legislation, the rules on multimodal transport, contained in Chapter VII COGLA, would have to be applied. This is so because one of the modes (inland waterways) is terrestrial (Article 67 COGLA), with the consequence that, in those cases where it was not possible to determine 'the phase of the journey in which the damage occurred', the liability of the carrier would be determined in accordance with COGLA (Article 68 (3) COGLA). A regime that, in addition, cannot be suppressed (Article 46 COGLA) and is therefore not subject to the autonomy of the parties (e.g., by including a Paramount clause).

This situation has changed with the entry into force of the Maritime Navigation Act. Pursuant to Article 1 (2) MNA, a navigation is considered to be maritime, although it is performed on rivers, canals, lakes, or natural or artificial reservations, in two cases: (*a*) when they are accessible for ships from the sea, but only as far as the effect of the tides is felt; and (*b*) where it is carried out on navigable sections of rivers, as far as where there are ports of general interest. Since the port of Seville is a port of general interest, navigation between the Atlantic Ocean and the port shall not be governed by the COGLA, but by the Maritime Navigation Act. This was also the position adopted by the jurisprudence prior to the entry into force of the Carriage of Goods by Land Act.[45]

Finally, given the limited importance of inland navigation in general and the physical impossibility of performing international carriage of goods by inland waterways, none of the relevant international treaties on these matters has been signed, ratified or acceded by the Kingdom of Spain.

§2. Carriage of Passengers by Inland Waterways

448. The carriage of passengers specifically by inland waterways has not received any attention by the Spanish legislator. As has been shown above, it should be borne in mind, however, that the 2014 Maritime Navigation Act applies directly to certain acts of navigation on rivers, lakes and other inland waterways. Where this is the case, it seems that the rules that govern the contract of carriage of passengers by sea (Articles 287–300 MNA) shall have to be taken into account, with the consequence that the liability of the carrier shall be determined pursuant to the 1974 Athens Convention, as amended by the Protocols to which Spain is a party (Article 298 MNA).

In those cases where the Maritime Navigation Act does not apply, the liability of the carrier is governed by Articles 1601–1603 of the Civil Code (that are, however, designed for the carriage of goods and could at most be applied to the passenger's luggage), as well as by the general rules on contractual liability contained in the Code.

449. Regardless of which regime applies, passenger rights remain subject to Regulation (EU) No 1177/2010 of the European Parliament and of the Council, of 24 November 2010, concerning the rights of passengers when travelling by sea and inland waterway, where the port of embarkation is situated in the territory of a Member State or the service is operated by a Union carrier. However, some situations that can typically be found in navigation on inland waterways are expressly excluded by Article 2 (2) of the Regulation: (*a*) where the ships certification does not allow to carry more than twelve passengers; (*b*) where the crew responsible *of the operation of the ship* is composed of not more than three persons, or where the distance of the service is less than 500 metres (e.g., river ferries); or (*c*) in case of excursion or sightseeing tours other than cruises.

45. *See*, e.g., the judgments of the Spanish Supreme Court No 1148/2002, of 29 November; and No 990/2008, of 7 November.

Chapter 4. Air Transport

by Maria-Victoria Petit-Lavall

§1. Introduction

450. In Spain, the determination of the law applicable to a contract of carriage by air widely depends on the object of the contract and legislation is different for passenger transport and air cargo.

451. As in all Member States of the European Union, passenger transport within the EU is governed by the Montreal Convention (MC) and by Regulation (EC) No 889/2002, together with the EU Regulations on passengers' rights. However, the law applicable to carriages between Spain and third countries depends on the itinerary and the nationality of the carrier:

A) As regards intra-Community and domestic air transport, the MC and Regulation (EC) No 889/2002 shall always apply where the carrier is a Community air carrier.
B) With respect to international air transport performed by a Community air carrier, Regulation (EC) No 889/2002 (and therefore also the MC) shall apply, regardless of whether the third State of origin or destination has ratified or not the Convention, as derives from Article 3 (1) Regulation (EC) No 889/2002.
C) International air transport performed by a non-Community air carrier shall be governed by the MC if the third State of origin or destination, as the case may be, has ratified the Convention (Article 1.2 MC). Otherwise, the Warsaw System applies. In this regard, Spain has ratified the 1929 Warsaw Convention, the 1955 Hague Protocol and the Montreal Additional Protocols Numbers 1, 2, and 4 of 1975, but not the 1961 Guadalajara Convention.[46]

Thus, Regulation (EC) No 889/2002 applies whenever a Community carrier, regardless of the flight itinerary (international, intra-Community or domestic carriage), performs the carriage (Article 3 (1)). The legal regime envisaged by the Regulation is, basically, a development of the provisions of the MC, although it lays down certain complementary provisions improving passenger protection and extends the application of its provisions to air transport within each Member State (Article 1 (2)). However, the European Regulation only applies to the carriage of passengers and their luggage and is complemented by the so-called passengers' rights Regulations.[47] In addition, the interpretation of the aforementioned provisions by the ECJ enables the establishment of a unified doctrine throughout the

46. Convention Supplementary to the Warsaw Convention for the Unification of Certain Rules Relating to International Carriage by Air performed by a Person other than the Contracting Carrier, signed in Guadalajara on 18 Sept. 1961.
47. Regulation (EC) No 261/2004, of 11 Feb. 2004, establishing common rules on compensation and assistance to passengers in the event of denied boarding and of cancellation or long delay of flights;

European Union, not only in matters directly envisaged by the Regulations, but also as regards the MC itself, since Regulation (EC) No 889/2002 incorporates a block reference to this text for air carriage by Community air carriers (Article 3).[48]

Nonetheless, the MC and Regulation (EC) No 889/2002 do not contain a complete regulation of the contract of carriage of passengers by air. Accordingly, in the case of internal air passenger transport, albeit the CM and Regulation (EC) No 889/2002 apply, those provisions of Act No 48/1960, of 21 July, on Air Navigation (ANA) that have not been tacitly repealed for being inconsistent with those texts must also be taken into account.

452. With regard to air cargo transport, there is no provision governing it at a European level. If the transport is international, either the Warsaw System or the MC will apply whenever the third State of origin or destination has ratified those texts (Article 1 WC; Articles 1 and 55 CM). In any case, MC is the rule applicable to all contracts for carriage between the Member States of the European Union, that is, to all intra-Community transport operations. On the contrary, it does not apply to domestic air transport, which remains subject to the Spanish Air Navigation Act.

Certainly, the Spanish legal regime of domestic air carriage is archaic since it is still governed by the 1960 Air Navigation Act, which remains in force. Although it was thoroughly analysed by the authors after its promulgation, it has been completely overlooked during the last decades. This is due, on the one hand, to the fact that the ANA rules on passenger transport, which is the true nucleus of the aeronautical sector, have been practically repealed by the relevant European and international legislation. On the other hand, although the ANA remains in force for the carriage of goods, this mode of transport has traditionally had little relevance in Spain, except in the traffic from and to the islands. The short distances and, especially, the high cost of air carriage compared to road and maritime transport may have been the cause of the little or no concern shown in the past years by the legislator or the authors.

§2. The Air Carrier

453. The contract of carriage by air is a bilateral contract concluded between two parties, the consignor or the passenger and the air carrier. The air carrier is defined by Regulation (EC) No 1008/2008 of the European Parliament and of the Council of 24 September 2008 on common rules for the operation of air services in the Community, as an undertaking with a valid operating licence (Article 2 (10)). Thus, air carriers must hold an authorization granted by the competent licensing authority that permits them to provide air services, that is, a flight or a series of flights carrying passengers, cargo and/or mail for remuneration and/or hire (Article 2 (1) and (4)).

---

and Regulation (EC) No 1107/2006, of 5 Jul. 2006, concerning the rights of disabled persons and persons with reduced mobility when travelling by air.

48. It should be noted, moreover, that the European Union itself has become a party to the Montreal Convention by depositing the corresponding instrument of approval on 29 Apr. 2004.

Regulation (EC) No 1008/2008 establishes all the essential technical-legal (Article 4) and economic (Article 5) requirements to obtain such operating licence. Among them, the granting and validity of an operating licence shall depend upon the possession of a valid Air Operator Certificate (AOC) specifying the activities covered by the operating licence issued by the competent licensing authority. In Spain, the authority that is competent to issue both the AOC and the licence is the Ministry of Public Works and Transport.

Moreover, air carriers are obliged to take out the compulsory insurance established in Regulation (EC) No 785/2004 of the European Parliament and of the Council of 21 April 2004 on insurance requirements for air carriers and aircraft operators.

§3. The Aircraft

454. Both the Warsaw System and the MC provide that they shall apply to international air carriage of persons, baggage or cargo performed by aircraft (Article 1 (1)). Accordingly, the air carriage contract and, consequently, the contractual liability regime of the airlines are subject to these international agreements (and also to the ANA) only when the transport is carried out by aircraft and not by any other means of air transport.

However, neither the WC nor the MC define what an aircraft is. Its legal concept and classification at an international level is found in the Annex 7 to the Convention on International Civil Aviation of 1944 (Chicago Convention), which defines the aircraft as 'Any machine that can derive support in the atmosphere from the reactions of the air other than the reactions of the air against the earth's surface.'

455. Under Spanish legislation, the concept of aircraft is contained in Article 11 of the ANA, modified in 2014 by Article 51 of Act No 18/2014, of 15 October, on urgent matters to promote growth, competitivity and efficiency. Pursuant to this provision, an aircraft is:

(A) Any construction suitable for the transport of persons or things capable of moving in the atmosphere thanks to the reactions of the air, whether or not lighter than air and whether or not provided with powertrains.
(B) Any remotely piloted machine that can be sustained in the atmosphere by reactions of the air other than the reactions of the air against the surface of the earth.

It should be noted that, on the one hand, contrary to the Chicago Convention, Spanish Law requires the aircraft to be capable of transporting persons or goods. On the other hand, the amendment has consisted in dividing the precept into two paragraphs, with the aim of adding a section b) to include remotely piloted aircrafts (UAV). A basic and transitory regulation of such aircrafts is contained in Article 50 of Act No 18/2014, even though it refers the establishment of the legal regime and the operations and activities to be developed by the UAVs to a future regulation (Second Final Provision), which has not yet been passed.

§4. THE CARRIAGE OF PASSENGERS

456. The Air Navigation Acts regulates the contract of carriage of passengers in Chapter XII, section 1 (Articles 92–101), and in Chapter XIII, on liability in case of accident (Articles 115 et seq.). The Act formally remains in force, absent any express derogatory rule.

Nonetheless, most of its provisions have been tacitly repealed as being contrary to Regulation (EC) No 889/2002 and, therefore, to the MC, as well as to other Community Regulations. This is the case, for example, with Article 101 ANA, which provides that the transport price will be fixed by the former Ministry of Air (a precept contrary to the freedom of prices currently contained in Articles 22 and 23 of Regulation (EC) No 1008/2008 of the European Parliament and of the Council of 24 September 2008 on common rules for the operation of air services in the Community). The same happens with Article 96 ANA, which regulates, in very vague terms, the justified denial of boarding for reasons of health or safety. This is a matter now envisaged by Regulation (EC) No 261/2004; by Regulation No 1107/2006; by Commission Regulation (EU) No 185/2010 of 4 March 2010 laying down detailed measures for the implementation of the common basic standards on aviation security (whose Annex details the checks to be carried out on passengers and cabin baggage); and by the Spanish National Civil Aviation Safety Program (ASP).[49]

457. Furthermore, all precepts on the carrier's liability regime for damages (injury or death) caused to passengers in case of accident, damages to luggage and delay (Articles 98, 100 and 115 et seq.) are no longer applicable (albeit not *de iure* repealed), since these matters are governed by Regulation (EC) No 889/2002 and by the MC.

Thus, the air carrier's liability regime applicable to domestic transport in Spain is the following:

a) The liability regime applicable to the injury to or death of passengers in case of accident is a mixed system, combining strict and *quasi*-strict liability, and limited with unlimited liability. Pursuant to this so-called two-tier system, the carrier is strictly liable in claims that do not exceed 113,100 SDR per passenger, and he may only be exonerated of liability if he proves concurrent negligence, that is, that the person claiming compensation has caused or contributed to the damage (Articles 20 and 21 MC). For any damage that exceeds the aforementioned amount, the carrier does not benefit of any limitation to the maximum amount of compensation, but his liability is only *quasi*-strict: he shall be liable unless he proves that the damage was not due to the negligence or other wrongful act or omission of himself or of his dependents or agents (servants), or that

49. Resolution of 16 Jul. 2012, of the Secretariat General for Transport, which publishes the Agreement of the Council of Ministers of 6 Jul. 2012, which modifies the Agreement of the Council of Ministers of 5 May 2006, which approves the National Civil Aviation Safety Program (*B.O.E.* No. 193, 13 Aug. 2012).

it was due solely to negligence or other wrongful act or omission of a third party (Article 21 (2) MC).

b) In case of destruction or loss of, or of damage to, checked baggage the carrier's liability is strict, but the maximum amount of compensation is limited to 1,131 SDR per passenger (Article 22 (2) MC). Furthermore, the carrier shall not be liable if and to the extent that the damage resulted from the inherent defect, quality or vice of the baggage (Article 17 (2) MC). On the contrary, the carrier shall lose his right to limit his liability if it is proved that the damage was caused with intent to cause damage or recklessly and with knowledge that damage would probably result (fraud or *dolus eventualis*). In the case of such act or omission of a servant or agent, it shall be also proved that such servant or agent was acting within the scope of its employment (Article 22 (5) MC).

c) In case of destruction or loss of, or of damage to, unchecked baggage, the carrier is liable for fault, with limitation of the maximum amount of compensation (up to 1,131 SDR per passenger), that is, it shall only be liable if the damage resulted from its own fault or that of its servants or agents. Once again, the carrier cannot avail himself of the limitations to his liability if it is proved that the damage resulted from an act or omission of the carrier, its servants or agents, done with intent to cause damage or recklessly and with knowledge that damage would probably result (Articles 17 (2), 22 (2) and 22 (5) MC).

d) In case of delay, both in the carriage of passengers or baggage, the carrier's liability is *quasi*-strict, that is, he shall be liable for fault, but with reversal of the burden of proof. The maximum amount of compensation is limited to 4,150 SDR and 1,131 SDR per passenger, respectively (Article 22 (1) and (2) MC). Article 19 MC parts from the base that air companies are liable for damages caused by delay, except they prove their lack of negligence, that is, that they or their dependents and/or agents have taken all reasonably necessary measures to avoid damage or that it was impossible to adopt them or that damage was caused by the concurrence of negligence or the exclusive fault of the passenger (Article 20 MC). In order to overcome the limitations of liability laid down in the Convention, the claimant has to prove fraud or *dolus eventualis* on the part of the carrier or its agents and servants (Article 22 (5) MC).

458. In addition to Regulation (EC) No 889/2002, the regime contained in Regulation (EC) No 261/2004 has to be taken into account, which regulates the obligations of air carriers and consequent rights of passengers in cases of cancellation, denied boarding, long delay and change of class. As a consequence, the domestic provisions on cancellation, interruption and delay of transport (Article 94 ANA), which are incompatible with the international regime, have to be considered tacitly repealed.

Article 95 ANA entitles the passenger to waive his right to make the journey by obtaining the refund of the fare paid. This is an aspect not included in Regulation (EC) No 261/2004, although partially contemplated in the Proposal of an amended Regulation[50] (new Article 4 (4)), which expands the regime of denied boarding to

50. Proposal for a Regulation amending Regulation (EC) No 261/2004 establishing common rules on compensation and assistance to passengers in the event of denied boarding and of cancellation or

the return journey when the passenger did not take the outbound flight or did not pay an additional charge for this purpose.

459. The projected EU Regulation incorporates the habitual practice of denied boarding on circular flights, that is, when the passenger is denied boarding on the return flight for not having used the outbound flight included in the same ticket. Nonetheless, it is admitted that companies may establish special rules in this respect, namely the charging of an additional levy in order to prevent companies from suffering losses due to the non-presentation of passengers. Consequently, it seems that the so-called no-show clauses will be forbidden. In this sense, Spanish Courts have already considered such clauses to be abusive and have declared that 'an automatic flight cancellation clause if the flight is not used has no reasonable justification'. Indeed, the loss of a bonus or discount might be considered to be justified, but this is not true for an absolute denial of the contractually agreed service, since this means that the contractually weaker party suffers intolerable damages[51] (Judgments of Commercial Court No 1 of Bilbao, 7 July 2008 and 3 July 2009).

Thus, Article 95 ANA continues in force. Together with this provision, other precepts continue in force, too, but their wording does not match reality anymore. This is the case of transport documents. Articles 92, 93 and 99 ANA regulate the passenger ticket and the baggage identification tag, but do not contemplate – as CM does – their replacement by electronic means, when the electronic issue of the passenger ticket has already been fully implemented by all airlines members of IATA.

460. It is striking that other precepts have recently been amended with a complete lack of success. This is the case of Article 97 ANA, which regulates both the checked and the unchecked luggage. Its current wording obliges the carrier 'to carry, together with the passenger, and within the price of the ticket, baggage with weight limits, irrespective of the number of packages and volume laid down in the Regulations'. This rule was introduced by the Sixth Additional Provision of Act No 1/2011, of 4 March, establishing the State Program of Operational Safety for Civil Aviation and amending Act No 21/2003, of 7 July, on Air Safety.[52] Nonetheless, it has been declared incompatible with the EU's legal order, in particular, with the freedom of prices in air transport laid down in Article 22 (1) of Regulation (EC) No 1008/2008 by the ECJ in 2014.[53]

---

long delay of flights and Regulation (EC) No 2027/97 on air carrier liability in respect of the carriage of passengers and their baggage by air, COM(2013) 130 *final*.

51. Among others, Judgments of the Commercial Court No 1 of Bilbao of 7 Jul. 2008 (AC 2009, 306) and of 3 Jul. 2009 (AC 2009, 1802); Commercial Court No 2 of Bilbao of 7 May 2013 (JUR 2013, 219445); Commercial Court No. 3 of Gijon of 10 Nov. 2015 (AC 2015, 1790); Commercial Court No 2 of Palma de Mallorca of 4 Dec. 2014 (JUR 2015, 283631); Court of Appeal of Palma de Mallorca (s. 4) of 4 Feb. 2010 (JUR 2011, 55378).
52. *B.O.E.* No 55, of 5 Mar. 2011.
53. Judgment of the Court of Justice (Fifth Chamber) of 18 Sept. 2014, case C-487/12, request for a preliminary ruling under Art. 267 TFEU from the Administrative Court No 1 of Ourense (Spain), made by decision of 23 Oct. 2012 (*Vueling Airlines, S.A. v. Instituto Galego de Consumo de la Xunta de Galicia*).

§5. THE CARRIAGE OF GOODS

I. Legal Regime

461. The 1960 Air Navigation Act, unlike what happens in domestic carriage of passengers, is still practically in force with respect to internal air cargo transport, with the sole exception of Article 104, contrary to the freedom of determination of the freight established in Regulation (EC) No 1008/2008. Thus, the legal regime governing the contract for domestic carriage of goods by air is contained in Chapter XII of the Act and, more specifically, in its section II, expressly dedicated to the transport of goods, as well as in the corresponding provisions of Chapter XIII, which regulate the liability of air carriers in the event of an accident.

The regime contained in the Act is quite unrelated to the various international texts in force. It is not entirely coincident to the one contained in the Warsaw System (prior to the ratification of Protocol No 4 of Montreal), which was in force in Spain when the Act was passed. Indeed, and unlike other European legislation, which incorporated the WC and its subsequent amendment by the Hague Protocol into their respective internal rules, it was not inspired by the principles contained therein. Nor does the regime contained in the ANA coincide with what would later become the MC. It can therefore be said that the Spanish Act contains a sui generis regime. On the one hand, it is different from the rules governing air transport within the European Union, where the MC is in force. On the other hand, it is also different from the regimes that apply to international carriages by air, that is, either the Warsaw System or the MC, depending on the States in which the place of departure and that of destination of the carriage are situated (Articles 1 (2) WC and MC).

II. Obligations of the Air Carrier

462. Not only can the regime applicable to the contract of carriage by air according to the Navigation Act be qualified as singular; it is also, incomplete and lacks any system.

The first striking issue is the absence of a definition of the contract. Nonetheless, what is even more surprising is that the Act configures the contract of carriage as a 'real' contract by providing that it is perfected with the delivery of the goods to the carrier (Article 102 ANA). The solution is different to that in international and comparative law, or to that which applies to other modes of transport in Spain, where the contract of carriage is a consensual contract and the delivery of the goods is the first obligation of the consignor.

463. However, albeit the absence of any definition of the contract, the Act does envisage the two main obligations of the carrier, that is, the transfer, as an obligation of result, and the custody of the goods (Articles 105–109 ANA). Accordingly, the carrier is obliged to transfer the goods in the time and conditions agreed with the consignor and to deliver them to the consignee unharmed or in the state in which he received them. Furthermore, the Act, although in a quite confusing way, establishes the space-time period of custody and, consequently, of imputation of liability.

Pursuant to Article 108 ANA, the carrier is obliged to preserve the goods he took over for transportation and is liable for their loss, damage or delay on account of the 'journey'. Although, in principle, it seems that the period of custody is limited to the 'journey', it must be concluded that, similarly to what happens in international legal texts, this period does not strictly cover the flight, but extends from the moment the cargo is taken over by the carrier until it is made available or delivered to the consignee (Articles 109 and 115 ANA). Nonetheless, the Air Navigation Act is silent on this issue, in contrast to Articles 18 (4) WC and MC, which more precisely limit the spatial aspect of the period of liability to the airport. Indeed, the carrier's liability has been extended not only to 'air transport' or to the strict flight period, but also to the operations of loading, unloading and to all the time during which the goods remain under the custody of the air carrier within the geographical limits of the airport, excluding all transports outside it.

On the other hand, unlike the International Conventions, the Air Navigation Act expressly exempts from the period of liability of the air carrier the time during which the cargo remains in the possession of the customs services (Article 108). Consequently, the air carrier shall only be liable while the goods are under his control or under that of his dependents or agents. Thus, the period of liability begins with the reception of the goods at the airport and concludes when the carrier makes them available at the place of destination (Article 115 ANA), but the time during which the goods are neither in possession of the consignor or the consignee, nor does the carrier (or its agents or dependents) have control over them (i.e., while they are under the custody of the customs authorities), is excluded from the air carrier's period of liability.

464. The air carrier is under an obligation to deliver the goods to the consignee immediately upon arrival. Article 107 ANA, in much stricter terms than the correlative international texts (Articles 13 (2) WC and 13 (2) MC), obliges the carrier not only to notify the consignee of the arrival of the cargo, but to its delivery immediately after its arrival to the place of destination. Pursuant to the Air Navigation Act, the period for the exercise of the relevant actions starts with the reception of the transported goods, without any protest by the consignee, instead of their arrival at destination, as established in Article 29 WC and in Article 35 CM (from the arrival of the aircraft to its destination or the day it should have arrived). However, the provision cannot be interpreted literally, as this would leave to the exclusive discretion of the consignee the determination of the *dies a quo* of the limitation period, which illogically would not start to run while he does not pick up the cargo. Such conclusion derives from Article 109 ANA, which establishes the obligation of the consignee to cooperate with the carrier by withdrawing the goods. If delivery is impossible because the consignee is not found or because he refuses to receive the goods or to pay the charges to be satisfied by him (cash on delivery, carriage or other charges), the carrier must communicate this circumstance to the consignor and assumes the custody of the goods during the period of one month, unless the goods are perishable, in which case the period may be reduced. At the end of this period, if the consignor has not disposed of the goods, the air carrier may sell them in public auction to cover his expenses and make the remaining amount available to those who are entitled to it (Article 109 ANA).

465. The Air Navigation Act requires the carrier to follow the consignor's instructions. Thus, on the one hand, Article 105 provides that if, by force majeure, the goods cannot be carried on the itinerary provided for in the air waybill, the carrier must deliver the packages to another transport undertaking at his own expense for their more rapid conveyance, following the instructions of the consignor or the consignee. Such obligation was not envisaged in the Warsaw System but has been included in the MC (Article 18 (4)), in order to legalize the usual 'substitutability clauses' whereby airlines reserved the right to transfer goods by other means of transport. In this case, the transport carried out by other means shall be considered within the period of air transport, and the ANA will consequently apply, if the consignor's instructions have not been followed. Thus, the carrier cannot exonerate itself from the liability provided in the Act for damage caused to the cargo in the event of force majeure when he decides to transport the cargo to destination by another mode of transport, without the consent of the consignor. On the other hand, Article 112 of the ANA regulates the right of disposal of the consignor, although much more sparingly than Article 12 WC and Article 12 MC.

III. Documents

466. The Air Navigation Act does not envisage the traditional documents of air carriage. On the one hand, the air waybill that must be extended by the air carrier is called transport ticket. On the other hand, it does not even contemplate the cargo receipt, which is obvious, as such receipt has not been regulated by the WC until the amendment introduced by the Montreal Protocol No 4, and is envisaged by the MC in case of failure to issue the air waybill or the electronic air waybill introduced by the MC in its Article 4 (2). However, like the air waybill, the transport ticket constitutes a document of preferential probative value, since it provides full proof of the existence of the contract, according to the terms contained therein. It is a document of legitimacy, too, as the carrier must deliver the cargo upon its presentation by any person (Article 103 ANA). It should be noted that, pursuant to Article 102 ANA, it is the carrier who shall issue the transport ticket (Article 102 LNA), which is what actually happens in practice, even though it is an obligation that is reserved to the consignor in the international Conventions (Article 6 WC and Article 7 MC).

IV. Liability of the Carrier

467. Similarly to what happens under the Warsaw System and the MC, the Air Navigation Act only envisages the air carrier's liability in case of material damages (destruction, loss or damage) and delay in the delivery of the cargo *vis-à-vis* the person entitled to compensation (consignor or consignee), regardless of whether the action for damages is based on contract or tort (Article 24 (2) WC and Article 29 MC). This regime applies also to the servants and agents of the carrier (Article 25 WC and Article 30 MC), provided that they prove that they acted within the scope of their employment.

However, the domestic liability regime does not correspond in any way to the content of the Warsaw System (WC and Hague Protocol), which establishes a *quasi*-strict liability of the carrier, that is, he shall only be liable for fault, but with a reversal of the burden of proof, combined with a statutory limitation of the maximum amount of compensation. The air carrier and its agents or dependents may be exonerated from liability if they prove their diligence or that the damage was caused by one or more of the grounds of relief provided for in the Convention itself. On the contrary, the limitations to the liability of the carrier cannot be invoked if the damage has been caused with intent or 'recklessly and with knowledge that damage would probably result', that is, in case of fraud or *dolus eventualis* or wilful misconduct (Articles 18, 19 and 22 WC, as amended by the Hague Protocol).

468. But the liability regime envisaged by the Air Navigation Act does not correspond to the regime in force in the MC, either, which incorporates the system of Protocol No 4 of Montreal. Indeed, the MC (as well as the WC, as amended by Montreal Protocol No 4) sets up a regime of objective liability for damages caused to cargo by destruction, loss and damage. Article 18 MC does not allow air companies to prove their diligence or that of their dependents and/or agents to become exonerated from its liability for damages caused by destruction, loss or damage of the goods, but establishes four grounds for relief (together with the fault of the person claiming compensation, or of the person from whom he or she derives his or her rights: Article 20 MC), the concurrence of which must be proved by the carrier. Nonetheless, it maintains the system of *quasi*-objective liability of the Warsaw System in case of delay, since the carrier shall not be liable if it proves that it has taken all 'necessary' measures (Article 19 WC) or 'all measures that could reasonably be required to avoid the damage or that it was impossible for it or them to take such' (Article 19 MC). Moreover, and surprisingly, the maximum amount of compensation for damages in case of destruction, loss, damage or delay in international air transport of cargo is always capped, even in case of fraud or wilful misconduct (Article 22 (3) and (5) MC).

469. Thus, in contrast to both international systems, the Air Navigation Act, in a somewhat confusing way, divides the liability regime in two and distinguishes between liability derived from an accident (regulated in Chapter XIII) and liability not derived from an accident, which is contained in some precepts of Chapter XII.

For damages caused in case of accident, a two-tier system of liability is set up. The liability of the air carrier and its agents or dependents for loss, damage or delay in the delivery of the cargo is strict, so that the carrier shall compensate such damages even if they are due to a fortuitous event or if the carrier proves that it acted with due diligence; the maximum amount of compensation, however, is capped (Articles 116 and 120 ANA). The air carrier and its agents or dependents lose their right to the limitation of liability if they acted with fraud or gross negligence (Article 121 ANA). Thus, it should be noted that:

(a) Contrary to the international provisions, the carrier's liability is always strict, even in case of damages caused by delay;

(b) The Act does not envisage exoneration from liability for damages in case of destruction, loss or damage of the cargo, as does the MC; and
(c) Unlike the MC, but similarly to what happens under the WC, the carrier loses its right to limit its liability in case of fraud or gross negligence, and not only in case of wilful misconduct, as it was introduced in the WC by the Hague Protocol, in benefit of air carriers. Indeed, wilful misconduct is a category situated in between negligence, even gross negligence, and fraud: the author does not want the damage but assumes that there is a high probability that it will occur.

However, as has been explained, the Air Navigation Act distinguishes between liability for damages caused by accident and liability for damages caused by any other circumstance ('fact') or incident. This derives from the provisions of Article 114 when it establishes that the provisions of Chapter XII will be understood without detriment to the provisions of the following Chapter on liability in case of accident. Thus, although Articles 116, 120 and 121 of the ANA, in the event of an accident, declare the liability of the air carrier even in case of a fortuitous event, Articles 106 and 108 ANA admit the concurrence of grounds for relief.

On the one hand, Article 106 ANA exonerates air carriers from liability for damages caused by the suspension, cancellation or delay of the flight, when such circumstances are due to force majeure or meteorological reasons that affect the safety of the flight. Therefore, under Spanish law, the causes of the delay or cancellation of the flight, which are many and many varied, are important. However, it seems that the interpretation of the provision should follow the orientations on the concept of 'extraordinary circumstances' in Regulation (EC) No 261/2004 as given by the Court of Justice, albeit with respect to the carriage of passengers.

On the other hand, Article 108 ANA also admits as a cause of exemption from liability of the air carrier the nature or vice of the goods. It establishes that the airline is liable for loss, damage and delay in the delivery of the goods, 'provided that they are not the exclusive consequence of the nature or vice thereof'. However, the wording is undoubtedly defective, since the defect of the goods as a disclaimer of liability is, pursuant to the Act, applicable only in case of loss, damage or delay, but not in case of destruction; on the contrary, Article 116 ANA considers the airline liable also in case of destruction, together with loss and damage. This terminological imprecision should not lead to the conclusion that airlines cannot be exonerated from liability due to inherent defects of the goods in case of destruction. Indeed, although the Air Navigation Act (as well as the International Conventions) does not define destruction (neither loss, nor damage), both destruction and loss produce the same result, that is, the absence or impossibility of delivery of the goods.

470. However, according to the Act, there is no other cause of exemption from liability for damages caused by destruction, loss, damage or delay in the delivery of cargo. It is logical not to have included an act of public authority carried out in connection with the entry, exit or transit of the cargo, or even an act of war or an armed conflict as grounds for exemption from liability (which are listed in the Warsaw and in the MC), as the Act only applies to domestic transport. However, since both issues constitute cases of force majeure, airlines will not be liable if they affect the safety of the flight.

It must be pointed out that, unlike the Warsaw System and the MC, the Air Navigation Act does not envisage the defective packaging of the goods, performed by a person other than the carrier or its servants or agents, as a ground for relief. Neither does the Act, unlike Article 21 WC or 20 MC, allow airlines to be exonerated from liability, totally or in part, if it proves that the damage was caused by the negligence or other wrongful act or omission of the person claiming compensation, or the person from whom he or she derives his or her rights, or that such act of omission contributed to the damage.

471. The Act also establishes a limitation to the maximum amount of compensation, although it shall only apply in case of damage to the cargo occasioned by accident without fraud or gross negligence on the part of the carrier.

It should be noted that the amounts have been amended by Royal Decree 37/2001, of 19 January, which updates the amount of damages envisaged by Act No 48/1960, of 21 July, on Air Navigation. The decree modifies Article 118 ANA, although not in a manner consistent with the MC (Article 22 (3) MC). Thus, in contrast to the Convention, which does not make any distinction, the Air Navigation Act differentiates between cases of loss, destruction or damage to the cargo (where the compensation due is capped at 17 SDR per kilogram of gross weight short or damaged) and cases of damage caused by delay of delivery of the cargo (where the liability of the carrier remains limited to the carriage charges); except – in both cases – when the consignor has made a declaration of value and has paid a supplementary sum, where applicable. In that case, the carrier shall pay a sum not exceeding the declared value, unless it proves that the sum is greater than the consignor's actual interest in delivery at destination (as in the WC and in the MC). On the other hand, it should be noted that the Air Navigation Act does not provide for a periodic update of the limits of liability, so that the limit remains at 17 SDR per kilogram, while it has already been updated to 19 SDR per kilogram for intra-Community and international carriages.

In short, the Air Navigation Act contains a regime of strict liability with limitation of the maximum amount of compensation in case of accident, similar to the one established by the MC. To the contrary, where the damage is not due to an accident, the Act does envisage grounds for relief, so that the situation is similar to that under the Warsaw Convention. However, it provides for the inapplication of the limitations to the liability of the carrier – like the Warsaw and unlike the MC – in case of fraud or gross negligence (which is not equivalent to wilful misconduct), even in the event of an accident (Article 121).

§6. Procedure

I. Right of Action

472. Article 24 (1) WC deals with the right of action, providing that 'any action for damages, however founded, can only be brought subject to the conditions and limits set out in this Convention'. Nonetheless, the Convention does not establish, neither in its original version nor after the amendment by the Hague Protocol, in this or in any other precept, which persons are entitled to file a claim for damages against airlines. This has become even clearer with the entry into force of Protocol No 4 of Montreal, that added a new phrase to Article 24 (1) and (2), in the sense that the liability of the carrier is to be determined according to the Convention, 'without prejudice to the question as to who are the persons who have the right to bring suit ... ' (*see also* Article 29 MC).

Thus, the determination of the persons entitled to file a claim corresponds to the *lex fori*, that is, to the law of the court seized with the case. Indeed, since the liability of the carrier envisaged by the Convention is for breach of the contract of carriage, it is the creditor of the obligation to carry the goods who can bring the action for non-compliance. Consequently, it is irrelevant if the consignor is or is not the owner of the cargo; it suffices to have concluded the contract on his or her own behalf, assuming the obligations of the consignor.

473. As a consequence, not only the consignor or the consignee are entitled to bring an action against the carrier, but – pursuant to Article 1257 of the Civil Code – it can also be brought by anyone who derives his or her rights from the former or the latter, for example an insurance company. It is indeed usually an insurance company who brings the action for breach against the carrier. The conditions for the subrogation of the insurer are established in Article 43 of the Spanish Insurance Contract Act, namely, that there is a valid insurance contract and that the insurer has previously paid compensation to the insured.

It should be noted that the insurer may not claim from the carrier more than the maximum amounts laid down in the Warsaw System or the MC, even though he has indemnified his insured – in accordance with the insurance contract – with a higher amount, except where the carrier is liable without any limitation.[54]

474. There are certain provisions in both the Warsaw and the MC from which it follows clearly that the consignor and the consignee are entitled to file a claim for damages in case of destruction, loss, damage or delay in delivery of the cargo. In case of successive carriage, Article 30 WC and Article 36 (3) MC allow the action to be brought by the passenger or the consignor against the first carrier, and by the passenger or the consignee against the last carrier; furthermore, any one of them may take action against the carrier which performed the carriage during which the destruction, loss, damage or delay took place.

II. Time Limits

475. Pursuant to Article 26 (2) WC and Article 31 (2) MC, a written complaint to the air carrier is an essential requirement to bring legal action for damages or delay in delivery of the cargo. Not so in case of loss or destruction, since no prior extrajudicial claim is required.

---

54. Judgments of the Courts of Appeal of Santa Cruz de Tenerife of 6 Nov. 1995 (AC 1995, 2255); Madrid (s. 14) of 1 Jul. 2006 (AC 2006, 1811); or Bizkaia (s. 5), of 17 Jul. 2000 (AC 2000, 4745).

In case of damage to the cargo, Article 31 (2) MC requires the previous written complaint to be submitted to the carrier forthwith after its discovery and, at the latest, within seven days from the date of receipt in the case of checked baggage, and fourteen days from the date of receipt in the case of cargo. In case of delay, the complaint must be made at the latest within twenty-one days from the date on which the baggage or cargo have been placed at the consignee's disposal. Pursuant to Article 52 MC, the expression 'days' means calendar days, not working days.

It should be noted that the Air Navigation Act requires a prior written complaint to the carrier also in relation to a domestic carriage. Nonetheless, the period is shorter both in case of damage and in case of delay: ten days following the delivery or from the date the cargo or baggage should have been delivered (Article 124).

476. Article 35 MC (and Article 29 WC) then establishes a limitation period of two years to bring an action for damages against the carrier, reckoned from the date of arrival at the destination, or from the date on which the aircraft ought to have arrived, or from the date on which the carriage stopped.

The method of calculating that period shall be determined, as provided in paragraph 2 of Article 35 MC, by the law of the court seized of the case. Where Spanish law applies, periods fixed for years shall be counted from date to date and, if in the month of expiration of the period there is no day equivalent to the initial day of the period, such period shall expire the last day of this month (Article 5 of the Civil Code).

For domestic transport, Article 124 ANA provides for a very short limitation period that clearly favours the air carrier: six months, reckoned from the date of arrival at the destination, or from the date the damage occurred.[55] Nonetheless, as has been explained, this period is only applicable to cargo transport but not to the carriage of passengers by air.

The two years' period provided for in the international Conventions (or six months for domestic transport) cannot be reduced, as derives from Articles 26 and 49 MC and Articles 23 and 32 WC. A clause establishing shorter terms shall accordingly be null and void.

477. It should be noted that for those actions not covered by the Conventions or by the Spanish Navigation Act, such as the claim for the payment of the carriage charges, the general limitation period established in Article 1964 (2) of the Spanish Civil Code applies, that is, five years, reckoned from the date the could be exercised. In this same sense, the Judgment of the European Court of Justice (Third Chamber) of 22 November 2012[56] declared that the time limits for bringing actions for compensation under Articles 5 and 7 of Regulation No 261/2004 are determined in accordance with the rules of each Member State on the limitation of actions.

55. Judgment of the Court of Appeal of Santa Cruz de Tenerife, of 6 Nov. 1995 (AC 1995, 2255).
56. Case C-139/11, *Joan Cuadrench Moré v. Koninklijke Luchtvaart Maatschappij NV*.

III. Jurisdiction of Courts

478. Article 28 WC regulates international jurisdiction in the following terms:

> An action for damages must be brought, at the option of the plaintiff, in the territory of one of the High Contracting Parties, either before the Court having jurisdiction where the carrier is ordinarily resident, or has his principal place of business, or has an establishment by which the contract has been made or before the Court having jurisdiction at the place of destination.

This rule, which allows the plaintiff to choose the forum that suits him best within the established terms (forum shopping), is mandatory and implies that the Contracting States are obliged to recognize a judgment entered by a competent court of a Contracting State, under the terms of the Convention. Nonetheless, it does not prevent from attending different fora and obtaining various judgments.

It can be said that the WC follows the principle of *favor actionis*, that is, it favours the exercise of an action for damages in the courts of those States that are closest to the interests of the injured person.

479. The MC, in its Article 33 (1), reproduces the content of Article 28 (1) of the Warsaw Convention, with respect to the courts that can be seized in case of destruction, loss, damage and delay in delivery of the cargo. It keeps these four jurisdictions, although with a terminological variation, since it replaces the word 'establishment' by 'place of business'. With regard to the carriage of passengers, Article 33 (2) MC added a new possible jurisdiction in case of damage resulting from death or injury of the passenger: an action may also be brought 'in the territory of a State Party in which at the time of the accident the passenger has his or her principal and permanent residence and to or from which the carrier operates services for the carriage of passengers by air, either on its own aircraft or on another carrier's aircraft pursuant to a commercial agreement, and in which that carrier conducts its business of carriage of passengers by air from premises leased or owned by the carrier itself or by another carrier with which it has a commercial agreement'.

480. The WC and the MC only determine international jurisdiction, i.e., the State whose courts are competent to hear the case, but not the court that has territorial jurisdiction within that State. With respect to the territorially competent court in Spain, cargo and passenger air carriage have to be distinguished. For the carriage of passengers, as the contract of carriage is a contract with general conditions in which the passenger is also a consumer, territorial jurisdiction lies with the court at the domicile of the consumer within the Spanish territory, which does not have to coincide with that of the air carrier. Clauses by which the passenger renounces to his own jurisdiction are null and void (Additional Provision 1.IV.27 of the Consumer Protection Act). By contrast, in air carriage of goods, even though it is a contract with general conditions, the airline can perfectly well establish within its clauses the territorially competent court within the State, which will normally coincide with the place where the carrier has its main establishment or place of business (or main office).

Article 28 WC and Article 33 MC are mandatory rules. This derives from the wording of Article 32 WC and Article 49 MC, pursuant to which all special agreements in the contract of carriage entered into before the damage occurred by which the parties purport to infringe the rules laid down by this Convention, 'whether by deciding the law to be applied, or by altering the rules as to jurisdiction, shall be null and void'.

481. Where international jurisdiction lies with the Spanish courts and tribunals, commercial courts are competent to hear claims based on both national and international regulations on (air) transport, as provided in Article 86*ter* (2) of the Organic Act No 6/1985, of 1 July, of the Judiciary (*Ley Orgánica 6/1985, de 1 de julio, del Poder Judicial*).

Chapter 5. Multimodal Transport

by Maria-Victoria Petit-Lavall and Achim Puetz

482. As mentioned above, no International Treaty relating to multimodal transport is in force as of today. On the one hand, the United Nations Convention on International Multimodal Transport of Goods, made in Geneva on 24 May 1980, has not entered into force. On the other hand, the United Nations Convention on Contracts for the International Carriage of Goods Wholly or Partly by Sea (known as the 'Rotterdam Rules'), adopted on 11 December 2008, has been ratified by only four countries (apart from Spain, Cameroon, Congo and Togo) and is not expected to enter into force in the near future.

There is no EU Regulation relating to multimodal transport, either. Certainly, Council Directive 92/106/EEC, of 7 December 1992, on the Establishment of Common Rules for Certain Types of Combined Transport of Goods between Member States, refers thereto. However, its main purpose is the liberalization of the sector in order to enable the development and further improvement of intermodality. As a result, it does not deal with private law issues linked with multimodal transport at all.

483. In the absence of an international or European regulation on multimodal transport, the law applicable to such carriages has to be determined, within the European Union, according to Article 5 (1) of Rome I Regulation. Pursuant to this provision, where there is no valid choice of law agreement between the parties, the law applicable shall be that of the country of habitual residence of the carrier, provided that the place of taking over of the goods or that of delivery, or the habitual residence of the consignor is also situated in that country. Otherwise, the law of the country where the place of delivery as agreed in the contract shall apply. Furthermore, in those cases where, absent a choice of law clause, it is clear from all the circumstances that the contract is manifestly more connected with another country, the law of that other country shall apply (Article 4 (3) Rome I Regulation).

§1. Multimodal Transport under Domestic Law

484. Where the applicable law is that of Spain, it should be noted that there is no global regulation of multimodal transport, either. There are, however, several legal instruments that govern the contract of carriage in the different modes that do refer to multimodal transport, although in an incomplete manner.

In particular, Chapter VII of the 2009 Carriage of Goods by Land Act, entitled 'Multimodal transport' (Articles 67–70), governs those multimodal carriage contracts where one of the legs is performed by land (by road, by rail or, arguably, by inland waterway). Multimodal transportations that are carried out wholly by other modes different from road or rail (or inland waterway) are excluded from its application. Pursuant to Article 67 COGLA, a multimodal carriage contract is a 'contract of carriage agreed between the sender and the carrier to move goods by more than one mode of transport, being one of them terrestrial, regardless of the number of carriers involved in its execution'. In short, the contract of multimodal transport must be configured in a single contractual relationship that may be expressed in a single transport document.[57]

Article 68 (1) COGLA clearly states that this type of transport 'shall be governed by the regulations of each mode, as if the carrier and the sender had concluded a different contract of carriage for each leg of the journey'. Nonetheless, if the leg where the damage occurred cannot be determined, the carrier's liability shall be decided pursuant to the provisions of the Carriage of Goods by Land Act (Article 68 (3)), that is, the liability regime of the land carrier shall apply.

The Carriage of Goods by Land Act thus contains a formula that respects the existing regulation for each mode of transport. In this context, Article 209 MNA establishes that, '(i)f the contract of carriage includes the use of means of transport other than transport by sea, the rules in this chapter shall apply only to the maritime transport leg, while the other legs shall be governed by the specific legislation applicable thereto, provided that it is mandatory'. In other words, this provision merely acknowledges the application of the so-called network system of liability. According to this system, the liability regime proprietary to each mode shall apply if the place where the damage occurred is known. However, at the same time it affords legal security to operators to the extent to which, if the place where the damage occurred is unknown, the liability regime of land carriers shall apply. The Carriage of Goods by Land Act has thus become a kind of 'general theory' of multimodal transport, since it shall subsidiarily govern those multimodal transports in which the place where the damage occurred remains unknown.

485. The regulation in COGLA is worth noting because, in addition to regulating multimodal transport, the Act refers to other groups of cases directly related to multimodal transport. On the one hand, it envisages the so-called undetermined transport, which is defined as a contract of carriage where the form of execution has not been specified in the contract, so that it is up to the carrier or transport operator to decide whether it will be performed by one or more modes. In these cases, pursuant to Article 69 (3) COGLA, where the contract does not specify the mode of transport and it is performed by land, 'the rules corresponding to that mode shall apply'. On the other hand, it also considers as being multimodal those contracts of carriage in which the carrier does not follow the instructions of the sender. Two are the possible cases: (*a*) the parties agree the carriage operation to be performed by two or more specified modes, but the carrier only takes recourse to one of them or to modes other than those agreed; and (*b*) the contract envisages a carriage by land, but it is carried out in one or more different modes. In both cases, the regime of liability corresponding to the mode of transport that is most beneficial for the sender shall apply (Article 69 (1) and (2)).

57. Judgments of the Courts of Appeal of Barcelona (s. 15) of 7 Jun. 2002 (JUR 2004, 14066); and Malaga (s. 5) No 1084/2003, of 28 November (JUR 2004, 13179).

§2. Multimodal Transport under Single-Mode International Conventions

486. Faced with the absence of any international convention on multimodal transport, most single-mode conventions do refer to at least some aspects related thereto. This is the case, for example, of the CMR, the COTIF and the MC.

487. As regards the international carriage of goods by road, Article 2 CMR contains a rule that is partially identical to that in Article 68 COGLA. Pursuant to that provision, the convention shall apply to the carriage as a whole 'where the vehicle containing the goods is carried over part of the journey by sea, rail, inland waterways or air, and (unless in the presence of an impediment to carriage) the goods are not unloaded from the vehicle'. In these cases (ro-ro and piggyback transport), the liability of the carrier by road shall be determined according to the legislation that would govern a contract of carriage for the leg different from road, provided that it is proved that any loss, damage or delay in delivery of the goods which occurs during the carriage by the other means of transport (sea, inland waterway or rail) was not caused by an act or omission of the road carrier, but by some event which could only have occurred in the course of and by reason of the carriage by that other means of transport (e.g., when the damage to the goods derives from the fact that they have been wetted with sea water).

488. The CIM Uniform Rules, on their part, contain three special rules on multimodal transport. Two of them are located in Article 1 CIM UR, dedicated to the Rules' scope of application. The third one can be found in Article 38 CIM UR. Pursuant to Article 1 (3) CIM UR, the Rules shall apply when an international carriage being subject to a single contract includes carriage by road or inland waterway *in internal traffic* of an OTIF Member State as a supplement to *transfrontier* carriage by rail. Article 1 (4) then declares the application of the Rules to those international carriages, subject of a single contract, that include carriage by sea or *transfrontier* carriage by inland waterway as a supplement to carriage by rail, although the carriage by sea or inland waterway has to be performed on services included in the list of services envisaged by Article 24 (1) of the COTIF Convention. Once the line has been entered in the corresponding list (and the Uniform Rules apply to the transport as a whole), Member States *may*, for this specific line, declare the application of the additional grounds for relief listed in Article 38 (1) CIM UR ('Liability in respect of rail-sea traffic'). The rule was introduced at the 1952 Revision Conference, as a condition for the United Kingdom to ratify the Convention.

The inscription of the mention regarding the application of the additional grounds for relief must be requested by the Member State concerned and not, as might be thought, by the carrier. The request shall be made to the Intergovernmental Organization for International Carriage by Rail (OTIF) and the relevant mention shall be recorded in the chapter corresponding to that country of the *List of maritime and inland waterway services*. However, when a State requests the inscription of the line, it is not obliged to make a declaration as to the application of Article 38, but if it does so, the grounds for relief will apply to all companies that serve the line

(Article 38 (4) CIM UR). If the same route is served by different States (international maritime transport), the liability regime must be the same for all of them, so that a prior agreement between the States is necessary.

The regulation contained in Article 38 CIM UR is substantially different from that provided for in Article 2 CMR, since it is not a condition that the whole vehicle is loaded on the ship (roll on-roll off traffic, although railway ferries do exist), so that unloading and trans-shipment does not prevent the application of the Rules (Article 38 (1) *a contrario*). Nor can it be said that the rule merely refers to the law applicable to a hypothetical contract of carriage by sea, concluded between the shipper and the sea carrier: Article 38 CIM UR establishes an autonomous liability regime. Be that as it may, it should be noted that Spain has not requested the inscription of any service in the List of maritime and inland waterway services.

489. Finally, the 1999 MC on carriage by air contains two rules on combined carriage. The first one is to be found in Article 18 MC, that delimits the period of liability of the carrier. Pursuant to the first paragraph, the carrier shall be liable in the event of destruction or loss of, or damage to, cargo 'upon condition only that the event which caused the damage so sustained took place during the carriage by air'. Accordingly, paragraph 4 indicates that such period of carriage does not extend to any carriage by land, by sea or by inland waterway performed outside an airport. There are, however, two exceptions: (*a*) where such carriage is carried out in the framework of a contract for carriage by air, for the purpose of loading, delivery or transhipment, the damage shall be presumed to have been the result of an event which took place during the carriage by air, although proof to the contrary is admissible; and (*b*) where the carrier substitutes the carriage by air agreed between the parties by carriage by another mode of transport, such carriage by another mode is deemed to be within the period of carriage by air.

The second provision that directly deals with multimodal transport is Article 38 MC, pursuant to which, where a combined carriage is performed partly by air and partly by another mode of transport, the Convention shall apply, provided that the carriage by air is an international carriage in the sense of Article 1 (2) MC. In such cases, the parties may insert in the air waybill conditions that relate to other modes of carriage, although the provisions of the Convention are to be observed as regards the carriage by air.

Selected Bibliography

ALBA FERNANDEZ, M., *Régimen jurídico privado del capitán del buque*, Tirant lo Blanch, Valencia, 2006.

ARROYO MARTÍNEZ, I., *Curso de Derecho Aéreo*, Thomson-Civitas, Cizur Menor, 2006.

ARROYO MARTÍNEZ, I., *Curso de Derecho Marítimo*, 3rd. ed., Thomson-Civitas, Cizur Menor, 2015.

ARROYO MARTÍNEZ, I./RUEDA MARTÍNEZ, J.A. (eds), *Comentarios a la Ley 14/2014, de 24 de julio, de navegación marítima*, Aranzadi, Cizur Menor, 2016.

CAMPUZANO, A.B./SANJUAN, E. (eds), *Comentarios a la Ley de navegación marítima*, Dykinson, Madrid, 2016.

EMPARANZA SOBEJANO, A./MARTÍN OSANTE, J.M. (eds), *Comentarios sobre la Ley de navegación marítima*, Marcial Pons, Madrid, 2015.

GABALDÓN GARCÍA, J.L., *Curso de Derecho marítimo internacional*, Marcial Pons, Madrid, 2012.

GABALDÓN GARCÍA, J.L., *Compendio de Derecho marítimo español (complementario al Curso de Derecho marítimo internacional)*, Marcial Pons, Madrid, 2016.

GONZÁLEZ-LEBRERO, R.A., *Curso de Derecho de la Navegación*, Vitoria, 1998.

GUERRERO LEBRÓN, M.J., *La responsabilidad contractual del porteador aéreo en el transporte de pasajeros*, Tirant lo Blanch, Valencia, 2005.

MARTÍNEZ SANZ, F., *La responsabilidad del porteador en el transporte internacional de mercancías por carretera – CMR*, Comares, Granada, 2002.

MORILLAS, M.J., PETIT, M.V. & GUERRERO, M.J., *Derecho aéreo y del espacio*, Marcial Pons, Madrid, 2014.

OLMEDO PERALTA, E., *Régimen jurídico del transporte marítimo de pasajeros: contratos de pasaje y crucero*, Marcial Pons, Madrid, 2014.

PETIT, M.V., *La responsabilidad por daños en el transporte aéreo internacional de mercancías*, Comares, Granada, 2007.

PETIT, M.V., 'El contrato de transporte aéreo de mercancías', in *La regulación de la industria aeronáutica* (ed. A. Menéndez), 2nd. ed., Civitas-Thomson Reuters, Cizur Menor, 2016, pp. 355–390.

PETIT, M.V., 'La conveniencia de una Ley sobre el contrato de transporte aéreo', in *Retos y tendencias del Derecho de la contratación mercantil* (eds Miranda/Pagador), Marcial Pons, Madrid, 2017, pp. 587–605.

PETIT, M.V. & ROSAFIO, E., 'La responsabilità del vettore in caso di incidente nel trasporto ferroviario di persone: la prospettiva spagnola e italiana', *Rivista del Diritto della Navigazione*, n. 1, 2015, pp. 93–131.

PETIT, M.V. & PUETZ, A., 'Rail Passengers' Rights Under Regulation (EC) No 1371/2007 and Their Implementation in Spain: Does the Spanish Rail Sector

Regulation Comply with the Acquis Communautaire?', *ZBORNIK, Pravnog Fakulteta u Zagrebu*, vol. 66, 2016, pp. 363–390.

PUETZ, A., *Derecho de vagones (Régimen jurídico-privado de la utilización de vagones de mercancías en tráfico ferroviario)*, Marcial Pons, Madrid, 2012.

PUETZ, A., 'Transporte internacional de mercancías por carretera y sumisión a arbitraje: problemas en la aplicación del artículo 33 CMR', *Arbitraje: Revista de Arbitraje Comercial y de Inversiones*, vol. IV-3, 2011, pp. 869-884.

PUETZ, A., 'Brussels Ia and International Conventions on Land Transport', in *Brussels Ia and Conventions on Particular Matters – The Case of Transports* (ed. Carbone), Aracne, Roma, 2017, pp. 141-179.

PULIDO BEGINES, J.L., *Los contratos de remolque marítimo*, Bosch, Barcelona, 1996.

PULIDO BEGINES, J.L., *La responsabilidad frente a terceros de las sociedades de clasificación de buques*, Servicio de Publicaciones del Gobierno Vasco, Vitoria, 2006.

PULIDO BEGINES, J.L., *Instituciones de Derecho de la navegación marítima*, Tecnos, Madrid, 2009.

PULIDO BEGINES, J.L., *El concepto de porteador efectivo en el Derecho uniforme del transporte*, Marcial Pons, Madrid, 2012.

PULIDO BEGINES, J.L., *Curso de Derecho de la navegación marítima*, Tecnos, Madrid, 2015.

QUINTANA CARLO, I., *La responsabilidad del transportista aéreo por daños a los pasajeros*, Universidad de Salamanca, 1977.

RECALDE CASTELLS, A., *El conocimiento de embarque y otros documentos del transporte: función representativa*, Civitas, Madrid, 1992.

RECALDE CASTELLS, A., 'Derecho marítimo, Derecho de la navegación, Derecho del transporte: concepto, sistema y especialidad', in *Diez Años de Derecho Marítimo Donostiarra*, Departamento de Transportes y Obras Públicas del Gobierno Vasco, Bilbao, 2003, pp. 199–232.

RUIZ SOROA, J. M. /GABALDON GARCÍA, J. L., *Manual de Derecho de la Navegación Marítima*, 3rd. ed., Marcial Pons, Madrid, 2006.

SÁNCHEZ-GAMBORINO, F., *La llamada culpa grave en el transporte de mercancías por carretera*, Marge, Barcelona, 2016.

VV.AA., *El contrato de transporte internacional de mercancías por ferrocarril* (eds. Emparanza & Recalde), Civitas, Cizur Menor, 2008.

VV. AA., *Manual de Derecho del transporte* (eds. Martínez Sanz & Puetz), Marcial Pons, Madrid, 2010.

VV. AA., *Comentarios a la Ley de Transporte Terrestre* (eds. Duque/Martínez Sanz & Emparanza/Petit), Aranzadi, Cizur Menor, 2010.

YTURRIAGA BARBERÁN, J. A., *Ámbitos de soberanía en la Convención de las Naciones Unidas de Derecho del Mar. Una perspectiva española*, Ministerio de Asuntos Exteriores, Madrid, 1993.

ZAMBONINO PULITO, M., *El régimen jurídico de la marina mercante*, Tirant lo Blanch, Valencia, 2008.

ZUBIRI DE SALINAS, M., *La responsabilidad civil del transportista en el contrato de pasaje marítimo*, Bosch, Barcelona, 1995.

Index

The numbers here refer to paragraph numbers.

Index

Made in the USA
Monee, IL
13 September 2026

62974284R10136